A Will to Learn

SRHE and Open University Press Imprint
General Editor: Heather Eggins

Current titles include:

A Will to Learn

Being a Student in an Age of Uncertainty

Ronald Barnett

Society for Research into Higher Education
& Open University Press

Open University Press
McGraw-Hill Education
McGraw-Hill House
Shoppenhangers Road
Maidenhead
Berkshire
England
SL6 2QL

email: enquiries@openup.co.uk
world wide web: www.openup.co.uk

and Two Penn Plaza, New York, NY 10121-2289, USA

First published 2007

Copyright © Ronald Barnett 2007

A catalogue record of this book is available from the British Library

ISBN-10 0 335 22380 X (pb)   0 335 22381 8 (hb)
ISBN-13: 978 0 335 22380 0 (pb)   978 0 335 22381 7 (hb)

Library of Congress Cataloging-in-Publication Data
CIP data has been applied for

Typeset by RefineCatch Limited, Bungay, Suffolk
Printed in Poland by OZGraf S.A.
www.polskabook.pl

The **McGraw·Hill** Companies

To my students
who have given and taught me so much

The Will warms an action, the mind receives it, and thought bodies it forth.
[Hildegard of Bingen (1098–1174), from Scivias, I, IV.]

The University is home to an indivisible inquiry in which the question of being ... and the question of value ... are brought together again under one roof.
[Martin Heidegger (2002b: 33) on the Art of Teaching.]

I am resolutely in favour of a new university Enlightenment.
[Jacques Derrida (2004: 132) *The Principle of Reason:*
The University in the Eyes of its Pupils.]

But does thought need an other air than the living do? More ethereal?
[Luce Irigaray (1992: 6) *The Forgetting of Air in Martin Heidegger.*]

Contents

Acknowledgements

I wish to thank Denise Batchelor, Angela Brew, Bruce Macfarlane, Stephen Rowland, Alison Phipps, and Paul Standish, each of whom read, commented and advised on the manuscript of this book. The care with which each of them took on that burden said so much about their generosity and their valuing of this project: I am much in their debt. I am sorry that I have not been able to do their comments full justice, but I hope each of them will sense our continuing conversations in this published text.

I should also like to thank Colin Syme, Michael Peters and Malcolm Tight, who acted as referees, in advising the publisher on my original book proposal (each of whom generously identified themselves to me via the publishers). I gained much from their commentaries.

I should also like to record my appreciation of conversations of various kinds with academic colleagues that I have had over the years and that bear on this text. Some of those conversations have been more in the way of my reading and valuing their own texts, although in many cases those readings and values have been wonderfully supplemented by conversations in person. Those conversations include those with Graham Badley, John Cowan, Steve Cranfield, Gloria Dall'Alba, Paul Gibbs, Beena Giridharan, Peter Jarvis, Ian McNay, Jon Nixon, Jan Parker, John Strain, Marilyn Strathern, Melanie Walker and John Wyatt.

I should also like to thank Rania Filippakou and Yu Ching Kuo, who helped me with the composition of the bibliography.

I remain responsible for any errors and omissions that there may here be.

Introduction

The jumper

In the ritual of the N'gol, an event full of power, the jumper hurls himself off the secure platform into the void. There is risk here. Yes, his ankles are secured by the thongs, but there is always some doubt as to the degree of elasticity of the liana vines, not to mention the reliability of the fastenings. The jumper has the courage to take off. Exhilaration, a finding of space, a rushing of air and uncertainty are in front of him: 'as the vines stretch at the end of the dive, the land divers' heads curl under and their shoulders touch the earth, making it fertile for the following year's yam crop'.[1] In the process, the jumper becomes himself and proves himself, as the event enables the jumper to move into a new phase of human being.

This image of the land jumper, made somewhat more benign in the modern sport of bungee jumping, will serve as a motif through the explorations to come in this book. For there are several parallels between the bungee jumper and the idea of learning in higher education for which I shall contend. Learning in higher education, too, calls for courage on the part of the learner and a will to leap into a kind of void. There is bound to be uncertainty. A pedagogy of air (as I shall term it) opens up spaces and calls for a will to learn on the part of the student; to learn even amid uncertainty. In the process, it is just possible that the student may come into a new mode of being.

'How is it that students persist?'

Over the last year or so, two students of mine have submitted their doctoral theses, one student having been registered for ten years and another for nine years. They were each well-advanced in their careers and, in each case, their studies and thesis writing had to be fitted in with their other professional and personal commitments. Nevertheless, neither student wavered in their determination to complete, notwithstanding some very considerable personal life challenges.

These are but two examples – albeit extreme examples – of what happens every day in higher education across the world. By and large, students keep going. How might we understand this phenomenon? Just how is it that students persist? Is it not, in fact, an extraordinary human phenomenon, that of human beings taking on a project of some personal challenge, and persisting with that project over three, four or more years. Whether students are relatively young or well advanced, whether they are taking full- or part-time degree courses, it is a phenomenon that, to my knowledge, has gone largely unremarked in the literature.[2]

Not only does this persistence towards students' own learning last over a protracted period of time, but it is also a project that calls for considerable effort and even anxiety on their parts, and it is a project where success cannot be assured. Yet many millions of individuals do this all over the world and the majority of them succeed. Just how is it that students keep going?

Much effort – valuable effort – is being spent across the world in addressing the question 'Why is it that students *fail* to complete their courses?' We need to understand the phenomena of failure or, as it more often is, non-completion (where student leave their programmes somewhat prematurely). Our question here ('How is it that students persist?') bears upon the question about non-completion, but is far from being the same question expressed in a different way. It is rather a different order of question. To pursue the matter of persistence with any seriousness is to bring into view three sets of further questions.

First, there are questions as to the kind of enterprise on which students are embarked:

- What is it to be a student?
- How do we understand the tasks and achievements of being a student?
- What are students called to be and to become?

Secondly, there are questions as to the educational journey itself:

- What kind of changes might students undergo in their educational journey?
- What is it to develop as a student?

After all, it is not unusual for a student at times of graduation ceremonies or even some time after their graduation – or even before it – to say to her tutor that the course 'has changed her life'. How are we to understand such a self-reflection? How is it possible for a course in a particular subject to change *a life*?

Thirdly, there are questions of educational responsibility:

- In broad terms, what kinds of pedagogies might help to sustain students on their educational journey?
- Are there educational principles that might help tutors and professors who might be reflecting as to ways they can be helpful to students?

- To use an idea that will warrant our critical gaze, what forms of 'student experience' are likely to prompt a student's continuing engagement with her studies?

Approach

My approach in this volume shall be primarily philosophical. Clearly, a text of this kind, which will focus on students and their learning, could adopt other perspectives:

- A psychological perspective could open up empirical insights into students and their 'learning approaches' and their motivational states (Prosser and Trigwell 1999).
- A sociological perspective could offer us insights into the students' wider learning environment, including the extent to which it characteristically reinforces or adds to their own social and cultural 'capital', and the ways in which it is shaped by contemporary discourses (cf HEA & OU/CHERI 2006).
- A biological approach could alert us to deep structures built up in the course of evolution so as to prompt tacit learning (Reber 1993).
- A management perspective could help us inquire into the conditions of the institutional environment and its facilities and services that are conducive to students' success.

Other perspectives, too, could have come into view, including those afforded by anthropology and economics.

I offer this text, therefore, as a contribution to what, ultimately, should become a multidisciplinary inquiry. However, I want to go further than that rather modest claim might imply. I contend that the philosophical perspective is fundamental in our present inquiry. In this book, I shall especially draw upon continental modern European philosophy. By 'modern' here, I refer to work over the last 200 years and, especially, to those writers who could either be said to be 'existentialists' in their offerings or to writers who advanced views that are akin to that form of philosophy.

Why turn to this range of literature and how might my earlier claim be justified, that this literature is fundamental to any serious understanding of the educational challenges facing higher education in the twenty-first century? It is simply that it is here, in these writers, that we encounter efforts to understand human being, that is *being* as such, and what it is to be in the world. Associated, too, with concerns about being, is an interest in being free and becoming.[3] This philosophical perspective, I shall try to show, is crucial to getting to grips with what it is to *be* a student in the contemporary world, and with the kinds of human being that are appropriate, indeed, called for, in a contemporary world that is full of perplexity.

In describing this book as primarily philosophical in character, I am doing more than pointing to the main kinds of writers on whom I draw or alluding to the kinds of ideas and concepts in play here. I am also saying something about the kind of text it is. In saying it is philosophical, I am saying that it is primarily conceptual in nature. It is also both critical and even utopian. In this book, I am holding out – often against the dominant ideas of our age – for a set of ideas of what it is to be a student, and what kinds of learning and teaching might be thereby implied. I shall try to show that there is a pressing case for such a critical utopianism.

In other books of mine, I have described my approach to understanding higher education as 'social philosophy'. My thinking has been that higher education is a social institution and that, therefore, any philosophizing, if it is to carry water, has also to take account of higher education in its contemporary manifestations as a social institution. An exposition of funda-mental concepts has to go hand-in-hand with a keen sense of the develop-ments and complexities of higher education, both across quite different institutions and disciplines in a mass higher education system. Otherwise, there will be the likelihood of concepts, on the one hand, being ideologically contaminated, representing unacknowledged interests and, on the other hand, lacking feasibility as they attempt to offer resources to the world for its development.

In this book, my philosophical approach is slightly different. Here, for the first time in my books, I am much less interested in higher education as a societal phenomenon, and much more interested in the student in herself, and in the pedagogical relationship that bears in upon the student's sense of herself and her learning. The unit of analysis, therefore, is much more localized than hitherto in my writings. However, it has an even more intensified relationship to the way things are in practice. This book, there-fore, contains quotations from students – from very different kinds of institu-tion of higher education and from a range of disciplines. Rather than being a social philosophy, therefore, I would say of this book that it is a person-orientated philosophy.

'Person' here is two-fold. On the one hand, it is acutely sensitive to the individual student, and his or her own personal challenges, while on the other hand, into it is necessarily injected my own experiences – with all their challenges and delights – as a teacher, for whom teaching has been crucially important in my own biography.

In his (2001 [1994]) book, *Difference and Repetition*, the philosopher Gilles Deleuze (1925–95) introduces the idea of 'transcendental empiricism'. In that idea, Deleuze is referring to a philosophical approach where 'we appre-hend . . . the sensible (as) that which can only be sensed, the very being of the sensible' (pp. 56–7). Transcendental and yet empirical, glimpsing reality with our senses and our imaginations, with our hopes and even our passions: this is my approach here. However, the stories that emerge should not be totally fanciful; rather, they should be testable and tested against experience. The ideas that I offer here should provide feasible scenarios: perhaps they will never be fully realized or even could never be fully realized. The ideas here may have a utopian quality, therefore, but they should have an empirical potential, being capable of being taken up perhaps as resources for imaginative actions.

I offer, therefore, the ideas in this book with a double *empirical warrant* (as I should like to put it). On the one hand, I suggest that the ideas that I develop here are already to be found, at least in some small part, in some of our pedagogical practices in higher education. On the other hand, the ideas I urge here have to be feasible as new possibilities; there should be a sense that they could be very much more realized, even in a mass higher education system. This concern for empirical realizability is one reason why I have sought to inject the voice of the students themselves.

The empirical and the transcendental realms will weave around each other in these explorations, therefore, and in ways perhaps not fully transparent. For instance, if I assert that 'Teachers and taught teach each other' (as I do in Chapter 10), that is both an empirical and a transcendent statement, and also a critical statement. It should not be taken *purely* as an empirical statement; rather, it is at once a suggestion that such a situation occurs not infrequently in higher education (though not necessarily commonly), that such a situation is representative of the kind of pedagogies for which I am contending, and that it should be more readily present than it is in contemporary higher education. It is also, therefore, a critical statement; it holds up critical standards against which contemporary practices may be tested.

I am wanting, therefore, the language that I draw on in this book to work in several directions at once. I mention this because some may be tempted to feel that I am offering simple empirical generalizations without sufficient empirical backing, but it is probably the case – in a particular instance – that I am not trying to offer a simple empirical claim. Essentially, I am trying to develop and hold up concepts, pictures, and stories that are indicative of ways in which we might take things forward.[4] The apparent empiricism of my propositions is a *muted empiricism*. The concepts, pictures and stories have to be feasible: there should be a sense that they are already at least embryonically present in higher education, and could be even more apparent, with a fair input of energy, imagination and resource, and even educational will.

I have said that this work is a critical work. In contending for a certain conception of what it is to be a student, and what it is to teach in order to encourage that kind of student being forward, I am also implicitly – and often explicitly – critiquing some contemporary conceptions of teaching. In this book, I distance my position here from 'outcomes'-based approaches to teaching. I am not concerned to rail against the idea of 'outcomes' as such; I am rather taken up with advancing a particular idea of higher education, but which I not infrequently observe, *en passant*, is in effect a repudiation of outcomes orientated curricula. The vocabulary, the ideas and the conceptualization of what it is to be a student and to educate for such student being do not live in the same educational universe as inhabited by the outcomes approach. If what I have to say here has any validity, then it implicitly provides an attack on the idea of 'outcomes'.

In the preface to the book I mentioned earlier, *Difference and Repetition*, Deleuze suggests that:

> A book of philosophy should be in part a very particular species of detective novel, in part a kind of science fiction.
>
> [Gilles Deleuze, *Difference and Repetition* (2001: xx).]

This book, too, may be seen both as detective novel and as science fiction. I have a puzzle – two puzzles actually – that I set out to solve, and I believe that I succeed in solving those puzzles. Is there a crime, though? Yes, in a way. Indeed, several crimes, in the way in which students are coming sometimes to see themselves as consumers, a process in which they are aided and abetted by the institutions in which they study; in the way in which curricula are being confined to the straitjacket of 'outcomes'; and in the way the pedagogical relationship is being subject to the laws of the market.

So far as this book being a work of science fiction is concerned, it is so in the following ways. My writing of this book is speculative, it tries to go beyond our dominant contemporary understandings and I try to use my imagination in conjuring a particular sense of how things might be. However, so often, science fiction has quickly been overtaken by real-life developments, and I hope that that may be the case here, too.

Two puzzles

I have just suggested that, in this book, I have set out to solve two puzzles (or, at least, to see if they could be solved). However, I omitted to identify those puzzles.

First, I am driven to write this book out of a concern for the idea of the will, and more specifically, for what I term 'the will to learn'. At once, a key puzzle arises: is the will to learn *particular or general?* In having a will to learn, is the student herself driven forward, on one hand, towards *certain* kinds of object or to satisfy *particular* kinds of interest or, on the other hand, is the will to learn *general* in character? Is it that the student simply has taken on a general will to learn and, perhaps fortuitously, that will, that spirit, just spills over into her particular studies so that she becomes enthused about them? Is the will to learn, then, general or particular? This is our first puzzle.

Secondly, in a previous book (Barnett 2003), I suggested that, in relation to learning, ontology trumps epistemology. That is to say, the student's being in the world is more important for her learning than her interests in developing knowledge and understanding in a particular field. I did not, however, explain fully how it was that – *educationally* – ontology trumps epistemology. That puzzle remains outstanding.

In this book, I tackle both of these two puzzles and, I believe, offer a resolution of both of them. Furthermore, I shall suggest that there is a combined way of resolving the two puzzles: the two sets of issues that give rise to those two puzzles – as to the nature of will and as to primacy of ontology – turn out to be inter-related. The two puzzles turn out to be different aspects of what it is to live in and to be educated for a complex and uncertain age. Perhaps I may be forgiven if, just like a detective story, I keep back for now the answers that I offer to those two puzzles.

A suitable vocabulary

If we are to advance an idea of higher education that is fitting for the contemporary world, it has – I shall try to show – to draw on a certain kind of vocabulary. It will have to be a vocabulary that includes such terms as excitement, passion, self-confidence, journey, travel, will, energy, engagement, being and becoming. It is a language that helps to advance the idea, central to this inquiry, of – as I shall term it – 'a will to learn'. If students are to develop the wherewithal not just to survive in, but to make an effective contribution to this challenging world, this world of the twenty-first century, they will need just such a 'will to learn', a will to learn not just while on their course – and so pursue their engagement with their programme of study – but also to go on learning throughout their lives. However, even to say that is slightly to skew things; for what is in question here are forms of human disposition, a readiness to keep going, a willingness to open oneself to new experiences, and a propensity critically to be honest with oneself and critically to interrogate oneself.

This may all seem straightforward, at least put like that. However, this is a radical agenda for higher education. For in advancing this language – of being and becoming, of will and dispositions (a language, we may note, entirely missing from major reports on higher education) – certain other vocabularies will be set aside. Notably, the mantra of 'knowledge and skills' has been missing from this introduction, and those terms and their associated discourses will be downplayed in our journey to come. In saying that, I do not want to be misunderstood. In themselves, knowledge and skills are not redundant: they must have their place in a 'knowledge society', which is also fast changing and calls for action that bears the mark of a concern for doing things well. However, 'knowledge' and 'skills', even when run together – ubiquitous as that mantra has become – cannot begin to offer us a sufficient set of ideas for a higher education for the twenty-first century. At best, even when understood generously – for instance, as ways of active 'knowing' and as forms of action shot through with first-handed authenticity – they offer just two pillars of an educational project. By themselves, these two pillars, which we may label the epistemological and practical pillars, will topple over: they need (at least) a third pillar – the ontological pillar – to ensure any kind of stable structure.

This book, therefore, is in part an attempt to balance the unstable framework of current educational thinking in higher education (cf Bone and McNay 2006). It is also an attempt to put the student back into the centre of such educational thinking. Surely, many readers of this text can recall, as I can, personal instances of participating in conferences and seminars about higher education in which not only were students not physically present, but they were not even mentioned in the conversation. Many seem to believe we can have intelligible debates about higher education without mentioning students. When the term 'students' does come into the conversation, so often it is uttered as a reference to social equity (in considerations of access and inclusion), or as units of resource or cost (as in considerations of non-completion rates), or as bearers of flows of income (as fees) or as ultimate contributors to the economy (in patterns of 'employability').[5]

Such perspectives tend literally to objectify students: they form students into objects, examined from a vantage point outside of students. Even the newly emerging discourse around 'learning and teaching' – including the 'scholarship of teaching and learning' – often falls surprisingly short in this respect. Much is offered about teaching approaches and its effect on student learning, but rather less is offered to us about students as such. Even then, when the term does come into view, it is the plural form 'students' that we tend to see. If it is not students *en masse* to which our attention is being drawn, it is students *en bloc*, in this subject or on that course with their collective levels of 'satisfaction'. Of the individual student with his or her own challenges and struggles, we gain little sense.

Certainly, there have been large efforts across the world – especially in Europe, Australia and the Pacific Rim – to inquire into students' orientations to their learning, principally through the research approach known as phenomenography (Marton *et al.* 1997; Prosser and Trigwell 1999). That that framework and research programme has yielded helpful insights can hardly be denied – for example, that an individual student's approach to her own learning is not solely a personal or psychological matter, but is a relational matter influenced by the (teaching and assessment) context in which she finds herself. A student on a modular or combined course may be determined to get to the bottom of things in one subject (a 'deep' learning approach), but in another subject may just find herself skimming over the ground, memorizing key points and facts (a 'surface' approach). However, if I may be forgiven for the observation, that research programme has largely left unasked and unexplored matters as to what it is to *be* a student.[6]

I want to make one other point about this text, a point about gender. I am insistent on talking not of 'students', but of 'the student'. Since there is no gender-neutral pronoun in English that is appropriate here, and since I am loath to use such constructions as 'his/her' or 's/he' or even 'they' or 'their' (which is now coming into use, even where the subject is singular), I am obliged to use simply 'she' or 'he'. I use both pronouns more or less interchangeably (though I make more use of 'she' than 'he'). It will be clear, I hope, than in resorting to this formulation, I have no particular student in mind; it is a linguistic device to refer to students as individuals.

An ontological turn

If, then, we are seriously concerned with students, a suitable vocabulary and a suitable line of inquiry have to embrace matters of 'being', 'self', 'will' and 'becoming'. How can these matters be avoided? If we are to tackle them, we are bound to embark on a philosophical journey, strictly, on an ontological journey, in which matters of student being are brought into view and engaged with.

This book, therefore, grows in part from my sense that we are urgently in need of an ontological turn in our thinking about higher education and, by extension, in our research into higher education. Matters of what it is to be a student, of the kinds of human being that tutors might be looking to nurture, and of the pedagogic possibilities and even responsibilities. These are some of the considerations before us.

Even though these matters and this way of trying to understand higher education have seldom been evident, they have a certain timeless quality to them. Whenever there will be institutions of higher education with tutors and students, matters of being are in front of us. However, these matters take on a particular resonance in an age of turbulence and uncertainty. For an age of turbulence and uncertainty itself imposes questions and challenges of being. The doctor, the nurse, the accountant, the politician, the professor, and, therefore, the student – not only does each have a right, but also a responsibility to ask the question 'Who am I?' Each of these concepts – of doctor, nurse, accountant and so on – change over time; but, in an age of instability, they are rendered intractably open. To ask the question permits of no clear answer, and any kind of answer can only be forthcoming with the insertion of values and hopes.

The student is doubly implicated in all of this. On the one hand, amid massive changes in higher education worldwide – the neo-liberal turn and the marketization of higher education *and* the repositioning of higher education for the learning economy – what it is to be a student is broken open. A market relationship with the student's host institution jostles with and even threatens to crowd out the pedagogical relationship. At the same time, *higher education as performance* comes to demand the student's attention ahead of higher education as a form of critical reflection (the agenda of 'skills' supercedes that of 'knowledge'). However, while these changes bring their uncertainties as to what it is to be a student so, too, are there uncertainties facing students in the wider society, indeed, in the wider world. So the being of the student is placed in question at two levels: the immediate being of the student and the student's being-to-be in the future.

These two dimensions of being – here-and-now and being-in-the-future – are not really distinct for the student's being-in-the-future enters into her being here-and-now. As Heidegger drew out in his (1998) monumental opus, *Being and Time*, being is in time and anticipates the future. This dimension of being is not just (!) a metaphysical aspect of the contemporary student's being; is not just a matter of alluding to an ultimate reality. Rather, a concern for *students' time* has also now become virtually a practical necessity. Most courses of study are now, to some degree, a preparation for the student's future, especially her economic future, whether for a particular occupation or for the world of work more generally. The student straddles time zones on the Internet, and grapples with assignments and timetables that have their own pacings. The student is in time and even lives in multiple horizons of time.

So the matter of being presses in upon us as we consider what it is to be a student. It presses upon us, too, as we consider the pedagogical responsibilities that befall tutors and lecturers, and others concerned with the student's development. The ontological turn not just beckons and invites, but sucks us in and compels our attention.

Journey

This book will be a mutual journey – for myself and for the reader. As we start this journey, we cannot be sure exactly what is in front of us, what we might encounter. The main stages of our journey are the following:

In Part One, we will explore matters of the student's being and becoming: how can we understand these ideas? Other large issues – of will and authenticity – will come into view. The primary term, indeed, is that of *will* and the key point I want to establish is that a student's engagement with her course of study depends on her will.

In Part Two, we shall explore matters of learning, of student development, and here, issues of voice and disposition will occupy our attention. What kind of journey does the student embark on? What changes are there before our student? What forms of human being is it that the student might come into? There is much concern these days about students using and passing off texts produced by others as their own. (They might be texts already existing or may be texts specially prepared by private 'for profit' companies.) What forms of student being are we looking for where such actions would be repudiated by students? Here, I shall suggest that such a student is one who has a will-to-offer, a will to proffer her own work. Such a will requires energy, a willingness to risk, and such a will requires human qualities – such as courage and resilience – and dispositions – such as those of care and authenticity. We shall, therefore, need to explore the qualities and dispositions that must accompany a will to learn.

In Part Three, we shall consider what it is to teach, if we consider that a part – perhaps the main part – of teaching is that of nurturing in the student a will to learn. Students like to say sometimes that they were inspired, but in using such a term, they normally have in mind their being inspired by a particular teacher or teachers. How do we understand this notion of inspiration? Is it bound to be only a rare phenomenon or might it even be ubiquitous in higher education? What *is* an effective relationship between teacher and taught? What are the responsibilities that befall the tutor guided by a concern to nurture the student's will?

This is a single voyage, but the different stages may be essayed by the reader in any order. Some may like to get their conceptual bearings at the start and so begin with Part One. Others will have a concern for the student and will want to engage with those central issues of student will, and student being; and so will want to start with Part Two. Yet others will be interested in the challenges on teachers and teaching in higher education, and will, therefore, want to join the voyage at Part Three. I shall conclude by offering solutions to our two opening puzzles and share some wider reflections on the possibilities for student becoming.

Part 1

Being and becoming

1

Where there's a will

What continues to fuel me? I don't know.

(4th year medical student.)

The will is the substance of man, the intellect the accident.
(Arthur Schopenhauer, *The World as Will and Idea*, p. 87.)

Introduction

'Will' is the most important concept in education. Without a will, nothing is possible. At any level of education, a pupil, a student cannot make serious progress unless she has a will to do so. Unless she has a will, a will to learn, she cannot carry herself forward, cannot press herself forward, cannot come successfully into new pedagogical situations.

As I observe, this is so at any level of education, but it is the case especially in higher education and for two reasons. First, students are adults; they are *there*, at least to a significant degree, through their own volition. They are students out of their own wittingness (as Richard Peters put it). They are there, as students, through their own will. Their presence is not formally required, whatever the tacit expectations in their own milieu might be.

Secondly, they are embarked on a major personal project of their own. We noted this phenomenon in the Introduction, for such it surely is that individuals should be prepared to give themselves up to a personal project of several years' duration. Whether they be younger or more 'mature' students, it is still an extraordinary matter. We shall unravel some of the structure of this phenomenon in the inquiry ahead of us, but we may here observe a couple of its features.

In the first place, embarking seriously on such a personal project involves a seeing into the future and some way into the future at that. Perhaps a better way of putting the point is to say that it involves the student seeing herself in a time horizon (of typically three or more years). Sometimes, a student may not survive to complete her course, either as a result of an accident or illness, and so university regulations often allow for an aegrotat degree, when a student is deemed to have merited a degree for the effort and achievements that fell just short of the final hurdle. Even more rarely still, a relative or partner may collect posthumously the full degree at the award ceremony. Here, the collecting of the degree is a mark of the effort expended by the deceased student *over time*, as much as it is testimony to the quality of the student's work. The duration of time is significant, therefore, in being a student.

In the second place, it involves a commitment on the part of the student. This commitment, we may in turn observe, is a commitment by the student to herself and of herself; that is, there is a double commitment at work.

On the one hand, the student commits herself to her studies over a protracted period of time; here, the object of the commitment is the activity of studying. The student is committing herself to making the time to study. The studying is a kind of object beyond the student. This is a *practical commitment*. On the other hand, the student also commits herself to herself. She promises to herself that she will give herself up to the challenges ahead of her. She displaces herself into the mode of being of being a student. This is, to put it formally, an *ontological commitment*: the student wills herself to accept the discipline that her studies will bring.

All this is a matter of will. It is a matter of the student having a will to learn, and that will being sustained over time. The moment that will drops, so will the student's likelihood of success on the course drop. It may wither altogether. At this point, the likelihood of the student leaving her course is surely likely to rise. Non-completion is an indication – in part, at least – of a lack of will.

Will and motivation

It will be noticed that I have not used the term 'motivation' so far or its associates, such as 'motive' or 'motivated'. This is deliberate. 'Will' and 'motivation' are entirely different concepts.

A motive, as Richard Peters (1969) made clear some time ago, is a reason of a kind for doing something towards an end. A motive is essentially rational. I run from the tiger because I am afraid. My motive in so doing is to avoid being eaten by the tiger. I believe that if the tiger catches me, things will not go well. Accordingly, I flee the scene, and I have reason to do so. The reason may be misplaced: I may have mistaken an antelope for the tiger, but I have a reason both for my fear and my hurried exit from the scene. I may – and, in this case, most certainly will – *feel* something. Here, I feel fear. I am in an emotional state of fear, but, again, the emotion stems from a rational judgement.

Furthermore, there is an object both of the emotional state and of the motive (of avoiding being eaten). The object – the tiger – stands separately from the emotion and the motive. There is an externality about this motivational state. Even if the object is internal to myself – I eat because I am hungry – it has an externality of sorts; the motive leads me on to a particular act and an end beyond myself.

For our story, motives cannot be far away. Students study for all kinds of motive: to gain a good job, to be close to a girl or boyfriend, to please a set of parents, to widen their skills and knowledge. Motives, therefore, are inevitably present, and loudly so, in higher education; but motives will not be at the centre of our story.

What is at the centre of our story is will. Why do we get up in the morning? Not because we have lots of knowledge or skills (to pick on the two main contemporary components in the educational rhetoric); we get up, we take on the world in all its craziness, because we have a will to do so.[1]

The structure of will is utterly different from that of motive. Whereas – as we have just observed – a motive calls on the intellect to furnish a reason for action, the will is non-rational. To a significant degree, the will is independent of reason. This does not mean that it is irrational; it may be in particular circumstances, but that is not its general structure. Will is simply not a phenomenon that can be caught by concepts of reason or intellect. Will works in a plane of being, separate from reason or intellect.[2] As Schopenhauer observed:

> . . . the intellect is so alien to the will that it is sometimes mystified by it.
> (Schopenhauer 1997: 94)

Not uncommonly, when someone has cancer and seems to us to be continuing to be involved in life, we may say 'she has a will to live'. We might also say that 'she has a motive to live', but then we would be saying something different. We might have in mind, for instance, that the person in question wanted to live in order to be present at the forthcoming marriage of a daughter or to run a marathon. This would be a specific reason for living that furnishes the person's motivation, but, to return to our earlier construction, if we say that 'she has a will to live', we are depicting something more general in character. We are saying something about the person as such, about her state of being, her hold on the world, her way of relating to the world.

Differences between will and motive, therefore, are emerging. Generalizations are notoriously difficult with such diffuse concepts, but we are already seeing that, whereas motivation is specific in character, will has a more general character. Whereas motive refers to an object or an interest that is external to the person, will is fundamentally interior to the person. Indeed, without will, we have no person before us; the same cannot be said of motive.

This interior–exterior distinction opens up another difference. A motive is instrumental in character. Of a motive, we can ask: Is she taking the right steps to fulfil her motive? Is she finding the best way of financing her degree studies that she wishes to undertake? Motive has a means–end character. A motive is an end, a purpose, a goal; however, it is embedded in an emotional state, and that emotional state may both help to energize the person towards her goal, but it may also cloud her judgement about the best means to achieving that goal. Will, in contrast, is not so specific. Certainly, as we shall see in this study, *will* may carry with it both orientation and disposition: a student's will to study may be associated with her interest in medicine. The will orientates and disposes a person in some way; it is not totally aimless, but it lacks the specificity of motivation.

Why is this? How do we explain this relative lack of specificity? An answer lies as follows. A motive, as we have seen, stands in a sense outside of a person: it pulls a person forward, towards some end. Will, on the other hand, as we have also seen, is internal. It comes from within. Will is the state of the person's being. It provides internal energy; spirit even. In some way, it is what is invoked when a student says of a teacher that 'he (or she) has inspired me'. (We must return later to the specific matter of inspiration.) Will propels the student forward.

If a motive is a pull, the will is a push. That formulation, however, is over-simple. It implies a symmetry between the two, between will and motivation. It suggests that the two are different, but equal. Such a conception is wrong and dangerously so. Motivation is not unimportant in education, but it is the will that is paramount, especially in higher education. Motives may be ephemeral, whereas the will has an enduring character, which is not to say that it is everlasting or solid. To the contrary, that the will may change and may even dissolve will be an abiding theme of our inquiries here.

Will is, to repeat, a matter of being, a matter of a person's hold on the world. Is this student engaging with her experiences? Is she putting herself into them such that she is opening up new experiences for herself? Is she energized? Is she carried forward in some way? Is she pressing on, regardless of the challenges and even disappointments that she faces? Does she really have a will to learn?

Will, we must say and not shirk from saying it, is ontological through and through. Without will, the idea of person cannot get off the ground. Without will, too, the idea of a student cannot seriously have meaning. A student is someone who gives something of herself, who throws herself into her studies. Underlying the famous 'deep'/'surface' distinction that has been the fulcrum of much international study of the student experience over the past 30 years (Marton *et al.* 1997) is surely the following sense (even if it hasn't been recognized as such by the adherents of that distinction): that a 'deep' orientation towards her studies is a personal stance on the part of the student in which she invests something of herself *as a person*; in a 'surface' orientation, by contrast, the student lacks such a will and subjects herself passively to her experiences. That is, underlying the apparently cognitive level on which the 'deep'/'surface' distinction works, is an ontological substratum. What is fundamentally at issue is whether or not the student is projecting herself into her studies, and whether she is taking an active stance in her experiences.

The idea of will, therefore, bears in on the student as a person.[3] It betokens that the student is alive as a student; its presence is a sign of student life. It indicates that a student is committed, is energized, is giving of herself in a firsthand way. It indicates much more, too; for example, as to matters of responsibility and other virtues that we must come onto. Where the will is present, everything is possible. Where it is absent, nothing, educationally speaking, is possible.

Will and energy

Will is intimately linked to energy, but it is not reducible to energy. Through will, a person is also orientated towards the future. Her being is in time. Only in this way can we explain the phenomenon – that will remain before us in these inquiries – of a student embarking on a course of study that may last three, or four or five or even more years (a course of study in architecture or medicine or engineering, say, or a part-time research degree study). Such a student projects herself forward in time, is willing to embark on such a long-term commitment, wills herself to do so.

The will, therefore, is a mode of being in the world. Through the will, one has a care (to use a term of Heidegger's) for something or other. It may be simply life itself – as with our earlier cancer patient – or, as a student, it may be a care for human health or for imaginative building design.

Characteristically, this will imparts energy, but it is not energy itself. Without will, there can be no energy; it is a necessary condition of energy, but it is not a sufficient condition. I may have a will that leads me to write this book, but I may have no energy to do so – at least, on a particular day. I may just be tired or the will may not be particularly strong. All manner of physical or psychological conditions may come into play that affect how the will may play itself out at a particular moment in time.

However, the will is the fundament of the necessary level of energy; the level, that is to say, associated with the student carrying herself successfully through her studies over a long period of time.

For Schopenhauer, will was an element in the universe:

. . . every force in nature should be thought of as will. (1997: 43)

It was in life – or, indeed, anything that had a life, even constituents of the natural world. We have just glimpsed how that might be so. Will is a mode of being in the world, it is teleological, bringing the future into itself. However, this metaphysical idea of Schopenhauer's – of will being a constituent of the natural world – goes beyond the idea than we require for our purposes here.[4]

With will, I want to say, is to be found energy of an especially human kind. However, we may depict energy in the animal and even the inanimate worlds, in human beings, energy takes on a purposive character. Through her will, the student is orientated towards the future and embarks on some large projects. She may even be looking beyond her degree to her life beyond, and may be forming a sense of some major life projects and her degree forming part of a pattern of such projects. She engages with the present, but holds herself in readiness for what the future may bring her. She is energized, if not to take on the world – though she may be! – then to commit herself to her studies and to all the experiences that go with them.

The will imparts a steady energy; it is not easily dissipated. Tutors may tacitly sense this, and become careless and unfeeling with comments in the classroom setting; they assume that their comments cannot have lasting effects. This may be the case, but this is a contingent matter. Depending on the character of the pedagogical relationship that has been established, the odd careless word can have a lasting effect. How many of us can remember specific words spoken about us by an unfeeling teacher, whether at school or university, even decades ago? However, for all that, the will, once established, will not be easily dissolved. Indeed, where it is firmly in place, the odd unfeeling comment, while initially damaging, may even be a spur to press on, to succeed 'in spite of' a set of impoverished student experiences.

Visiting parties engaged in national evaluations in higher education have not infrequently been able to put aside concerns about a programme of study during the meeting with a group of the students: the students were succeeding virtually in spite of the teaching staff, partly because the students were willing each other on. The students each had a will to succeed, separate from and despite the immediate quality of their presenting experiences.

Losing the will to learn

Interviewer: *The modules that you have failed . . . do you think anybody could have done anything to help you?*
Student (having withdrawn from the course): *No, it was me. I just lost interest. I believed it wasn't for me and I didn't want to do it.*
(Quinn et al. 2006, RAB's emphasis)

The will is the foundation of educational energy. It brings a sense of the future, and a purpose in that time horizon. Through her will, the student is propelled forward, and is given the courage to engage with the unknown (for, no matter how well planned are her curricula, there are bound – at the level of higher education – to be major elements of unpredictability). The will supplies a steadiness that sustains the student over time, amid its vicissitudes.

How do we account for the steadiness that the will helps to impart? I suggest that the steadiness can be accounted for through the will being a constituent of the student's identity. Not unusually, a student may sense, very soon after embarking on a programme of study, that it isn't for her and, instead, at the same time, wants to opt for a completely different programme: the student on the theology course turns to sociology or even the other way around. We can say that the student has lost the will to proceed with her first choice and has even found a new will, but we could also say that the student has come to a new sense of herself, of how she understands herself, of how she wants to be in the world. She has come to 'comport' herself differently (to use a term of Heidegger's).

So the will and the energy that flows from the will are liable to be of some durability, but the will is, as we have just noticed, not immutable.[5] The will can dissolve, as Emmanuel Levinas observed:

> In affirming that the human will is not heroic we have not declared for human cowardice, but have indicated the precarity of courage, always on the verge of its own failure by reason of the essential mortality of the will.
>
> (Levinas, 2005: 236–7)

Here, we arrive at a matter of the profoundest importance for higher education. If it is the foundation of what it is to be a student and if it can dissolve, then we have to ask:

- What are the responsibilities of tutors as individuals and of universities as institutions towards the nurturing of this will?
- What might they do – whether as individuals or as institutions – to develop and to nurture this will?
- How, in turn, can that will be turned into positive energies?

Will and intellect

For Schopenhauer, in understanding the world:

> ... the difference between the will and the intellect [can be understood as] ... the primacy of the former and the subordinate position of the latter ...
>
> (Schopenhauer 1997: 94)

If this is right, and I believe it is, it surely heralds a revolution in how we understand higher education. For historically, the project of the western university has evolved as one around knowledge. Old-style endorsers of this project saw, indeed, the university as a bastion of 'the aristocracy of the intellect'. Certainly, that depiction of the university has received a battering of late and from various directions. Separately, but contemporaneously, the university has been told by the wider society that to the dimension of knowledge, it should add that of 'skills' (NCIHE 1997). Some philosophers have critiqued the idea of objective knowledge, suggesting it reeked too much of modernist universal claims that could no longer be seriously sustained and that we should instead content ourselves with 'conversation' (Rorty 1980). Social theorists have declared that the university's functioning as a site of national culture has been undermined by a homogenizing discourse of 'quality' and 'excellence' (Readings 1997). Lastly, modernizers have urged that the university's definitions of knowledge were so narrow that they were being superceded by a new practical form of knowledge [so-called 'Mode 2' knowledge (Gibbons *et al.* 1994)].

All of these critiques have some merit on their sides and they are self-evidently different, but taken together, they have a peculiar effect in that they leave the student vulnerable to a performative slide. It is not that they are not radical: on the contrary, their collective force is absolutely radical, but it is a radical agenda that undermines higher education as an *educational* project.

These ideas often spring from big battalions. They will not be easily put asunder. Instead, we need to see if there is a large idea available to us that just might presage an oppositional force in its train. Schopenhauer's idea, that the will is primary and the intellect is secondary is, surely, just such a radical idea. If Schopenhauer is right, we need to rethink utterly what we take higher education to be. No longer can we construe it as a mainly epistemological project, even if we supplement it as a practical project in which we explicitly embrace an agenda of skills. Following Schopenhauer's lead, we have, instead, to put the will *first*. It is worth emphasizing that point – not merely that it should be placed alongside the projects of knowledge and skills, but that it should be placed before them. *Primacy should be given to the will*: if we have the will of the student, then we have much. If we do not have the will of the student, we have nothing.[6]

How can this be? That the will should occupy such a commanding position in our educational thinking, especially in the university? Can this really be right?

We have already touched on two of the considerations that must lead to this view: that the will helps to impart a propulsion towards the world; and that the will enables a student to embark on a large and enduring project such as is constituted by a programme of studies in higher education. These are, it might be admitted – or alleged, depending on one's taste – to be metaphysical points, but there are more educational considerations to hand.

Will and commitment – or the devil's advocate

In higher education, ultimately, even in group projects, an individual student has to give something of herself. This giving of oneself itself has two components. First, the student has to involve herself with or engage in the project in question. There has to be some degree of personal identification with the task in hand. Of course, empirically, this does not always happen: students fail to become involved, but then, in turn, just such a lack of involvement is likely to lead to disenchantment or even to the student's withdrawing from the course. To acknowledge any of this is tacitly to accept that the matter of engagement is the default position: if we are in the presence of a genuine higher education, then a measure of personal identification has to be present. A condition of such personal identification with the students' learning challenges is that of voluntariness on the part of each student, which is a particular feature of higher education.

Secondly, the giving of oneself involves – as we have already seen – a commitment on the part of the student. The student signs up to what she has said or done: she is accountable for it. It is hers and no one else's. Again, this does not always happen. These days, in mass higher education, there is more pressure on students to acquire good degrees, which can then be used – so it is hoped – for subsequent enhanced life chances. The so-called commodification of higher education leads inexorably to students seeing their higher education in instrumental terms.[7] Under such conditions, it is hardly surprising if students resort to paying private companies to produce their essays or incorporate without attribution chunks of material downloaded from the Internet. Clearly, here, there can be no personal investment of the student in her work. So, again, the default position has to be that the university is a pedagogical space in which students commit themselves to their work.

This point about commitment is particularly important to our immediate inquiries, and will remain as a theme in these inquiries. In making a knowledge claim, a student forms an identity between the claim and herself. She wills herself into her claim. The claim is hers. Even if the claim has been made thousands of times before, by other students, in other universities, on other courses, still the claim is hers. She not merely identifies with the claim; the claim has its particular status precisely because it carries with it this student's identity. She not merely states it, but *believes* in it; the claim is hers.

By itself, if it could hang in a metaphysical space, it would be nothing. The claim has arisen out of a particular pedagogical situation, involving this particular student. Even if many other students in this student's cohort are making the same claim, still this claim, in this essay, in this classroom, in this studio, is this student's. The claim carries force, so far as the student's educational development is concerned, in direct proportion to the student being committed to it.

Is this possible, that the idea of commitment can or should be expected to bear so much weight? After all, suppose our student has been reading Feyerabend and wants to stir things up intellectually; or has encountered even some post-modernist writers of a so-called ludic persuasion, and simply decides to have some fun; or has imbued a penchant for the critical spirit, perhaps as a result of a casual encounter with critical theory. In any of these cases, the student may put something into the pot simply to generate a response: this particular student may be keen on academic debate and wants to do her bit to help matters along.

It may be said that, here, in any of the possible cases so identified, our student is precisely *not* committed to her utterance: far from being committed, the student is engaged in a form of insincerity and the insincerity is *intended*. The student is acting out a social role of make believe, in which she is distant from her utterances. Each of the examples, to use a shorthand, is the devil's advocate in operation: the student is advancing a case in which she precisely does not believe. 'Commitment', it would appear here, cannot be a necessary condition either for a genuine higher education to be present or for the student's development to be possible.

There are two points to make here. First, the examples gain their weight on the basis of committed utterances being the norm. The role of the devil's advocate only makes sense providing that most of the other participants in the discussion are playing things straight and can be relied upon to mean what they say. Debate would break down immediately if everyone tried to act the role of devil's advocate. Secondly, the role of the devil's advocate is a highly sophisticated and demanding role. It implies that the devil's advocate can distinguish truth from falsehood *and* sincerity from insincerity. The person who can play to good effect the role of the devil's advocate has an acute sense of what it is to be committed to one's claims.

The devils' advocate example, far from undermining our general thesis, supports it. The case that I am urging is that the will is primary; all other aims and concerns in higher education are secondary. If it is to be effective, the devil's advocate role itself depends on the student's will: the student has to throw herself into the role, has to take it on wholeheartedly, so as to be convincing. Even if she precedes her interventions with cautions, such as 'let's put another point of view and see what happens' or 'I wonder what we happen if we did such and such', still the offering has to be put so as to command plausibility: the student has to play the part. However, this is to say that the student's will has to be present, in order that the necessary energy and commitment to playing the role can also be present. No will, no commitment, even to a devil's advocate role.

The fragility of will

For the most part, in higher education, we take will for granted. We assume that students will attend on the set days at the appointed times, will engage with their studies, will listen intently to their lecturers, and will participate in the group tasks that are set. The student's will is assumed to be present: the students, after all, can be seen moving around, often in quite animated ways. They may even be observed to be engaging with all manner of tasks at once, some that are part of the formal curriculum and others – using the mobile phone during a lecture to pass each other text messages about their thoughts on the lecturer – that are not. Their will is evident; they could not be so engaged, on all sorts of levels, if their will were not present.

In any event, students are adults and are participating on their programmes of study voluntarily: their will towards their learning can hardly be questioned, surely. Since their will can be assumed, their lecturers and tutors can concentrate on other things, on imparting knowledge and frameworks of understanding, on helping students to acquire skills and on preparing for the examinations to come.

This taken-for-grantedness character of the student's will bedevils higher education. It is surely part of the explanation of student non-completion across the world. That the concept of will is pretty well entirely absent from the literature on higher education is testimony to this taken-for-granted status of the will. No one gives it any thought, however, it is the supreme element in higher education.

Let us be charitable. Let us assume that this taken-for-grantedness is not so much a sign that lecturers and tutors are either unaware of its importance or indifferent to it; let us – in this spirit of magnanimity – make the further assumptions that lecturers and tutors are alert to the presence and the significance of the student's will in relation to their participation in their programme of study. In that case, two options are before us to explain tutors' diffidence in the student's will entering into the tutor's own educational thinking and practices.

The first option is that they consider that the will, while significant, is not a matter for the educator: the tutor is here drawing a tight boundary around his responsibilities and determining that he has no responsibility towards nurturing the student's will. Students, after all are adults: surely, their will is their own affair. Lecturers have enough on their hands worrying about the development of the student's knowledge and skills, and perhaps even some of her attitudes as well. But her will? That must lie with the student. The tutor can only come into play if the student has brought herself to the start line; then the tutor can help the student round the course. The will – that brings the student to the start line – is not and should not be a matter over which the tutor should concern himself.

The second option is that the tutor considers that the will can be taken for granted because the will is always present. If the student is alive, then the student's will is present. There is a durability to will such that it can reasonably be taken-for-granted.

We may address these two options more or less together, and begin with the second one. The second option is taken-for-grantedness in full flight. It assumes that the will is always present. Some lecturers may believe that their students will always be with them and, with those presences, so will the students' *will* be always present. It can just be assumed to be present. However, this is an unwarranted assumption. It assumes a durability to will that cannot be justified. The will in general is pliable. It is liable to wane. The *student's* will – qua student – may dissolve. It may not always be present.

The second option – that the pedagogical will is always present – can, therefore, be set aside. If that is the case, the first option also falls by the wayside. If the will can wane and even dissolve, the prospect arises that tutors and lecturers may be said to have a responsibility towards nurturing the student's will and even towards enhancing it.

Conclusion

In this chapter, we have thrown out some opening salvoes along the following lines. As an idea in educational thinking, the idea of the will is pretty well nowhere to be found. This is a serious omission, for the will is fundamental to any serious construal of higher education. In saying that it is fundamental,

I want to put the will ahead of both knowledge and skills. Without the will, nothing will be learnt by the student and no claim will be made by that student that can be bear any weight. Correspondingly, without a will in place, no serious effort can be made to acquire a new skill or to exemplify itself once it has been acquired. The will is the foundation upon which all else rests in higher education.

This is a crucial matter, for the will is fragile. It is often taken-for-granted, assumed to be ever-present, but its apparent ever-presence is beguiling. If only tutors would look, they would see clues all around them as to the significance and to the mutability of will. As we have noted, students may say on graduation that 'the course has changed my life' or even that 'coming across so-and-so in the literature changed my life'. Students also often say in questionnaire surveys that they look to their tutors to be 'enthusiastic'; they may even say of a tutor that she has been 'inspiring'. All these are signs of the students' will being nurtured and enhanced. In these and other ways, students are saying that their will towards the course and their studies was given a boost. They came to care more about their studies; their will to learn was lifted.

We may summarize these opening reflections in the following way. For over a hundred years, until the middle of the twentieth century, for higher education, knowledge lay at the centre of its educational mission. As the twentieth century drew to a close, with the onset of rapid economic growth and change worldwide, higher education was urged to broaden its ambit to include a skills agenda. It was important that graduates not just knew things – no matter how deeply or broadly, or with what critical insight; it was also important (perhaps even more important) that students should be able to do things with some degree of competence; and preferably, those acts of doing should be transferable in the wider world. In short, and more formally, an epistemological project (of knowing and knowledge) has been or should be joined – some would even say overtaken – by a project of doing; of performance or action or practice or praxis or *phronesis* (the terminology one uses depends on one's own educational politics, and their similarities are more important than their differences).[8]

These two projects – epistemological and practical – are important, even in the twenty-first century. The 'even' is there because, in an age of change and uncertainty, it is debatable in any event how far the world can be known and how far actions can be identified that are going to be sure in their ethical basis and their likely outcomes. Even when nuanced and put together in some way, the two projects – of knowing and acting – have to be insufficient. What they leave out is the student as a person, especially her will and her being. Here, we have been concerned with the will. In short and maintaining our formal way of putting things, what we can say by way of a conclusion in our opening reflections is that both our practices *in* and our thinking *about* higher education are in urgent need of an ontological turn. To put it more straightforwardly, we are in desperate need of thinking and practices that take the student as a human being seriously. Let us, therefore, having just touched upon the student's being, turn precisely to the idea of being.

2
Being

Being has not been given its due.

(Sartre 2003b: 16)

... *Being-towards-possibilities* ... is itself a potentiality-for-Being. [It] has its own possibility – that of developing itself ...

(Heidegger 1998: 188)

Introduction

What is the being of the student? How do we understand this? This what? Is there another word, other than 'being' itself that will help us here? If there is, I do not know of it.

The being of the student is the way the student is in the world. In the first place, the student is a person in the world, and has her hold on the world as a person. However, the student is also a student. She is embarked on a course of study with its challenges, with its time sequences and with its situations. The student moves, and is amid these challenges, sequences and situations. She is embedded in all of this, but this student is not to be read off these educational moments – of challenges, sequences and situations. She brings her own wherewithal to bear on all of that.

A characteristic term to bring to bear here would be 'relational': the student stands in a relationship with her educational setting. Certainly, that way of putting the matter can be put more subtly, even in its own terms. It might be said that the student stands in sets of relationships with her educational settings and those relationships are dynamic, always on the move (Engestrom 1999) The student's sense of herself fluctuates, depending on whether she is just about to embark on an assignment or has completed it; on whether a tutor made complimentary remarks or her marks fell short of those she was expecting. The way in which she stands varies, from one course to another and, therefore, even from one time of the day to another.

Such an invocation of a relational account of the student in her educational settings has merit on its side, but it is also misleading. It sets off the student from her settings. It sets up the issue as to the relationship between the student and her educational settings. However, as Heidegger showed us, such an account is misguided. We do not properly understand the student as separate from her educational settings, even if related to her educational settings. Rather, we understand the student more properly as being *in* her educational settings. The question is: what is the nature of that being?

Being itself

In setting out his ideas on the matter, on the nature of being, Heidegger turned to the term '*Dasein*'. Strictly, *Dasein* does not mean being as such, but rather being-there. The term points to, picks up, as we may term it, the 'placedness' of being. Being is not just there, but is *in* there.[1] In being *in* an educational setting – walking down the corridor with her friends, carrying out a procedure in the laboratory, being put somewhat on the spot in a seminar – the student is there, in a particular place, being part of that place, at least, to the extent that she feels herself to be part of that place. However, as we began to note, the student is herself in any such place.

No-one can feel the student's feelings, however much, say, her friends may empathize with her (as she struggles with a problem-solving procedure in the chemistry lesson or wrestles with a statistical exercise in psychology), but even if complete empathy was possible, this student's feelings, her being, would be hers alone. Her being is hers, in each situation and it is unique. Her feelings, attitudes, worries, anxieties, hopes, understandings, priorities, values, capabilities and felt certainties, are all bound up in her being. Many of these carry over across all of her studies and so there is a continuity of being across her educational settings.

Coming into view are the beginnings of a sense as to the complexity of the student's being. It is both specific and general; both enduring and even fragile; both barely felt and fully conscious. We have already begun to touch on these three matters so let us take them quickly in turn.

Pedagogical being

The student is a human being, has being *as* a human being, with all the hopes, relationships, projects, joys and anxieties that are part of human being itself. However, the student is a student: she has being as a student. She is put into curricular settings and pedagogical relationships, and also puts herself into such settings and relationships. In higher education, those settings and relationships are coloured by their own locale, in particular disciplines and institutions. The student's being has forms of particularity about it, therefore. The student has being as a *student*, as well as a human being more broadly.

The student's being as a human being and as a student are not, of course, separate from each other: each infuses the other. The student as a human being takes up stances towards her studies, her pedagogical relationships and the other students. Is she characteristically a lively person or hesitant? Is she normally optimistic about how things might go or she is anxious? Her temperament will dispose her in certain ways towards her studies, but her studies, their characteristic pedagogical relationships, the openness and the challenge in their curricula, and the social codes within her institution, will encourage forward certain modes of being. For students on modular courses, those modes of being may differ from one disciplinary setting to another. There are interplays between the student as a human being and as a pedagogical being (as we might put it). In other words, there is both generality and particularity that help to fill out the student's being at any one time.

Fragility

This *being* – to turn to our second aspect of a moment ago and as we noted in the first chapter – is enduring and fragile all at once. Characteristically, in most parts of the world, students keep going on their courses. They are associated with their courses. They have their being, to a greater or lesser extent, in their courses. There is an enduring character, not only to their larger being, but to their pedagogical being. However, the apparent continuity of a student's being is deceptive. A student may hear that a beloved grandparent has died, or even a parent, or the student may contract a serious disease or suffer an accident that confines her to a wheelchair. An event such as that may cause her to come into a new relationship with her life, with her own mortality. Such reflections may cause her to see her studies in a new light: she may form a new set of goals and even leave her studies or she may renew her efforts on her course, becoming absolutely determined to succeed. Here, we see not only that her human being and her pedagogical being are bound up with each other (our previous point), but we glimpse, too, the fragility of her being.

However, the pedagogical being has a position of its own. A word insensitively written in the margin of an essay – perhaps 'nonsense' – may cut deeply into a student's being such that that one word may shatter her educational sense of herself. The pedagogical being is fragile.[2] It may appear to be relatively robust, but it is brittle, liable to shatter suddenly.

How may we account for such brittleness? The student's being is susceptible to shades, to being embedded to a lesser or a more pronounced degree; that is to say, it permits of degrees of firmness. Yet, it also bears this brittle quality, such that it may vanish entirely and at an instant. Suddenly, the student may just not show up for her classes, having been a regular attender. Are we simply to ascribe such transformations in the student's pedagogical being to some kind of psychological weakness – perhaps a temperamental flaw? That may be the case, of course; but I do not think that that should be our first port of call.

Being goes all the way down; it structures human beings and places them in relationships with the world, and so it is liable to have an enduring character, carrying a student, say, across the duration of her programme. However, precisely because it reaches in and out, precisely because the student is her being and is in her being, that being is liable to shatter if it stressed at its most vulnerable point. That single word in the margin of an essay or a word casually uttered in a classroom by a tutor – 'nonsense' – may have just such a shattering effect precisely because it reaches into the fulcrum of the student's being. This is not just psychology at work; there is both a logical and an ontological aspect to this process. The student is affected by a word such as 'nonsense' because it affects her pedagogical being in higher education.

A pedagogical being in higher education rests on such moments as integrity, truthfulness and sincerity. [The pedagogical being has to heed something approaching Habermas' (1979, 1991) validity claims.] A term such as 'nonsense', therefore, *has* to affect the student's being for her pedagogical being is constructed around senses and feelings, which implicate making sense, rather than forming nonsense. That the student loses interest in a course through an experience of such a careless utterance coming her way is entirely explicable, even if it is 'the straw that breaks the camel's back', riding on the back of other negative experiences. The logic of the situation cuts deeply into the student's being: there is a logic to this ontology.

Explicitness

This takes us nicely to the third aspect of the student's pedagogical being that we identified earlier, that between tacit and fully conscious being. Here we may resort to a (1998/62) distinction of Heidegger's, that between that which is 'ready-to-hand' and 'present-at-hand'. The 'ready-to-hand' are those entities in the world that are there, in, say, the student's world, of which she is barely aware. The experienced student, in, say, the second year of a science course, will be familiar with most of the instruments in the laboratory and will take them for granted; they will not form as definite objects as she makes her way around the laboratory. Her thoughts, instead, will be on her immediate project, and its procedures. The present-at-hand, in contrast, is that dimension which is much more explicitly present to the mind. Our student here, for example, will have certain formulae to mind in carrying out the particular procedures, or certain indications on the instrumentation. These entities are now present-at-hand. Clearly, there are processes at work of transference between the two domains: the student may become aware that an instrument is not performing as it is expected to perform and so what is in the pre-conscious may be raised to the explicitly conscious as the student investigates the problem.[3]

We see here how the student's pedagogical being works at once at the levels both of the tacit and the fully aware, of the ready-to-hand and the present-at-hand. Higher education, we might say, is precisely a process in which the ready-to-hand is raised into the present-at-hand. At least, the ready-to-hand is put under perpetual surveillance, is called to account, is put on notice that it may have to declare itself and place itself under critical examination, and so be called into the 'present-at-hand'. This, after all, is what is surely implied by the idea of criticality: that the student's presuppositions are liable to be put on trial; that, ultimately, no personal belief can be taken-for-granted. Every belief is liable to put on trial.

We are reminded here of the Greek idea that the process of knowing lay in bringing forth what was already intuitively known. This pedagogic process (set out especially in Plato's *Meno*) was termed 'maieutic' (from the Greek, *maeivtikos*, meaning midwifery; Rowland 2005). Knowing cannot be stamped in or assimilated from without: it has to come from within.[4] Can we make sense of this idea, amid mass higher education, and the sheer technicality of many disciplines and courses in higher education? We do not have to call in aid of such a reflection those courses – such as those in medicine or civil engineering or even accountancy – that are linked to life threatening situations: each course has its own disciplines and challenges that the student has to give himself to. Many of those experiences will be entirely new; so how might the ideas of the ready-to-hand (as distinct from the present-at-hand), of presuppositions and of pre-conscious knowing, have any purchase?

They gain their purchase because they remind us that knowing is a process in which the student's being is brought into new relationships with the world. Through knowing, the student comes to stand in new relationships to the world. Her hold on the world is changed. Richard Peters (1970) used to talk of a changed 'cognitive perspective', but it is not just a changed cognitive perspective that is involved. Through knowing, a student comes to stand anew in the world. Epistemological processes call forth ontological processes. The student is changed in her pedagogical being. She feels herself to be in a new place.

But these ideas only make sense – if they do – in virtue of the student being involved in her own knowing. The forming of an utterance, of a practical act of knowing or a textual proposition, is the framing of ideas, sentiments and murmurings that lay within. The forming of the paragraph is a dredging up and a creative ordering of inner movements in the student's being. This is a necessarily creative act: even if the substance of the paragraph has been evinced by others before, still this is a creative act in its own right. No one will have formed a paragraph exactly like this before: it will be original and the resources for that act of creativity lie within the student. Even if the student is drawing on existing data or scholarly resources, still the orderings, the analysis, the commentary, will be the student's. The framing of a paragraph has to come from within the student. It is a struggle – in which sentiments and murmurings are turned into textual utterances – that may bear some scrutiny.

Newman spoke of 'the bodily pain' that writing caused him. The process of writing is liable to produce discomfort precisely through its requiring this scouring of half-felt sentiments and murmurings as they are turned into sequences of sentences that are coherent, and stand scrutiny by the standards of the student's discipline or professional field. The transforming of the ready-to-hand into the present-at-hand is likely to be a painful process.[5]

The student's thought is always an afterthought – an afterthought to the presentiments that impress themselves in response to the student's curricular experiences. Her ideas are felt, are embodied. The ideas are a conscious formulation of feelings, of discomforts. We might call these discomforts 'cognitive discomforts', but that merely underlines the emotional side of thinking. To talk of 'emotions' here mistakes the way in which being comes into play in the formation of ideas. Given that the student is in a particularly formative stage of the forming of authentically held ideas, the student's being is implicated through and through. Consequently, discomfort is a necessary part of a genuine student experience.[6]

It is hardly surprising, then, if students struggle to keep up with their curricula timetables, especially if – as in modular courses – they are having on a fairly continuous basis to produce work for assessment. Not only do they have to contend with the anxiety that accompanies assessment, but they have the discomfort of the process of producing writing that makes propositional claims from within their own resources; from within their own being. No wonder, in this process of rendering half-felt presentiments within into explicit and public sets of ideas ('arguments'), that being a student – the being of the student – is fraught with anxiety.

Anxiety

Being a student is to be in a state of anxiety. In the first place, the student is to be examined and on the outcome of those examinations stand life chances. This is a matter of importance to most students. Empirically, it is clear that students' readings of the assessment regime shape the way in which they approach their studies. If they sense that the forms of assessment are calling for factual knowledge or for descriptive accounts of situations, then students will mirror those perceptions in their knowing accomplishments: their learning, too, in other words, will be more a matter of assimilating items of knowledge for subsequent recall. They will exemplify Freire's (1978) 'banking' idea of learning, in which learning is a matter of banking in a deposit so many items, which may then be brought out into the light.

This concern with the nature of the assessment processes to which they are subject is apparent in students' often insistence on transparency. The criteria by which they are to be assessed may be explicitly set out in their course handbook – even in neat bullet points – but still they may press with their question: 'but what are the real criteria by which we are to be assessed?' The transparency is mistrusted: surely, there is a hidden set of criteria that is in use and could be declared? Such mistrust, we may surmise, arises in a context of student anxiety. Their anxiety is not easily dissolved. Efforts to dissolve it – the neat bullet points – are met with scepticism. The students' anxiety has taken a deep hold.

There is, then, anxiety rooted in the assessment regime. The student is *ipso facto* plunged into a state of uncertainty as to the outcome of the assessments. That uncertainty is necessarily the case. If the outcome was entirely predictable, the assessment would lack point. No matter how well the student prepares for the examination, or how much effort is put into her assignments, or project or laboratory tests, still, the outcome will be uncertain to some extent. The uncertainty arises through that work being characteristically assessed by others. In assessment, the student yields her work to others; she places it in their hands, for their evaluations (cf. Strathern 2007). (Clearly, such a pattern does not hold in cases of self-assessment, but the situation in which others judge a student's work remains the default position in higher education.) The student lets it go and, in that letting go, surrenders any control that she might have had over it.

We may note, too, that in higher education, procedures – such as double marking and even double blind marking – have been evolved, so as to secure a measure of reliability and objectivity, and those procedures paradoxically have, from a student perspective, an unpredictability of outcome. If assessment outcomes were predictable, then we might think we were in the presence of forms of partiality that could be predicted in advance. However, the student cannot know her fate under such socially controlled forms of assessment and so the potential for a heightening of her anxiety level rises.

Anxiety over the outcome of the assessments, then, is to be expected and, in an age where more and more hangs on the outcomes or, at least, where students understandably impart ever greater expectations onto assessment results (given the perceived link to their life chances), anxiety may well again be heightened.

Yet, substantial as this assessment-grounded anxiety is, it is not the only or even the most significant form of anxiety that comes to students as students. All manner of anxieties, indeed, may break into the student during the course of his study.[7] There may be self-doubts about his ability to comprehend the key concepts, and to remember the many facts, terms and entities encountered (especially in the technological, bio-medical or natural science domains). There may be anxieties over the sheer workload, over one's capacity to perform effectively in front of others in group tasks or over one's capacities to master particular skills (such as essay writing, problem-solving in chemistry, playing a musical instrument or drilling teeth). There may be yet other anxieties over one's relationships with other students or the tutors and lecturers – or, indeed, especially under conditions of mass higher education, over one's lack of such relationships. There may be anxieties that befall a student over her contiguous concerns, whether over her family and other extra-mural relationships or her material infrastructure (such as her accommodation, and her funds – or her doubtless rising level of indebtedness).[8]

Were we engaged on a study of anxiety, it would be worth pausing to sift and to classify these forms of anxiety; for example, as between the material and non-material; between the cognitive and experiential; or between the personal and interpersonal. That is not our task here. Instead, I want to explore yet another set of related forms of anxiety.

While the forms of anxiety on which we have just touched are doubtless much to be seen and may well be rising in their severity, still they are empirical phenomena. Despite their ubiquity, they are not *necessary* phenomena of an individual student's being; they are contingent and, where they are present, will be so to a greater or lesser extent. They are properly phenomena of psychological study.

In contrast, there are aspects of student being that are more logically linked to forms of anxiety. The task of the student is to grapple with uncertainty, to come into a felt relationship *with* uncertainty. The idea of critical thought – so central to the Western idea of higher education[9] – gains its purchase out of a sense that the world is not given in any sense and that a valid higher education is, in part, that of taking up a critical stance towards the experiences to which one is exposed as a student.[10] So there is an *exterior* sense of uncertainty, albeit in relation to the student's field of study; a sense that the world as known is not stable, but is open to one's own interpretations. Even in dentistry? Even in dentistry, the enthused teacher senses that the student dentist still has to form her own experience and to make her own judgements (not only about the presenting situation but about the optimum treatment). However, the forming of schemas and judgements attest, in addition, to an *interior* mode of uncertainty; a mode of uncertainty that is imposed by the idea of higher education.

The idea of higher education calls upon students to come to their own interpretations, actions, judgements and arguments. They are required to be their own agents. They are examined on their own accounts. This is an idea of higher education that celebrates not just human being, but each human being as such.

This means that the student has to reach into herself, to draw something out of herself. She is bombarded with new terms, ideas, concepts, theorems, procedures, situations, experiences, all of which come out of lectures, books, papers, seminars, the laboratory, the studio, the workplace. She may feel that she is drowning in this world and yet, despite these impositions, she is called upon to make her own interventions, creations, propositions, offerings of one kind or another. For Heidegger, 'being' in general is in any case unstable: 'Dasein is constantly uprooting itself'; and, since, a higher education pedagogy is intent on 'uprooting' the student, there is a double uprooting that is before us here. It is hardly surprising that the student feels anxiety welling up inside her.

Anxiety in being a student

Being pulled in a large number of different directions . . . [is] not easy to cope with . . . (beginning the student journey) is [an entry into] a scary, exciting and fascinating world . . . We need . . . self-belief to survive and prosper . . . I remember thinking . . . this is amazing, exciting, exhilarating and downright terrifying . . . Working with a complex world is also about attitude . . . not giving up when you feel overwhelmed . . . You can never be totally prepared.

[Natasha Thomas (a recent graduate), 'Preparing students for a complex world: the harsh reality of being a student', talk at University of Surrey, June, 2006.]

. . . What's fascinating about Alison's courses is the amount of panic, you know, that surrounds the essays and I felt it personally . . . It was a very, very scary thing to do because . . . there were no right answers.

(Postgraduate student commenting on courses taught by a particular tutor.)

At one level, this interior anxiety can almost be explained away as a kind of intellectual immaturity: it is the outcome of the situation in which a student, qua student, is characteristically plunged. It is a situation in which the student is overwhelmed with the tasks confronting her. There are huge amounts to read and to comprehend, material to sort, terms and concepts to understand, and skills to acquire, and to bring it all together in an orderly fashion. The complexity and compression of tasks would be daunting for anyone; for someone who is, by definition, at an early stage in this journey of becoming – in all its intellectual and practical modes – this is an understandable source of anxiety. The student is plunged into complexity-within-time: time bears upon the resolution of this complexity. If anxiety is a state of being that is a combination of uncertainty, significance and pressure, then the being of a student is necessarily a *being-for-anxiety*.

However, there is yet a further and linked form of necessary anxiety into which our student must be plunged. Higher education imposes a severe set of demands on the student. Out of the maelstrom of experiences and time-bound tasks, the student is required to come forth with his own offerings. He is required to give an account by himself, in himself. He is required to come in contact with himself. There is no hiding place. The sentences, the paragraphs, the propositions, the arguments – and their equivalents in the studio, the laboratory, the clinical situation – have to be his. This – as Heidegger observed – is the very ground of anxiety. It is *being* being confronted with itself, as the student wills himself into the world:

That which anxiety is anxious about is Being-in-the-world itself.

(Heidegger 1998: 232)

It is the realization on the part of the student that he is being pulled and, at the same time, is propelling himself into the world, to be authentic in the world.

How can the student not be anxious? For his being declares its anxiety. In the one act, of framing the paragraph in the essay, the student is thrown into both an epistemological and an ontological anxiety. The epistemological anxiety is that of framing something orderly, something grounded, out of the chaos of the entities – terms, concepts, theories, procedures – that are swirling in his mind.[11] The ontological anxiety is that of the student's being protesting this call to declare itself, to stand in the world. Being a student is necessarily a lonely affair, no matter how extensive group project work may be or how much encouragement there may be to establish a 'community of practice' among the students. The student, in any circumstance, has to haul himself out of himself and come into a new space that he himself creates.

Anxiety, then, as Heidegger urged, is 'a potentially "enlightening" event' (Watts, 2001). Anxiety, especially in its ontological form, is a necessary mode of being through which the student struggles to come into himself, to find a new place in which to *be*. There is a dual struggle here, with which this ontological anxiety is associated. And there is the forming of the preparedness to move into a space of one's own. There is the forming of a preparedness to struggle into one's own utterances. (This is not a matter of originality, but, as stated, of authenticity.) These two struggles – of the forming of a readiness for authenticity and of the realizing of that authenticity – are testimony to the emergence of an acceptance on the part of the student of *responsibility*. Through anxiety, the student may eventually emerge into a responsible mode of being.

We must take up these notions of authenticity and responsibility in later chapters. What we may usefully observe at this juncture is that a *pedagogical task* of higher education lies in helping students to understand that anxiety is a condition of what it is to be a student (or, indeed, of what it is in general to offer defensible utterances to and interventions in the world). Accordingly, a *pedagogical achievement* of higher education is that – on the student's part – of coming to live purposefully with anxiety.

Complexity

Today's student has a tough time of it. For the present age is one of super-complexity (Barnett, 2000). It is an age in which it is reflexively, albeit intuitively, understood that there are neither end points nor beginning points; that is to say, there is dispute even over the descriptions of presenting situations. This is an age that is replete with multiplying and contradictory interpretations of the world; it is a world that is discursively open. If complexity is a term that we may apply to the open-endedness of systems, supercomplexity is a term that we may apply to the open-endedness of ideas, perspectives, values, beliefs and interpretations. This is the world with which students have to struggle to come into a new relationship. The student's being is perpetually unfolding:

> ... as Being-possible, ... Dasein is never anything less; this is to say, it *is* existentially that which, in its potentiality-for-Being, it is not *yet*.
>
> (Heidegger, 1998: 186)

Without too much of an extrapolation, then, the view surely suggests itself that an educational task in such a milieu is that of ushering in *both* being-in-and-for-complexity *and* complexity-in-being. The student's being has to reside within a felt sense of complexity and, in turn, that being – if it is to be adequate to its situation – has itself to become complex.

Think, for instance, of what it might be to be a student doctor in the contemporary age; not only does the student have to grapple with (presumably often) bewildering and fast expanding arrays of 'beliefs' (concepts, ideas, understandings) and fast-changing practices, technologies and interventions (in different clinical situations), but the student has to grapple with the question 'What is it to be a doctor?', precisely when, in the modern age, such a question can permit of no clear or indisputable answer. (Consider the challenges that arise of specifying the doctor–patient relationship in a post-deferential age or in an Internet age in which the patient can know more about her condition that the doctor that she consults.) So the student doctor prepares for a profession and a role that is literally incomprehensible. At once, therefore, both a being-in-complexity and a complexity-in-being are called for.

There is another form of complexity that we should note *en passant* here. It is that form of complexity that arises out of what we may term *fast learning*. Robert Hassan (2003) has observed that, for all the talk about globalization being accompanied by a compression of time and space, much analysis has focused upon the compression of space; rather little has focused upon the compression of time. He has gone on to point out that time itself is subject to change and that shortening – 'chronoscopic time' – is leading to changes that we have hardly begun to comprehend.

We may note that these chronological phenomena have invaded the university, and are having impact upon the lives of both academics and students. The university environment (in its widest sense) is requiring of its personnel that they inhabit different time frames and live according to different rhythms simultaneously. In particular, all members of the academic community are characteristically subject to multiple information streams, in various media, which have to be processed rapidly and their associated tasks completed swiftly. Within the student experience, such chronological phenomena are aided and abetted by the ubiquity of modular courses, which call for a continuous sequence of assignments.

Such phenomena can be placed against an even larger set of stories of the modern university, caught as it is worldwide amid forces of globalization, neo-liberalism and the information technology revolution. However, for our story, they also reach down deeply into the individual student's being. The 'abbreviated thinking' that Hassan observes finds its way into students' modes of thought, compelled as they are to assimilate rapidly huge quantities of information and often in different modes. In turn, we may say, students will adopt modes of *fast learning*, as a coping strategy in such a situation. However, this suggests, too, that the student's being is likely to alter. Now it is turned out even more into the world, displaced into the world of speeded-up information flows and quickly-to-be-completed tasks. It is a being that is liable to be hollowed-out, forgetful of itself and losing the interior space with which to come into a relationship with itself.

These two sets of reflections are in tension with each other. On the one hand, a world that is increasingly complex, requiring an evermore complex and nuanced form of student being; on the other hand, a world so speeded up and so insistent in its demands for rapid responses, that the student being is being robbed of its interior resources with which to form any kind of secure hold on the world. There is the prospect that student being is heading, if not towards nothingness, then towards emptiness.

Conclusion

'Being' has to be claimed as a key concept in any serious reflection on higher education, especially any thinking concerned with students and their experience. It is through her being that the student comes into a relationship or, rather, a set of relationships with all that she encounters. It is through her being that the student makes or declines to make her own interventions into those experiences, and so make those experiences partly her own.

This general and even timeless reflection is compounded by considerations about the present era. The student's being is facing a fork, albeit a fork in which one prong is stronger than the other. On the one hand, a splintering *or*, even worse, a hollowing out, as her being struggles to find means of ways of accommodating to infinite amounts of information and experiences within compressed timeframes. On the other hand, the rapidly receding prospect of a reflexive being that is adept to this age, a being-in-complexity and a complexity-in-being.

If this thesis is granted, even in its bleakness, it at least is testimony to the significance of the idea of 'being' for any serious educational thinking, especially amid the challenges of the contemporary world. The thesis points, in short, to the absolute need – such language can be used without flinching – to install, in the context of the university, an ontological dimension in our educational thinking. Ultimately, a genuine higher education is none other than a transformation of being (cf. Freire, 1978), and the transformation is complex, for it is not so much a transition from a mode of being for one kind of life to a mode of being for another specific kind of life (for empire or the state). Rather, the transformation is the taking on of a mode of being for uncertainty; for no substantive form of life other than one in which all bets are off and all is contestable. A key aspect of the mode of being in question is that it be authentic and it is to this idea, therefore, that we turn next.

3

Authenticity

Introduction

A higher education that does not call, does not insist, on authenticity in the student is no higher education. 'Authenticity' is perhaps the key concept within the deep structure of the idea of higher education, even if it is seldom evoked. It is a complex concept, however, and we cannot unravel it fully in a single chapter. However, if we are to advance an idea of student being that has any pretensions to being adequate, let alone to offering a declaratory idea for the twenty-first century, we cannot evade the concept.

A mirage?

We have already encountered the idea of authenticity, in our discussion of anxiety. There, it will be recalled, we noted the challenge of becoming authentic as a source of anxiety. That observation already gives us a clue to an important aspect of authenticity: that, in higher education (as more generally in life), it has to be fought for, won and sustained. Two questions arise:

- Can authenticity ever be attained?
- What would it mean to attain it?

We may start with the first matter – as to whether authenticity can ever be attained – but in a somewhat roundabout way, as it may seem. 'Authenticity', we may note, has gone out of fashion or, at least, the use of the term has gone out of fashion. One reading of this situation is that its falling into desuetude is a sign of post-modernism having gained some supremacy. Post-modernism, after all, has notoriously declared the end of the self as a coherent unity. If that nostrum has any weight, then what is left of authenticity? For authenticity surely requires a self that wins its authenticity. If there is no self that we can hang onto, no stable self, then authenticity gets no purchase. Its substance disappears.

Two responses urge themselves. First, we may wonder how those urging such an idea – as to the end of the self – might reconcile it with the responsibility of teaching a student (or group or class of students) and the privilege of working with a student (or students), in support of their work and their assignments. As this student engages in a conversation to discuss her assignment, is this not a singular individual before me, whatever might be said about the complexity of her identity? Do I not have responsibilities towards this student in this setting as distinct from some generalized responsibilities concerning my larger set of teaching activities?

Secondly, the claim that a term such as authenticity may have gone out of fashion can be read in different ways. It may be that the term has gone out of fashion, but that many of the ideas that are invoked in the name of 'authenticity' are vividly present. For example, as we observed in Chapter 1, there has been for around the past 30 years an emphasis on encouraging 'deep meaning' in students' approaches to learning (within the 'deep-surface' research framework in research into student learning). Here, we have a sense that students' learning should be theirs and, in any case, is unlikely to be fully effective if it relies on other sources; there is an implication at work that students' offerings should have a measure of self-ownership.

By way of a second example, we may bring into view simply the explosion, again over the last 30 years or so, of efforts to discern students' views on and attitudes towards their educational experiences – whether at the level of the course or in relation to their perceptions of the university more widely in which they are registered. Such student 'feedback' exercises can be ritualistic and lead to 'questionnaire fatigue' (as it is sometimes termed). Even so, there surely lies here a consideration that students matter as persons, and that their perceptions of and attitudes towards their educational setting are likely to be significant for their progress. Students are potential educational agents in their own right and, all things being equal, the more that they are able to realize their own hopes, and live their educational lives free of undue encumbrances, the more they are likely to be successful, educationally speaking.

A third example is current and lies in the awkward term 'personalization', which is to be seen in policy moves at schools level and will surely find its way to some degree into the higher education sector (NFER 2005). Doubtless, the term springs from the positioning of education in the market and, in contemporary 'mature' markets, attempts are being made to give each customer what he or she wants (or so the rhetoric goes). However, notwithstanding this political and economic hinterland, 'personalization' contains within it, surely, a sense that the education experience is particular to individuals as such. Students, on this reckoning, are not to be bracketed simply in the plural – as 'students' – but have their own identities, their own hopes and their own ways of accommodating to their experiences.

So ideas of agency, of ownership of one's experiences, of self-meaning, of being free of undue restrictions and of particularity are present in contemporary research, institutional practices and political agendas. All these ideas could be said to be associated with the idea of authenticity.

The idea of authenticity in higher education, therefore, may be closer to hand than may at first be apparent. It may yet turn out to be a mirage, always out of reach, always receding as we think we are approaching it. However, it may lie nearer to us that we may think.

Yet still, the question invites itself: why worry about a term, then, if its associated ideas are with us in any event? Would much be added if 'authenticity' was brought into the general lexicon in higher education? Would it help if, say, debate over the higher education curriculum was to start to employ the term (just as it has begun to use to term 'creativity')?

My answer is two-fold. First, the use of the term itself invites thought *about* the concept of authenticity. In deploying the term 'authenticity', we open ourselves up to debate as to which idea or ideas we may have in mind and which aspects of authenticity are especially significant in today's higher education. Secondly, in authenticity being a concept with a long pedigree in the work of major philosophers (such as Nietzsche and Heidegger), we also – through its deployment as a term – open up the prospect of finding a route back to that lineage of thinking, and in opening up that backward path, we open up, too, the prospect of coming into contact with a pool of ideas and considerations that may otherwise remain occluded from our view, saturated as it is bound to be with the sentiments and ideologies of our age.

The pool of ideas that is here represented by 'authenticity', then, may be a mirage (cf. Adorno 2003). It may always be out of reach, but, if so, it would be good to understand in what sense it may be out of reach. Is it out of reach because the concept of authenticity stands for ideas of human being that can never be fully satisfied by human beings, *or* is it that the empirical circumstances of our age and of higher education in particular are likely to thwart its realization, *or* is it both sets of circumstances are acting contemporaneously? As we reflect on such matters, it may just turn out that a better metaphor than that of mirage is that of dream. Dreams may be benign or threatening but, in either case, they point backwards even as they project forwards. They convey sentiments and murmurings, possibly suppressed, of unrealized states of being. Being authentic is a matter of living out at least certain of one's dreams, though which are likely to lead to a state of authenticity is a further matter.

But what is 'authenticity'?

Having had a preliminary go at the first of the two questions that we raised earlier – as to whether authenticity can be obtained – we must now turn to the second of those questions: what would it mean to attain authenticity? In other words, what is 'authenticity'?[1]

We can do no better, surely, than to begin by turning again to the thinking and the words of Heidegger. For Heidegger, 'the *authentic Self* [is] the Self which has been taken hold of in its own way' (1998: 167). This is a Self that we may 'distinguish' from 'the Self of everyday Dasein', namely 'the *they-self*

(Heidegger, 1998). The 'they-self' is the self that is the self given up to the 'they', the everyday world inhabited by the community in which one finds oneself. When Dasein, or being, 'discovers the world in its own way and brings it close, [at the same time, it] discloses to itself its own authentic Being' (Heidegger, 1998):

> Authentic Being-one's-Self does not rest upon an exceptional condition of the subject, a condition that has been detached from the 'they'; it is rather an existentiall (sic) modification of the 'they'.
>
> (1998: 168)

But this reconciliation with authenticity is not lightly achieved. On the contrary, Dasein tends to flee from itself: we are faced with the 'phenomenon of Dasein's fleeing in the face of itself and in the face of its authenticity' (p. 229) In other words, authenticity is a severely challenging state of being and is one from which human being naturally shrinks: one would rather go along with the accepted views of others.

There are a number of ideas here that we should pick out, in the context of the contemporary nature of higher education. At the heart of this particular sense of authenticity is the idea of discovering the world in one's 'own way', unencumbered by other voices and messages. Isn't this idea central to the Western idea of higher education, that we look to our students acquiring this capability of coming at things in their 'own way'?[2] There lies, surely, one of the central responsibilities of teachers in higher education, to encourage the formation of just that capacity.

However, in Heidegger's conception, coming at things in one's 'own way' is not to be achieved in isolation from other voices, but, on the contrary, in their company. It lies not in personal 'detachment', but in a 'modification' of those voices. Again, do we not have here two other ideas that are central to Western higher education, namely those, on the one hand, of students immersing themselves in the major voices, texts and conversations relevant to their studies, and on the other hand, of being in critical dialogue with those voices? The student's educational being becomes itself, wins itself, partly through that critical dialogue.

The winning of the student's own authenticity is not easily or lightly achieved: it calls for hard work, yes, but also for courage, for the capacity to stand alone, independently of those surrounding voices and texts. The winning of authenticity calls for a combination of personal qualities of courage, persistence and resilience; and it calls for a state of being of – as we might put it – willing-to-be-disencumbered, of a preparedness to be oneself.

We must try to disentangle in a moment what 'being oneself' might mean, but note here that it means neither autonomy nor originality. Authenticity is to be distinguished from both concepts. Autonomy is here an unhelpful concept in two respects.[3] First, as we have seen, authenticity is to be won intellectually through the student's keeping company, albeit critical company, with her intellectual environment. Her arguments, her findings, her problem-solving, are achieved in presenting situations – of already present theories, concepts, data and procedures, but, secondly, autonomy is close to being otiose pedagogically: many desirable educational qualities can be developed through the student working with other students. That authenticity may be partly won through close interaction with others, will be a matter to which we must return throughout this book (*prima facie*, it may seem contradictory); for now, I just want to make the dual point that authenticity is to be distinguished from autonomy, intellectually and pedagogically.

Authenticity is also to be distinguished from originality. In making this distinction, it is important first to distinguish originality and creativity: I may be creative, but not necessarily original. I may come up with an idea or a design or a procedure that I have not personally encountered and which is personally creative, being something that I have brought forth from my own resources, but it may turn out that others have got there before me, and come up earlier with just the same idea or design or procedure. The fruits of my intellectual and practical labours may be creative, but not original. So, having established the distinction between creativity and originality, let us now go back to the distinction between authenticity and originality.

To speak of authenticity being won independently of other voices, even dominant voices, may conjure up a sense of originality. However, except at the level of research or other advanced students, we do not *require* originality; we do, though, if only tacitly, look for authenticity.

What is this authenticity that we look for? It is, surely, the taking 'hold of in [one's] own way', as Heidegger puts it. We want students to come at things in terms that are at their command. We want them to use the resources that they have acquired and with which they identify. The idea of 'ownership', present there in that phrase of Heidegger's, is inescapable. We determine how to use and, indeed, if to use, what we own, but there is here, too, the idea of 'taking hold of'. Here is a sense of being involved, of being active, of not just having resources at one's command, but of taking command of those resources (however meagre or rich they may be). This authenticity is liable to be creative, then, but originality has nothing to do with it, however worthwhile – for other reasons – originality may be.

On breaking free

In this section, I want to make three further points.

First, in drawing out Heidegger's idea of authenticity, I have used the term 'disencumbered'. I have used this term to bring out the sense of coming-into-oneself, of breaking free of surrounding voices and texts, which I think is present in Heidegger's thinking – and which is surely part of the heritage of the Western tradition of higher education. In fact, Heidegger himself uses a similar term, namely that of being 'disburdened' (1998: 165). However, Heidegger uses the term in precisely the opposite way to that in which I am using 'disencumbered', namely to refer to the way in which the 'they' lightens Being; in other words, to a situation of *in*authentic being.

This phenomenon is not unfamiliar in university life: not only students, but academics hide behind the 'they', for there lies a sense of security. The bibliographies grow ever longer; the quotations proliferate; and the commentaries on what B said about A multiply. This tendency to self-effacement is not purely self-induced. It may often be a rational response to the pedagogical environment that students sense around them. Students will be making their appraisals and interpretations of the educational situation in which they find themselves. If they glean that there are certain expectations of them, the students are likely to mimic those expectations. For that way, lies high marks or so the students may intuit. So the pedagogical environment may unwittingly encourage inauthenticity: the students naturally hide behind the 'they' that the students may sense is lurking close by.

The 'they' 'disburdens' those who shrink from working their way towards their own offerings, their own claims, their own ways of going on. Given this use of 'disburdening' by Heidegger, it makes sense to employ a different term for the contrasting situation – a situation of authenticity – I want to insist on here.

In a recent book, David Cooper has advanced the term 'dis-incumbencing' to identify the stance of the authentic person (Cooper, 2002: 153). Justifying the term – which Cooper admits is 'ugly' – Cooper observes that the second 'i':

> is coined from the Latin word meaning 'to lean on', not from the French word meaning 'to block', from which encumber comes.

For Cooper, then, authenticity betokens an absence of leaning or, as he puts it, in quoting a phrase from William James, the authentic person 'leans on nothing'. This is a powerful idea, that of 'leaning on nothing': in the end, authentic persons have only their own resources with which to tell their own story. Yes, they draw on others, on others' ideas, findings and ways of going on, but they do so because they freely assent to them – those that they take on, at any rate. However, even then, they take on those other resources in their own way. Ultimately, the authentic person is her own author; what authority she gains comes from herself, not from those who have gone before her. Some students find it especially difficult to develop their own authorship in this way: they would rather submit to the authorities with which they are presented (whether visibly in front of them, in the lecture room or laboratory or more distantly, in the textbooks).

Cooper's term, that of 'dis-incumbencing', suitably understood, is not, therefore, without its merits. However, for my taste at least, it does not exactly roll off the tongue. 'Disencumbering' may hardly be much better in this regard, but I shall stick to it, for I would prefer to err on the side of some more immediate intelligibility than largely obscure precision.

The second point I want to make here (in drawing out the idea of authenticity) derives from an earlier book by David Cooper (1983) on *Authenticity and Learning: Nietzsche's Educational Philosophy*. In that book, Cooper identifies two interpretations of authenticity, both of which – he suggests – are to be found in Nietzsche. On the one hand, is the 'Polonian' idea (as in Polonius' advice to his son: 'To thine own self be true'). Nietzsche, for example, asks and answers his own question: 'What does your conscience say? – You should become who you are' (Cooper 1983: 13). On the other hand, there lies in Nietzsche's work a 'Dadaist' view of authenticity, which contains the sense of 'total absence of constraint'. This leads to a bold, even imperious, conception of selfhood:

> I am the first to hold in my hand the measure of 'truths': I am the first who is *able* to decide … I contradict as has never been contradicted before…

Cooper observes that both the Polonian and the Dadaist conceptions of authenticity have their exaggerated versions. On the one hand, there is a sense of an enduring and stable self (in the Polonian version); on the other hand, there is a sense of it being possible for human being to sequestrate itself from one's environment (as in the Dadaist version). Neither – I suggest – are variants of authenticity to be encouraged in higher education. A genuine higher education is to be attained neither by a sense of a fixed self to which one has to be 'true' nor by the prospect of isolating oneself from one's educational environment (potentially worthwhile as that may be).

Where, though, one lies as between these two variants of authenticity is a matter for further consideration. Partly, it will be a matter of personal preference – between, as we may put it, the conservatives (the Polonians) and the iconoclasts (the Dadaists). Partly, it will be a matter of the character or stage of the intellectual field. The space for authenticity in the natural sciences (and subjects based on them) may be more Polonian in character, while the space for authenticity in the humanities and the performing arts may be Dadaist in character, their paradigms being more open and iconoclasm being at least more tolerated than in the sciences.

My third – and final – point in this section builds upon two earlier points. My first point was that authenticity is a form of student becoming that is disencumbered from its educational setting. This form of being, we may add, is both a quality and a disposition of being. It is the way we want students to become – a quality. However, it is also the way we want students to *be* – a disposition. My second earlier idea on which I wish to draw is that of Heidegger's, of authentic being involving a 'taking hold of in one's own way'. These two ideas are related: 'taking hold of in one's own way' and being disencumbered are, we might say, two sides of the same coin. A student is able to take hold of that which she encounters owing to her being disencumbered; and taking hold, she enhances her state of being disencumbered.

There is, however, a little more that can be said here, via an aspect of the notion of creativity that we commented on earlier. Then, we left open the matter of the relationship between authenticity and *originality*. We noticed that authenticity and originality were quite separate concepts: unless one holds the Dadaist and iconoclastic conception of authenticity in a strident form, originality cannot be said to be a condition of authenticity.

It is different, though, with *creativity*, as we may see if we bring into view our two previous ideas. Taking hold of an educational experience, and being disencumbered from the theories, concepts, data and procedures that help to constitute the student's experience, point to the student's being creative.

If the student is disencumbered and takes hold of her educational experience in her own way, she will *ipso facto* be creative. In this situation, the student wills herself into her experiences; she infuses her being into those experiences. And her orderings of those experiences, so as to make them her own, will be creative. (This is not, as we saw earlier, to say that those orderings will be original.) The student imparts her own framing to her experiences so as to bring them into herself and so as to have some degree of command over those orderings. This is a creative moment; and it is a moment of authenticity.

Commitment, engagement and authenticity – a medical student's story

I had some very negative experiences . . . in one case I was attached in a hospital to a consultant surgeon . . . and he just refused to speak to us medical students. I'd ask a question whether that would be in the theatre or would be somewhere else, and used to be totally ignored. So I just didn't go. I sat in the library throughout my ten-week attachment and did all my work there because I wasn't getting any stimulation. . . .

I needed to therefore find a way to drive myself. . . . This opportunity came . . . at [. . .] hospital, which does not have a great reputation. . . . I used to spend all my time in [the] accident and emergency department, encouraged by my consultant who on our first day said, I don't want you on the wards or doing any of the traditional things, I want you down on accident and emergency. . . . So I started working down there and I would turn up in the morning and the doctors who were there, who tended to be locums, [would see my arrival] as an excuse to go away. So I would arrive . . . and the doctors would leave. And there were a couple of occasions when I was the only person in the resuscitation room when a patient came in . . .

And I still have that feeling of being there, I had a nurse as well, and having to do something. Of course, I couldn't prescribe drugs, I couldn't . . . you know. The anxiety . . . 'Was I taught that?' 'What am I meant to do?' 'Quick, get a doctor. Oh no, he's not coming.' You know, 20, 25 minutes I'd be there trying to get this line into the patient's arm . . .

So early trepidation . . . but this turned into furthering, or . . . fuelled, my interests. I would see a patient . . . They would say some things that perhaps didn't fit into my schema of a disease or a condition or a presentation. I'd then go away and say, well, why? I think a lot of medical education has turned into lists. What are the 25 causes of chest pain? And students learn the lists. . . . I can't learn like that. I have to think of what's going on . . .

Commitment

We noted in chapter one that there lies, in the Western tradition of higher education, the idea of commitment as part of the student's becoming (Wyatt 1990). Precisely in that context, commitment is part of authenticity; and so we should delve into the inter-relationships between the two concepts and we can come at that inter-relationship through the concept of belief.

We look to a unity between the student's offerings, be they utterances, texts or performances, and the student herself. The student is expected to identify with those offerings, whatever they may be. They are not just to be hers, but they are to be *felt* to be hers by the student herself.[4] The truth claims are *believed*.

We can observe that, in getting clear about knowledge, philosophers have understandably put heavy qualifications around belief; belief has no warrant in itself as a mark of truth. Belief only gets going when it is justified, and justification comes outside of persons (cf. Popper 1975). However, from an educational point of view, things are entirely around the other way. For truth to have educational value, it has to be believed. Students advance through their coming to believe the truth claims they evince. Here, belief is supremely important. There has to be an identity between truth claims and the student; and beliefs and commitment to those beliefs, provide that identity.

The point begins to insist on itself in the realm of actions, whether they be actions in the laboratory or in clinical situations or in the design studio, or musical performances. Of course, the action has to be the student's, but what of a simulation of a historical episode or the playing out of a scenario of a situation in business life: where is the identity between the student and her actions there? The identity lies precisely in the idea of commitment: we look to the student to be committed to her actions, even if she is playing out a script to a large extent. That is to say, to draw on one of our earlier formulations, we look to the student to bring to bear her own resources, whatsoever they are. However, even more than that, we expect the student to invest herself in the expenditure of those resources.

One might be tempted to draw again on the language of existentialism at this point. One might say that at issue here is whether or not there is an existential moment present: does the student become her actions or are we in the presence of 'bad faith'? However, a phrase such as 'existential moment' only raises more questions than it addresses; it is in danger of becoming a slogan. It appears to be capturing something of the 'human subjectivity', which, for Sartre, constitutes 'the deeper meaning of existentialism' (Sartre 1973: 29), but what work might the phrase 'existential moment' be doing for us? What is the relationship between a person and his or her actions to which it is pointing? It is unclear.

Let me state the matter directly. The idea of commitment is, I contend, central to the idea of higher education; it lies as a fundament to our practices in higher education. (Its embedded presence can be seen, for instance, in the contemporary angst over plagiarism.) *However*, the idea of commitment is elusive.

We can press towards an understanding of it. The metaphors of investment, of the student having resources and even capital of her own in which she invests herself, such that she has a personal stake in what she does or writes, are helpful (despite their economic overtones). We may press the metaphors even further and observe that with investment arises the prospect of risk: the student's efforts – even though they be her own – may not please the examiners. However, the metaphor of personal investment has further limitations. It still implies some separateness between the student and the investment; it also conjures up a sense of calculation. So the separation of mind and being that the metaphor of personal investment is intended to close remains open.

Yet, does not the idea of commitment, especially in the context of authenticity, point us to just that: in being committed to her offerings, the student is involved as a person – she commits *herself* to what she says and does? These are not just offerings of her intellect, but of her being. The proper operation of the intellect is partly, but inescapably, ontological in character.

Part of the difficulty in becoming clear about 'commitment' in higher education lies surely in the ontological dimensions of education remaining still awkward territory for many. Concepts of being, becoming and self are discomforting to the Anglo-Saxon mind and a concept, such as commitment, that not only invokes an ontological dimension but points to an interplay between the intellectual and ontological sides of student development, is doubly awkward.[5]

One way forward lies in the sense that what is involved in commitment are ethical qualities on the part of the student. In being committed, a student is expressing her own thoughts or actions; the personhood of the student is put into the thought or action. The student has not merely integrity, but even has courage in projecting her thoughts or actions, and she has determination to press herself so as to yield that expression of herself. A corollary of these three ethical qualities of integrity, courage and determination is that the student is sincere in what she does or utters. It may be false or inappropriate, but it is still sincere.

In sincerity, we recall, lies one of Jurgen Habermas' (1991) validity claims (alongside truthfulness and appropriateness), but we should rather see this as an ontological condition of a truth claim. In higher education, we look to see that the utterances or the actions are the student's own; they are to be neither plagiarized nor simply second-hand. The authority of the utterance or action is depleted in its being purely a replica. That is to say, we detect that the student has failed to invest herself in the action or utterance. In making a claim, I propel myself forward. I inject not just the utterance, but myself into the world. I commit myself to it; I stand with it. For the moment, at least, I am wedded to what I say or do. I am identified with it and I identify with it. The thought or utterance could not happen without me and takes on its status partly through it being identifiable as mine. Truth claims, in other words, have an *ontological substrate*. The degree in history confirms that the student has *become*, if only embryonically, a historian.[6]

Possible corruption – and the wager

As with all human virtues, commitment may take a corrupted form. The student can be overly committed. This pathology appears in two variants. On the one hand, the student may be so taken up with her own perspective and understandings that she cannot entertain other possibilities. She is saturated with her own way of looking at the world; there is no room for any other view. This is a student who is opinionated. On the other hand, a student may be disinclined, in an almost conscious way, to engage with other voices, or traditions or methodologies other than those she favours. This is a self-indulgent student.[7] We may, respectively, term these pathologies an *exclusive commitment* and an *excluding commitment*.

In either case, the potential of commitment is lost. Commitment gains its spurs when it calls, to use a term from Kierkegaard, for a 'leap'.[8] In venturing forth with her own claims and actions, the student reaches out into a void: she leaps into she knows not what. She asserts her freedom, but at what cost? At cost to her stability, to her self-assuredness: she hears the other voices, sees the information proffered by others, empathizes with the actions of others, but yet struggles into her own self. Bungee-jumper like, she commits herself, throwing herself off the platform. The commitment, then, is not just to the assertion or the action; it is also to herself and of herself. She believes in herself.

To commit oneself is to reach for one's freedom; it is to break free, even in the midst of otherness. It is a journey into oneself; commitment contains an inwardness. Patrick Gardiner, commenting on Kierkegaard, puts it thus:

> [Kierkegaard's] stress on inwardness ... manifests itself in self-commitment and the spirit in which such commitment is undertaken: a person exhibits inwardness through the resolutions he forms, the sincerity with which he identifies with them, and the degree to which they govern his approach to the situations that confront him.
>
> (Gardiner 2002: 97)

In committing herself, the student breaks her own mould. She fashions herself into a new person. She places herself where she was not previously. Hardly any wonder, then, that many students shrink from putting themselves into a state of commitment to their utterances and actions. This is not to say that all that such students utter or do is 'reproductive'; much of what students offer is a careful weighing of the available evidence, a considered rehearsal of relevant views or a judicious exemplification of contemporary procedures. However, it often lacks that personal leap beyond the known; the wager is not made;[9] the risk is not taken.

Conclusion

The suggestion that a true higher education might be inauthentic would be given short shrift by many; the idea of authenticity lies deep within our presuppositions as to what counts as higher education. However, giving a sound and clear account as to what authenticity might mean in higher education is far from straightforward: authenticity is an elusive concept.

There are eight planks to the concept of authenticity as worked out here, with a pedagogical setting in mind:

i The authentic student is one who 'takes hold' of her educational experience in her own way. She takes hold of the resources at her command (at once, epistemological, practical and psychological) and makes something of them on her own account.

ii Authenticity announces itself not necessarily in originality, but in creativity: the student breaks free, with orderings and significations that are hers.

iii To do this, the student places herself such that she is 'disencumbered' by other voices and messages, which is not to say that she ignores them; to the contrary.

iv Authenticity is never fully achieved (except by Nietzsche's Overman): for most, it is a matter as to the extent it is realized. However, while authenticity can always be more fully developed, still there is a minimum state of being that attaches to it. This is the phenomenological condition intimated by Kierkegaard's idea of 'leap'. In being authentic, one leaps into the unknown. One puts oneself forward into a new place, not being sure of what one will encounter. Authenticity calls for an existential expression of one's freedom, risky as that may be.

v One measure of authenticity is the presence of the student being in a state of *commitment* to her offerings, be they in writing or in action.

vi In being committed to her utterances or actions, the student infuses herself into them: both knowing and practices have an ontological substrate.

vii In the presences of authentic claims, we are in the presence of four ethical qualities of integrity, courage, determination and sincerity.

viii While there are often outward signs of authenticity (in words or actions), authenticity has an inward quality: the student is committed not just to her words or actions but also to herself. The student believes in herself.

The idea of authenticity, then, can be used as an attribute of thought or action: in assessing an essay or a student's action in a clinical setting, we may feel that the work in question is authentic. So it may be, but it is so in virtue of the student herself *being* authentic. The student has willed herself into a new place to produce what appears before us. She is in process of becoming anew. It is to the idea of becoming, therefore, that we next turn.

4

Becoming

Become what you want to be.
(From advertisement for a post-1992 UK university, April 2006)[1]

Becoming is a verb with a consistency all its own; . . . It is . . . a creative
line of escape that says nothing other than what it is.
(Deleuze and Guattari, quoted in Guattari 2005: 75)

Introduction

It has long been understood that a genuine higher education is a process of
personal development, but what might be meant by 'personal' development
is ambiguous.[2]

Is it that the student's development is supposed to be particular to the
individual student or is it that the student is expected to develop as a *person* –
as distinct, say, from her powers of reasoning or her understanding of an
intellectual field or her capabilities in a professional domain? However, even
if we opt for the latter connotation, that the student is expected to develop as
a person, yet more options open out. Is it that the student is expected to take
on broad intellectual and moral virtues – of respect for others, respect for
evidence, turn-taking in conversations, fairness, due humility, persistence
and so on? In other words, acquire the personal qualities associated with the
English idea of liberal education or is it that the student is expected to be
immersed in processes of 'self-transcendence', of her being itself being
transformed, of her undergoing the process associated with the German idea
of *Bildung* (cf. Lovlie *et al*, 2003)?

I do not intend to go into all these matters here in a systematic way; but we
shall be obliged to touch on each of them. Instead, I want to come at the idea
of personal development through the idea of 'becoming'.[3] In so doing, I shall
continue to press our examination of the ontological dimensions of higher
education.

Becoming

RB: *You were saying that even at the age of fourteen, you were beginning to think of yourself as possibly becoming a doctor, and here you are. You are working away at a long course, at least five years. You know that there is a long postgraduate training ahead of you and all of that. You are seeing yourself in almost a twenty-year timeframe. You know it is quite extraordinary in some sense that human beings embark on these sorts of long journey. Do you want to say anything about that? How do you sustain yourself?*

Student: *Completely. This bears on every medical student's mind. Certainly, when I first started at medical school, I became a little . . . 'depressed' would be too strong a word . . . but a little bit down about the length of the thing I was embarking on. Not because I lacked motivation to start the process. I didn't . . . I was hugely motivated when I started at medical school, but it seemed like a huge mountain to climb. Staring at the bottom, I had a fear of this journey and what it was going to involve . . . There was a dichotomy, because on the one hand, I was really driven and on the other, I was wondering, is this really for me?*

The student comes into the classroom or the laboratory or the tutor's room. She is not only on time, but is *in* time.[4] Time passes: characteristically, a particular period of time is set aside for the task or commitment on hand. There attaches to her education a horizon of time; pedagogic time, as we may term it. However, the student is in time in another sense: as a subject, her being moves through time. This was one of the fundamental insights of Heidegger's magnum opus, *Being and Time*. Being is not fixed, but moves through time and, in that movement, may achieve its own transcendence beyond time:

To be a subject means to transcend. This means that *Dasein* (or *being* [RAB]) does not exist as something that transcends from itself from time to time – the fundamental meaning of his existence is the transcendence beyond the given.

(Heidegger, quoted in Gur-Ze'ev 2002: 69)

The idea of transcendence is important for our theme here. As we have noted, it is not unusual for the student to feel – and even orally to admit – that her time at university has changed her as a person. In saying such a thing, the student implicitly confirms her own self-transcendence. She has moved herself into another place, a place in which she not only understands the world anew, but also understands herself anew.

This self-transcendence is a *process* and an *achievement* of becoming: the student becomes herself as a person. Here, is a phenomenon to be explained: how is it that a higher education can have such a *self*-transforming effect – even possibly in 'pure subjects' in the sciences and humanities? How can it be that what may seem a largely intellectual and possibly practical set of developmental processes can enable a student to become herself? What does that *mean?*

Becoming itself

A genuine higher education puts students on the spot. It does not let them evade themselves. It not merely encourages the student to develop her own point of view, but requires the student to state *her* reasons for her point of view. The student is pressed relentlessly and, ultimately, the pressing is done by the student herself. She internalizes the interrogative voices. And in the process, takes on her own voice. (We must return to the matter of voice.)

A higher education, then, that is worthy of the name will not allow the student into her comfort zone (to resort to a modish phrase). The student is forever being challenged. The challenge is that of giving an account of one-self, first, of its continuing series of instances and, secondly, of its being anticipated as a possible rejoinder to any utterance or action. Such a pedagogy of challenge calls for qualities of resilience and fortitude, in addition to the capacity to take the side of the other and so be prepared seriously to address any challenge that comes the student's way.

The formation of such personal qualities of resilience and fortitude is necessary to being disposed to take up one's own positions or adopt one's own ways of going on. To recall part of our discussion in the last chapter, to speak of 'one's own way' is not tantamount to saying that it is particular to the student. Rather, this utterance or this action is owned by the student; she identifies with it. There is an *ontological substrate* to the student's intellectual and practical offerings. She even *feels* her own thoughts. Ultimately, her thinking is an afterthought to, and a recreation of, her feelings.

Through such a formation process, the student is set off – *even unknowingly* – on winning her own authenticity. There is here, to recall from our last chapter, a process through which the student becomes disencumbered from her experience, is able to break free of it (while still responsive to it) and is able to impart her own orderings of it. However, there is also the existential moment in which the student leaps into those experiences with her own daring. It is a bungee-jumping moment or, as Kierkegaard puts it more formally:

> Becoming oneself is a movement one makes just where one is. Becoming is a movement from some place, but becoming oneself is a movement at that place.
>
> (From Kierkegaard 2004: 66)

This leap of becoming is – again, just like the bungee jumper – paradoxical: it is a leap into a void, into a new space, but it is, at the same time, a leap by the student into herself. Through the leap, the student throws herself into newness. She ventures into a new place, which she discovers for herself, but in so doing, discovers herself. She comes to know herself, albeit in that place. Because she has willed herself into that space, she can identify with her new self in that space. There is personal satisfaction to be obtained here.

This is not just a new becoming; it is becoming itself. This is the promise of higher education, that it offers the prospect of a self-won position of '*authoritative uncertainty*' (Goodlad 1976). The student did not know how it would be before the leap and now, having come into the new place, still cannot be sure of its validity. However, she has won this space and this place for herself. Through the learning processes, which she has undergone, she is able to defend her new place. There is security amid insecurity. She can be confident about her new position.

Voice

We have just come upon the idea of confidence and that is a concept to which we cannot help but return. First, however, we must begin to engage with the idea of voice. The idea of confidence, after all, presumes that one has a voice over and through which one can be confident. Voice comes before confidence, temporally and logically.

Denise Batchelor (2006a) has asked the question: to what degree is each of the three terms – uncovering, recovering, discovering – helpful to us in understanding the student voice? To what extent is the student voice 'uncovered', 'recovered' or 'discovered'? What different nuances might be intended by those terms? Who is the agent of the verb? Even if each of those ideas is equally appropriate (albeit in different situations), is it always the student who is doing the uncovering, recovering or discovering?

We do not need to pursue these matters in detail here, but we may observe some distinguishing features *en passant*. The idea of 'recovering' the student voice implies a voice that was there, but has been suppressed (whether by the student herself and/or by an oppressive learning environment); the idea of 'uncovering' the voice implies a voice that has had difficulty in being heard, it being overlain by other presences, even other voices; while the idea of 'discovering' suggests the possibility of a voice that no-one dreamt about and yet was there, even if as a potential, just waiting to emerge.

Different as they are from each other, each of these voice situations contains certain aspects in common. Each implies a latent potentiality, not fully realized; each looks to a process of becoming, in which a voice is realized over time; and each implies a backwards horizon of student being – unfulfilled at that – but each also has a future horizon written into it, holding open the possibility of a better or truer or even a new voice.

The idea of 'discovering' a student voice is itself ambiguous. The term could imply that the capability, the talent, was always present and just needed a favourable set of circumstances for it to flower: here, the term holds both past and future together in equal measure. On the other hand, the term could be looking forwards much more, the idea being that an entirely new voice might emerge, given favourable circumstances; or at least a voice that no-one had known was even potentially present, not even the student herself. The idea of 'recovering' the student voice, as we just saw, is weighted entirely in the other direction, being largely concerned with the ways in which the voice has been suppressed in the past, perhaps by an authoritarian learning environment.

The metaphor of voice offers further snares for the unwary. The voice to be encouraged in higher education is not a solo voice, but neither is it one in unison with all others. It is more like the improvization of the jazz player in an ensemble. The student finds new possibilities in her own self, those possibilities being realized *in situ*, in company with others. The student takes account of the rhythms and styles of the work at hand, and of the tones and offerings of those around her, and yet is able to come forth with her own offering, fresh and vital, adding to the totality of voices and sounds. She listens and catches experiences almost unawares. After all:

> . . . 'learning' always takes place in and through the unconscious.
>
> (Deleuze, 2001: 165)

The student hears she barely knows not what and yet, through this interplay with her surroundings, resources come to dwell within her from which may come original (not just creative) offerings.

This idea of unison can be overplayed, however, and perhaps we see such a position in Paul Ricoeur, in his suggestion that:

> . . . every advance made in the direction of the selfhood of the speaker or the agent has as its counterpart a comparable advance in the otherness of the partner . . . Interlocution . . . is revealed to be an exchange of intentionalities, reciprocally aiming at one another.
>
> (Ricoeur 1994: 44)

This, perhaps, is the dominant form of one particular ideal of voice, that is, it is realized in concert with others and brings an 'exchange of potentialities'. So it may and one sees just this when things take off as students come together in a joint project or task. For example, engineering students gain much from a 'constructionarium', working together on substantial projects (see Ahearn *et al.*, 2007). However, the idea of authenticity also calls for the courage to stand outside the dominant voices. The idea of 'interpersonal skills', now often heralded as a desirable 'transferable skill', can be pernicious if it is interpreted so as to rob students of the potential of finding their own voice, which may be distinct from those around them. Ultimately, if necessary, in order to be authentic to her own insights, the student must find the courage to renounce the surrounding voices.

Whether in harmony with others (while voicing her own 'line') or as a soloist, the student has to go into herself, to hear, train and articulate her own voice. This process of developing one's own voice is long and arduous, in listening to one's own presentiments and bringing them forth. Georges Bataille has a bleak and a stark way of putting the matter:

> If one proceeds right to the end, one must efface oneself, undergo solitude, suffer severely from it, renounce being recognized: . . . to undergo things without will and without hope . . . One must bury thoughts alive.
>
> (Bataille 1988: 155)

This view has empirical warrant but, as a philosophy, it is surely unduly and even damagingly pessimistic. Sometimes, students get themselves into just this frame of mind: they encounter difficulty in developing their own voice and they shrink from the project. They are 'without will and without hope', and they falter as a result. Students have often been far too effaced; sometimes, that effacing has come from without, from their 'learning' environment; sometimes, it has been self-induced. If the student's own voice is to develop, indeed be discovered, the student has to have hope, will and self-belief. However, the student also needs self-confidence.

Self-confidence

> But the highest passion in a human being is faith . . .
>
> Kierkegaard, *Fear and Trembling* 2001: 105)

Taking our cue from Kierkegaard, we may say that the highest passion in a student is *self*-faith. Self-faith is belief in oneself and is a necessary condition of the kind of prolonged learning demanded by a genuine higher education.

Self-*faith* is a particularly apt term here. It points us to the ineffable character of the belief in self that is required of a student's continuing adherence to her course of study.[5] The course of study characteristically stretches over some years and is undertaken wittingly. The student has not merely to believe that she will stay the course, but she has also to believe in her personal engagement with her studies and experiences. However, this is a set of faiths. Even though the object of these beliefs is also their subject – namely, the student taking a view of herself – still, she cannot be sure that she will persist with the course. The student wagers on herself. Her belief in herself cannot be fully substantiated; again, she leaps into herself, giving herself strength and self-conviction.

A student's self-confidence

I have always lacked self-confidence . . . You worry about what other people think, and are they going to read this and completely disagree? . . . I was afraid of saying the wrong answer.

(Student at an ancient university who had just obtained a good 2:1 degree.)

There is a psychological literature that bears on these themes, connected with 'self-concept' and 'self-image'.[6] Much of it has been built up through research in the school sector, but some is also now being seen in the higher education sector. That research offers empirical evidence for the power (we may use the term) of self-confidence and of a positive self-image on the part of the learner. A paper by Abouserie (1995) is particularly telling: it suggests not merely that, in higher education, the student's preparedness to learn or that the student's persistence in her learning may be affected by her level of self-confidence, but it suggests also that the actual quality of a student's learning may be influenced by her level of self-confidence. Is this not crucial for our purposes here? The involvement that a student has in her learning and its meaning for her springs, in part at least, from her confidence in herself in that domain. To put it differently, the quality of a student's learning is affected not only by the 'learning environment', but also by the student's mode of being:

> We never know in advance how someone will learn; by means of what loves someone becomes good at Latin, what encounters make them a philosopher ... There is no more a method for learning than there is a method for finding treasures, but a violent training [or] a culture ... *which affects the entire individual ...*
>
> (Deleuze 2001: 165)

Being first, then learning, knowing, and effective practices: this is the principle that keeps bearing in upon us in our enquiry. *In her becoming,* the student has to be right within herself, has to believe in herself, have faith in herself, and have a measure of confidence in herself before anything of worth can happen in her learning. This is the fundamental principle of higher education.

It was always thus, but is now, in our present age, even more so. For our present age is one of ineradicable ontological uncertainty. In a situation in which there are no stable descriptions of our world, we cannot know with security who we are any more, and yet we want students to commit themselves to their studies over some years. In these circumstances, a self-belief is a necessary foundation of the acquisition of some kind of personal anchoring.

From where does this self-belief come? From the student herself or from her tutors or from an even wider array of presences that constitute 'the learning environment'? All of these together! Her tutors have no more significant responsibility than that of helping the student to acquire a proper level of self-belief (and, that being so, this is an issue to which we must return later in our enquiries, when we turn to matters of teaching), but the student also bears a measure of responsibility in the matter. Nietzsche, it seems, might have felt as much too:

> Whoever has preserved, and bred in himself, a strong will, together with an ample spirit, has more favourable opportunities than ever.
>
> (Nietzsche 1968: 79)[7]

Note that 'and bred in himself' – the individual can develop a self-belief in himself. Admittedly, there is no mention here of self-belief, but is not a strong self-belief required by both 'a strong will' and 'an ample spirit'? One cannot instruct oneself to have a strong self-belief; but it can be acquired over time, through one's own persistence and observations of one's own developing powers, supplemented by affirmation from those who count;[8] there is a pedagogical interplay, therefore, between the student's own pains-taking efforts and the support that she receives. The student is the author and artist of her own self-belief, but is advanced in that patterning of self-creation by the encouragement of her tutors and any other 'significant others' in her educational endeavours.

Passion and ecstasy

A strong self-belief may be accompanied by the student having a 'passion' for her subject. Whether it is that the self-belief opens the possibility of this passion emerging or whether it is that the passion prompts the self-belief is a further matter, but can we, in any event, speak seriously of passion and even of ecstasy in higher education today? Do they have any place in a mass higher education system, and in a setting that is increasingly marketized and even 'commodified'? (cf. Naidoo, 2005) Are such terms – 'passion' and 'ecstasy' – important or are they without purchase?

Here is Nietzsche on passion:

> Passion is degraded (1) as if it were only in unseemly cases, and not necessarily and always, the motive force; (2) in as much as it has for its object something of no great value, amusement – The misunderstanding of passion and reason, as if the latter were an independent entity and not rather a system of relations between various passions and desires; and as if every passion did not possess its quantum of reason.
>
> (Nietzsche 1968: 208)

Here we see it: for Nietzsche, reason is 'a system of relations between various passions and desires'. Anathema as this will be to many, if not most, in higher education (for whom the only greater dimension than reason is 'skill'), actually Nietzsche might have gone even further. For his formulation here puts reason and passion on a level with each other: reason is to be understood through passions and desires; and passion is to be understood, in part at least, through reason, but it is passion that fuels reason. The will to reason springs from passion, or 'various passions and desires'. It is the passion for a subject, and the desires to understand and to express oneself that energizes reason. Even to say that reason is inert without passion would be to underplay the significance of passion. For enduring and steadfast reason does not start to come into play in the absence of passion: it is passion that ignites such reason.

Teachers in higher education, it is said, have a double object (Elton 2005)

– their subject and their students. A proper orientation towards both is that of love, and what is that if not passion? In turn, we may say of students that they, too, have a double object: their intellectual or professional field and themselves. They have to have a concern for themselves if they are to prosper in their programme of study. But passion?

Passion is merely the manifest form of the will to learn.[9] By manifest form, we do not need to invoke a behavioural form in a straightforward sense. Passion is the way in which will declares itself, and carries itself forward in the world in an enduring way – as in a student's programme of study. Passion is evident in the student's continuing commitment to her course, her efforts, and her own development; and that commitment is an interplay of self-commitment and commitment to her intellectual or professional field.

And ecstasy? Characteristically, there are two forms of ecstasy evident in higher education. There is the *ephemeral* kind, the kind that is present as when a student passes her examinations or receives a particularly glowing set of comments from a tutor (perhaps after a prolonged period where a topic or set of skills had proved difficult to master). This form of ecstasy may be intense; it may even give rise to exaggerated behaviour in which the student shares her delight with others. The champagne is opened, and even spilled, but this ecstasy is ephemeral – motivating and even exhilarating as it may be at the time – and in itself does not advance the student in her being.

Against that may be distinguished an ecstasy that provides a sediment for the student's development. This is the ecstasy that forms when the student comes into herself anew. She becomes aware that she has understood something that had been posing a challenge or she realizes that she has enacted a set of actions that beforehand were daunting. She becomes herself and is aware of that new becoming. This *durable* ecstasy has a sure foundation. While it may just be possible for the student to regress, that is unlikely. The student has gone forward – she has won for herself and her being a new place. This ecstasy is associated with a durable new being that the student has attained for herself through her own efforts (however much aided by the other students and her tutors).

Admittedly, to distinguish these two forms of ecstasy does not entirely lay bare what ecstasy *is*. After all:

> It is easy to say that one cannot speak of ecstasy. There is in it an element which one cannot reduce, which remains 'beyond expression' . . .
>
> (Cooper, 2002)

What we *can* say is that ecstasy is a profound and intense human experience; it is a heightened form of being-with-the-world. For the student, it may spring from the student's new knowledge but, being an experience, it is:

> Non-knowledge [that] communicates ecstasy – but only if the possibility (the movement) of ecstasy already belonged, to some degree, to one who disrobes himself of knowledge.
>
> (Bataille 1988: 123)

We can also say this, I think (drawing on a distinction that Sartre made famous), that the ephemeral form of ecstasy leaves the student where she is; she is left as a 'being-in-herself'. She does not move forward, but the durable form of ecstasy is a reflection of the student becoming 'for-herself'. She realizes that in the knowing claim or in the action that led to the ecstatic moment, she has become authentically herself, but now in a new place. She has journeyed; she has changed her life and the ecstatic experience is that experience of being in a new place; it is not *reducible* to her new knowledge or capabilities. The ecstatic experience is the justifiable experience of reflection *that* the new knowledge or actions have been achieved, and that the new place has been won.

Becoming a different person

Overall, the four years I spent at [university] have been tiring and frustrating at times but mainly exciting, challenging and immensely rewarding . . . I have graduated a different person from who I was when I entered . . . better equipped for all aspects of life.

(Extract from a female engineering student's story.)[10]

Taking off

In undergoing a process of educational development, the student comes to understand matters, sees anew into topics, comes to be able to perform all manner of operations and engage in hitherto strange activities. Many of these knowledges and actions are intertwined – to those in other subject areas – in extraordinary interdisciplinary combinations. In fact, we do not have a vocabulary with which to describe the combination of capabilities and states of knowing that some contemporary programmes of study in higher education call for. The term 'interdisciplinary', for example, is quite inadequate in some domains, where practices and new knowledge domains have been brought together (as in music design technology). So students may be extended in a wide concatenation of ways. Their humanness is stretched in multiple directions.

However, put in question is the extent of the transformation of their beings. Higher education achieves its apogee when the student becomes authentic. 'Authenticity', we have seen, is but a shorthand for a number of ideas. Perhaps the principal idea that we have touched on is the Sartrean distinction between a self in-itself and a self for-itself. The being in-itself is the self that is largely the subject of other voices; the being for-itself has come into itself and now takes responsibility for its utterances and actions.

This is a journey of becoming, but crucial is the point that this becoming, this coming into authenticity, is never finally accomplished. The journey is never over. On the contrary, new rocks appear on which the being can founder. New tasks, new situations, new topics, new ideas and new techniques present themselves anew, on an almost daily basis. Accordingly, new energies have to be found continually with which to propel the student forward; the will has to be regrouped, over and over. The sustaining of that will to learn is, therefore, an ever-continuing pedagogical challenge and responsibility for the student's tutors; for without this will, knowing and action cannot be accomplished at any serious level.

'At any serious level' is, of course, if left unqualified, a sleight of hand. It evades the issue: what constitutes 'a serious level'? We see it in two forms, in the being in-itself and the being for-itself. The student's will is necessary simply to enable her to engage with her studies and to develop even where that progression is largely a matter of working within the confines of pre-given understandings and practices. Where the student's being is largely held in these confines, the student's being remains in-itself, an enhancement of the being that presented itself at the start of the programme of study.

If the will is necessary here, in the case of being in-itself, it is doubly necessary where the student reaches out to make her own claims, to form her own representations and to inject her own practices into presenting situations. For here, the student's being becomes for-itself; the student takes off, takes flight and flies; she is herself, driving herself, with her own intentionalities and aspirations. The course has become a resource for her own journey. In writing her essay, does she venture forth and even try to take off, or does she remain on the same ground, hesitant and even paralysed by fear of undue risk?

Conclusions

In a genuine higher education, the student not merely undergoes a developmental process, but undergoes a continuing process of becoming. This becoming is marked by the student's becoming authentic and coming into herself, which are two depictions of the same phenomenon. In this coming into herself, the student finds for herself a clearing that is hers. The staking out of the clearing brings with it freedoms, but also responsibilities; for the student can now be called to account on her own account, not that of others.

Here lies an extraordinary potential, indeed a requirement, of higher education: that, through its developmental processes, the student cannot just become herself anew, but can become herself *for the first time*. Her being can move from merely in-itself to for-itself. She discovers her own voice, is able to articulate it and deploy it to effect. She brings to bear not just her own intentionalities, but her own will. She not just is carried forward, but carries herself forward. However, this being for-itself is grounded; grounded in reason. Our student can furnish reasons for her claims and her actions. And her reasons are *her* reasons. The voice has its reasons, as well as its tone.

However, this is a becoming that is never finished. The challenges keep coming; the student is called by her programme of study to displace herself into yet another place. Here, we see an ontology in-the-making, but it is continually in-the-making. Here, perhaps, Sartre is a more sure guide than either Schopenhauer or Heidegger: for both of the latter, being was in time, was never still, but it was Sartre who saw the possibility of an entirely new kind of self emerging. Yet, even there, I am not sure that Sartre recognized the continuing challenges that higher education presages to human becoming. Our student never quite reaches the security of *being for-itself* fully. She is always aware of her shortcomings, of her incompleteness and this is necessarily so in a genuine higher education.

This is a rocky voyage and it is never-ending. It is also a lone journey. No matter the extent of interaction with others, of dialogue or of collaboration, still the student's development, anxiety and becoming are hers, and hers alone. Higher education is a voyage of perpetual self-differentiation, but self-differentiation is not self-individuation, for others are essential in assisting this solo journey. The discovery of the student's voice brings out modulations and dynamics not found in any other student; the student becomes herself and no other person.

A supreme test posed to higher education is that of living continuously with anxiety, of gaining a measure of contentment, and even ecstasy, knowing now that one's thoughts and actions can never be fully grounded. A measure of self-authority amid incompleteness and yet still to press forward. Here is a stubborn will-to-learn: it will not be quelled.

Part 2

Being a student

5

Travel broadens the mind

It's been a huge learning curve and building process as a person. I am completely different from how I was in the first place.

(Languages student, having just graduated.)

Introduction: taking stock

Having grappled with some fundamental concepts, it is time that we turned our attention more directly to the student and her learning. However, let us first capture some of our key points so far made.

The student has her educational being only insofar as she has a will to learn. The will to learn may not be everything, but without it nothing is possible, no knowing of any profundity, no acting with any seriousness, no meant engagement with those around her.

Will is the primary constituent of educational being, therefore, and it is that which must concern educators – even at the national level – as they wrestle with educational matters. At a national level, policies in relation to quality and to non-completion cannot seriously be developed in the absence of this recognition. However, more especially, this contention bears in upon curricula and pedagogical matters, and we shall come to them in due course (in Part Three). For now, we must unravel more explicitly what a will to learn implies for the individual student.

The student's educational being is not given, is not presented as such. It has to develop, to emerge, to be discovered. The student's educational being is always in a process of becoming. This process of becoming is delicate. It has continually to be worked at. It can be injured, and very quickly so, even lost forever. One casual word from the teacher in the classroom situation (or its equivalent in the laboratory or in the clinical setting or in the studio) may crush this process of becoming. So the student's becoming is itself a fragile process.

But what is this process of becoming? My contention here has been that 'becoming' is a process in which the student comes into a mode of authentic being, comes to that point, that realization of being in which she stands by herself, but with justification. She stands on her own ground that she has made her own. She achieves this moment, becomes herself authentically, through her own resources. Of course, she draws on all the relevant aspects of her experience, including the support of her tutors and other students, but ultimately, the resources on which she depends are hers. Those personal resources – of relevant qualities and dispositions – have to be built up. This is the process of becoming, and in this process of becoming, the will itself is not just reaffirmed continually; it is made anew as the student comes into a new place, a new sense of herself, her capacities and her relationships with the world. It is this process of becoming that allows the successful student, as a tutor is introduced at the graduation ceremony to her family (even in their multiple generations), to attest to the life-transforming impact that her university experience has had on her.

Strange places

A genuine higher education is a paradoxical process. It is a process in which the student becomes herself, becomes a self that is uniquely hers, yet, simultaneously, it is a process in which the student, as a self, is displaced from herself.

In a higher education that is worthy of the name, the student encounters strangeness. Intellectual and professional fields, with their perspectives, ways of going on, offer the student a new hold on the world. This is not a reflection on the student's intellectual immaturity; it is, rather, a reflection on the significance of the fields. The fields may be orientated around familiar matters, but as organized 'disciplined' fields of systematic endeavour, they have come to provide each a deep slicing into the world; their truths are their truths. Moreover, in higher education, the student's studies are 'research-informed' and, that being the case, the student is cast into a pedagogical situation of perpetual strangeness. Her knowing experiences are never settled; (new) strangenesses threaten to break in; or may even be desired.

The student, then, is in a process in which she is, in a sense, being estranged from herself. This is not a psychological phenomenon, but arises out of the confluence of epistemological and ontological movements. The student is asked to submit to the strangeness of new worlds opening before her. If they were not strange worlds, there would be question marks over whether we were in the presence of higher education.

In encountering this strangeness, the student is being asked to surrender her beliefs and understandings, or at least to bracket them; and be open to new representations of the world. Such a readiness is – as we have seen – an ontological as much as it is epistemological journey. The student announces – to herself at least – that she is ready for this challenge, to dislodge herself into a new place.

Yet, this is also a process of coming into oneself. In the newness, there is a self-becoming. Here, we may call up the words of Hegel:

This ambiguous supersession of its ambiguous otherness is equally an ambiguous return unto itself . . . through the supersession, it receives back its own self . . .

Self-consciousness . . . has come out of itself . . . it finds itself an other being.

(Hegel, 1977: 110)

Through the grappling with the new, the self moves into a new space. Only thus can it come into itself; it could not possibly come into itself if it remained at the same place.[1] This is the promise, the daring, the challenge of higher education – that it offers, it threatens even, to dislodge the student's self into a new place. In being so dislodged, the student's self may become itself. This self-becoming does not necessarily happen; it will only happen if accompanied by a movement into authenticity. When this happens, the student may come haltingly into this new space, but will emerge into it gladly, for she now knows herself in a new and pleasing way.

Still we have not got to the crux of the phenomenon at hand. It is not so much that the self becomes a new self; in a sense – at least, this is the claim and the promise of a higher education – the self finds itself truly for the first time. This is so through the moment of authenticity that the student reaches, and that is so, in turn, because the student now has reached a position of being able to form understandings of the world and with (more or less) sound warrant. That, to repeat, is particular to higher education, insofar as it is rooted in research and scholarship. In such an environment, the student moves epistemologically onto firmer ground, in that she has grounds for her understandings and claims.

Even in an uncertain world, the ground holds for a moment. That this ground may open up and give way at any moment is not a problem here, for the student's authenticity is founded on her newly found ability to take up a position with some authority, even if there is provisionality now always attaching to that authority. That the student's newly emerging authority may be challenged is, in a sense, all to the good. The student moves now in favour of 'the better reason', makes her judgements accordingly and she comes to being used to perpetual challenges to her position.

We have here, then, not so much a displacing of self as a finding of self; a coming-into-self.[2] Of course, this work, this movement, is never over, never settled. There can be no settlement here, but that is understood. Once set off on this course of self-becoming in this way (through understandings in dialogue), there can be no resting place.

To press the point, it is not just that the student's understandings are perpetually on the move. It is even more significant that the student's self, her being, is now always being tested in its place, that new abodes are being glimpsed and even accepted as successive new homes, and even, in multi-disciplinary programmes of study, new homes simultaneously. This self-becoming, then, is ontological as much as it is epistemological. It is a matter of the student as a person – her self, her being – being tested and of its coming into a new place – a new place, with all its excitement, challenge and, even, foreboding.

But the ontology is prior to the epistemology. That is perhaps the fundamental point of this book. The student's being, her will to learn, her strong self, her willingness to be authentic: all these are a set of foundations for her knowing and her practical engagements. Without a self, without a will to learn, without a being that has come into itself, her efforts to know and to act within her programme of study cannot even begin to form with any assuredness. Educationally, ontology does not so much trump epistemology and praxis as it provides the frame for them.

However, ontology is admittedly enhanced through one's knowing and practical efforts, especially where they are affirmed by the student's tutors or other significant others. New sights that are opened out and that afford some recompense for the struggle strengthen the will to travel further.

Venturing forth

What courage, what daring, we require of our students in higher education. A willingness to venture forth into they know not what. Of course, these days, students can be beset with course prospectuses, course descriptions and course 'outcomes'. However, if they are intent on gaining the most from their experiences, they will realize that these texts are essentially fictional. In a genuine higher education, texts such as these have to be chimerical in character. There comes the recognition that, rather than their higher education experience being simply given to them, students are self-creators of their own experience and have to give of themselves. Indeed, they come to understand that they have to be willing to venture into strange and challenging places. In turn, some students shrink from these challenges and resort to plagiarism, or some such strategy; anything that allows them to evade themselves.

This fear, this 'fear of freedom' – as Eric Fromm (1960) put it – is understandable. For the challenge being put to students in higher education is that they be willing to venture forth even into situations that their tutors cannot foretell. How could it be otherwise? How can one individual, in an educational space of freedom and autonomy, be sure how another individual will go forward and where she might end? To be able to give sure answers to such questions would amount to manipulation, to domination, to overbearing control. To the contrary, if we wish our students to fly, to become themselves, to take off, to take on the world, we have to let them go. Each student is a unique being, and her or his unfolding, accordingly, must lead to yet a furthering of that uniqueness.

Each one's ontology is particular and evades description. The idea that an individual's being, her hold on the world, can be captured in a set of 'intended outcomes' is tantamount to educational totalitarianism. (This is but one reason why talk of 'intended outcomes' has to be repudiated as any serious kind of educational thinking.) However, then, we see again the awesomeness of the personal challenge we put before students – to voyage into a new place, to place themselves into new experiences, that may test their very hold on the world.

Higher education, a genuine higher education, calls for the student to have a will to travel. This will to travel is not an aimless will, is not a propensity for globetrotting (though it is just possible that some modular courses in particular may prompt such an educational orientation). Rather, this will to travel is a will to explore with a purpose. It is a will to engage purposively with the experiences that present themselves and into which the student is plunged.[3]

This exploration is not, it will be clear, purely in the mind. This educational travel does not just broaden the mind; it opens up the self. It brings the self into a surer sense of itself. It allows the self to unfold. Is this not a common occurrence: that the student who was shy and inarticulate begins, through her course of study, to emerge: her self forms, and takes on stronger hues.

This is not an empirical point, which, after all, could only implicate a particular kind of student. This is a point about what it is to be a student in the higher education in front of us here. It affects the strong-willed, as well as the more hesitant. The voyage may be undertaken with great élan and confidence, and with great vigour and even enthusiasm, but what kind of personal becoming is on the cards? Is it a coming-into-authenticity? Is it a winning of one's oneness, one's own particularity, one's capacity to stand for oneself (if not by oneself)?

Let us try to be a little clearer about the venturing forth that a genuine higher education offers. It is not a rootless wandering, but a bounded voyage of discovery. It is also a voyage in which the self is implicated. When we speak of authenticity, what is meant is the emerging capacity of the student to be for-herself, but taking her bearings from the high points of the territories encountered. Here, again, we see some backing for our earlier suggestion that Sartre beckons more than Heidegger; for this authenticity is more a matter of coming into one's own space, rather than having that space identified by the surrounding traditions (even if Heidegger's authenticity was a breaking free of the 'they'). However, the coming into one's own space is only possible through the compass bearings that are available, through the student's course, its standards, the student's tutors, her co-journeying students and even the wider environment of the institution.

The spaces in which we must ask students to move these days are fluid spaces; 'liquid' spaces, as Bauman (2000, 2005a,b) might term them. There are few, if any, fixed compass bearings. Many are engaged on multidisciplinary courses, where the formations and integrations of knowledges and practices yield an infinity of positions, and of modes of being. Somehow, the student has to manoeuvre and come through safely in all of this, to reach some point – if not one of equilibrium, then of a capacity to hold the strands of those experiences and responses in some kind of tolerable tension. This capacity to live with inner tension may just open up spaces for temporary respites, for sojourns, to the student traveller.

These tensions are felt tensions, and are not just cognitive in character. The student may feel that she is 'at sea' and even feel that she is drowning; or, at least, that the lack of an assured and stable position is too much to bear.

There is, then, opening up here a large pedagogical task in encouraging the student to voyage forth into this milieu. It is a task of engendering the human capacity to live with uncertainty, to press forward when there can be no sure direction. Each student, after all, has to be his or her own voyager for he and she are different; their self, their sentiments, their experiences are theirs. In such a pedagogical setting, responses are likely to vary from fear and hesitancy to delight and wonder: it is the latter set of dispositions that our pedagogies are challenged to elicit.

Ultimately, we want our students to jump off the platform, to bungee-jump into the void, to venture into new experiences that will be emotionally disturbing, and that will challenge their being and move them into a new place. Will they have the courage to do it? What pedagogical forms are likely to elicit such preparednesses, such predispositions, among our students? How might they be enabled to gain that will to learn, to encompass the continually unsettling?

The oscillating self

The strangenesses that students encounter in a genuine higher education are not just cognitive, but are also, and more fundamentally, to do with their being. If we can use a language of 'delight', 'wonder', 'engagement' and even 'love' to begin to do justice to the meaning that a student's studies may have, then we are implicitly saying that the very being of the student is implicated in this educational journey.

Certainly, the value of such a language is threatened in a marketized age in which we invite the student to have a market relationship with her studies, valuing it for whatever capital it will return to her (whether financial, social or otherwise). So, to remind ourselves of a language in which the student's being is implicated is to remind ourselves of an alternative conception of higher education. The language in which we cast our educational practices itself predisposes us in pedagogical directions that may open and close certain educational possibilities.

Let us, for now, hang onto a language of delight, wonder, care, excitement, fun, engagement and love – the language in which a student is caught and even entranced by the experiences that her course has opened to her. How might we understand the ontological implications of such a language? I have suggested that the Sartrean idea of a self coming to be for-itself is helpful, but I think we need to go further.

Finding energy in one's studies

The new energy, in my case . . . is when I'm doing my studies well. So new energy mainly comes from the studies itself.

(First year Physics student, pre-92 university)

We have here a trajectory, in which the student implicates, indeed fuels and ignites herself. The student propels herself forward. Certainly, the student can be inspired and energized by her tutors, and many, if not all, of the experiences that she encounters (and we must come to the matter of inspiration later), but this energizing is also self-injected. The student's energies have to be hers, to a significant extent. The formation of the will has to be, in part, the student's.

The will in question here is a will, a preparedness, as we have noted, to move into a different place. We have here an extraordinary and surely largely unnoticed human phenomenon: a disposition to forget oneself. This self-forgetfulness is called for as we ask the student to yield herself to the curricula experiences that we put their way. Wherein comes the yielding? The yielding comes not just in the immediacy of the pedagogical situations, but even more in the giving oneself up to the forms and contours of the intellectual and professional fields that give substance to the student's course of study. Those intellectual and professional fields have their own ways of seeing the world, and of making legitimate claims about and even interventions in the world, and it is these perspectives and forms of understandings we term 'standards'.

It was the existence of such perspectives and standards that led Richard Peters (1975) to speak of the 'givenness' of educational situations. Where, perhaps, Richard Peters went askew was in over-focusing on that side of educational situations; rather lost sight of was the student as a human being being asked to engage with those perspectives and standards; and the very term 'givenness' perhaps implied a fixity of that external world that was overplayed.

The self, in this encompassing of the new, of the strange, does not lose itself as it extends itself. It oscillates between itself and this new world – or set of worlds – to which it is exposed.[4]

Helpfully, for us here, Rudolf Arnheim (1988) distinguishes two universal space systems, centric and ex-centric. In the centric space system, the self is concerned with itself, its own interests and predispositions. In the ex-centric, the self is prepared to reach out to other centres. In the mature educational orientation, there can be no signing up solely to either orientation; on the contrary, what is called for is a continuing oscillation between the two orientations, with both being held in tension with each other:

. . . the interaction between both tendencies represents a fundamental life task . . . the tension between the two antagonistic tendencies, trying to find the balance, constitutes the real spice of the human existence . . . Neither centring totally on yourself nor totally opening up for the exterior powers can constitute an acceptable image of human motivation.

(Arnheim, 1988, 18–19)

Flavia Vieira comments on these ideas of Arnheim with perspicacity:

If the space of the human experience is in the tension and balance between the centric and the ex-centric tendencies, two things (we) will be unable to do: looking inside and looking outside alone. *The space of our look will always be between 'here' and 'there', 'now' and 'then', 'me' and the 'other'. Only that space will enable dialogue and connection. Only that space will enable true knowledge power: the power to free and unite.*

(RAB's emphasis; Flavia Vieira, undated note)

This is an internal dialogue that encompasses the other; and it is a dialogue between oneself and the other, between self and knowing. In this dialogue, at its best, the student can feel herself growing in good ways: she gains in confidence. It is not just a confidence in relation to her studies, but a self-confidence, a heightened sense of herself as a person. The new enthusiasm is, in part, an enthusiasm for self, a new valuing of self. Being 'hooked' on one's field – history, physics, engineering, sociology, say, or the challenges opened up by interdisciplinary programmes comprising innovative mixes of comprehension and practice – is an indication of a displacement of self into the other (the intellectual or professional field), but it is also a sign of new self-belief. The self has grown, and continues to grow, precisely by displacing itself outside of itself.

In this interior movement, the centric is displaced to make room for the ex-centric. The concern with self is reduced as new worlds are encountered and new powers emerge to come into an authentic relationship with them.

In turn, new energies are created and the will to learn grows. In the process, the student expends energies, but this energy capacity is not finite, new energies can continually be created. The student's excitement need never wane. The voyage may yield continuing delight, producing new energies. Whether it does or not depends partly on the pedagogical situation: is it one that is likely to energize the student or, to the contrary, deflate those energies?

As the student's interests take hold, they take her over. The self is forgotten, in a way, as it gives itself to the demands of the educational situations. Yet, paradoxically, the self is expanded as it comes into an authentic relationship with the fields of interest. What may we conclude? That, surely, we have a new kind of self in the making. This is a learning-self, a self that is prepared continually to be tested by new experiences. Such a learning-self has to be energized – no energy, no learning. It is a self displaced into (intellectual) fields and (professional) regions, but yet that keeps itself within the student's being.

Accordingly, we may conclude not merely that this travel broadens the mind, but that it also widens the self and offers a new state of being.[5]

Getting lost

Students sometimes feel 'at sea'; they feel 'lost'. The travel metaphors that they themselves use to describe their situations are testimony to the voyaging aspect of their studies. In voyaging, they travel to new lands, and they may never return to wheresoever they started. However, sometimes, the travel does not go smoothly; how might we understand that, in terms of our recent reflections?

Perhaps two dominant possibilities lay behind the student saying that she is 'at sea' or 'is lost'. There is, on the one hand, the situation of impenetrable thickets, namely the possibility that the challenges being put the student's way are just too demanding either intellectually or practically. On the other hand, there is the situation of overly dense thickets. Here, the student may feel not so much that any particular aspect of the course is too demanding, but that the proliferation of ideas or experiences is such that she is in a state of some confusion, and is unable to see any way forward into a clear space. She is stuck fast in a wilderness.

We should note that the student might find difficulty in some other way. For instance, she may be unhappy with the ethical principles underlying the programme, but she would surely be unlikely to use the travel metaphor in this way. She is more likely to say that the course was going 'in the wrong direction' or in a direction with which she felt uncomfortable. I shall return to this possibility in a moment; for now, let us focus on the metaphors of being lost or at sea; in other words, of an overload of experience of some kind.

Here, we are faced with a student who is wanting to go forward, and is wanting to reach a firm understanding of the phenomena that confront her. For the moment, the will to learn is there, but now, at least, there is a blockage, whether of an insufficiency of understanding (the impenetrable thickets syndrome) or of an incoherent understanding (the overly dense thickets syndrome).

An issue that arises in a situation such as this is whether the blockage – in either case – can be released sufficiently quickly as to maintain the will to learn. There is, after all, precisely in this situation the very real possibility that the student may become frustrated if the blockage is not released in reasonable time. Of course, what counts as 'reasonable time' will vary from student to student and over generations. It may be that, in this age of 'chronoscopic time' (Hassan, 2003), students' propensities to 'stick with it' may be shortening. If that release does not come in an acceptable timeframe, the student's will to learn may dissipate. At such a moment, the student is on the cusp:

if the blockage is cleared, she can go forward; if it is not cleared soon, she may become disillusioned and lose her will to go on learning. She may even drop out of her course.

The educational voyages that we wish students to embark upon are bound to cause ontological discomfort. Far from such discomfort being uncommon, however, it is difficult to imagine that it could be avoided. One tacit aim of a genuine 'higher' education, as we have noted, is to displace the student's being into not just new, but strange places. This is almost certain to cause discomfiture. A tacit educational aim in higher education, it might even be said, is to bring about a measure of discomfort; the discomfort is a necessary condition of 'disjunction' (Jarvis, 1992), out of which a higher learning might arise. Accordingly, a key pedagogical task is that of enabling students to live with this discomfiture. After all, it will not be dispelled: one discomfiture, once overcome, will be replaced with another. A higher education, indeed, may be felt to be an initiation into continuing discomfiture or, at least, a series of sojourns between successive discomfitures.

The lost traveller looks (to draw on a theme favoured by Derrida in his later works (e.g. 2001) for hospitality.[6] So, too, with students in higher education. What succour might they hope for when lost? Hospitality is to be found in pedagogies of strangeness.[7] That is to say, the student may find a way of accommodating to her sense of being lost. She is lost. The thickets cannot suddenly clear. So she has to be enabled to live with this sense of being lost. She has to come to know that, with her will and effort, they will clear, at least sufficiently for her to go on with renewed confidence. However, it is a hospitality that enables her to understand that this sense of being lost cannot ever be entirely dissipated forever. A hospitable pedagogy is an honest pedagogy, enabling the student to understand and to find ways of living with uncertainty. Such a pedagogical sanctuary offers the student a temporary respite; a sojourn from any serious travail.

Conclusions

A genuine higher education is not just a matter of intellectual travel or even a movement through new kinds of practice, but is also a matter of self-travel. Using terms bequeathed to us by Sartre, we may say that the student may come into a position of authentic self-for-itself. This may come about through the authenticity that the student reaches over time in her intellectual and practical engagements. In the process of this self-travel, the student's being may itself change. Her hold on the world may change. Her essence as a human being may change.

In a genuine higher education, there is a process, as we put it, of ontological displacement: the student moves into another place as a human being. Her life, her relationship to the world, was changed. But she did not temporarily abandon her being as she became excited by her course: her engagement, her being caught by her course experiences, were only possible through her being immersing itself in those experiences. Her being evolved through those experiences. Her encounters with the intellectual fields and professional regions of her course prompted a continuing inner dialogue between those experiences and her self.

It was an educational journey in which she became more fully herself. This unfolding was possible because of the achievement of authenticity, in which our student came to see the world in certain ways and was able to offer accounts of the world with some authority (she could give her own reasons for what she said and did). She caught the wind and sailed on.

Things did not always go smoothly. The travel was halted at times, but pedagogies of hospitality encouraged her to persist, to maintain her will to learn and to go on. Those pedagogies included the formation of the student cohort into 'learning communities', where students extended hospitality to each other. Energies were sustained. Enchantment in the new, in the strange, was continually renewed.

6

A will to offer

Putting forward

The student not only has a will to learn but also has a will to offer. The will to offer takes double form. He offers his texts – in whatever form they take – *and* he offers himself. At least, this is one of the tasks of higher education: to bring the student to this point. Its achievement, the achievement of higher education, is to have brought this about, this willingness on the part of the student to put his texts *and* himself forward.

How do we understand this phenomenon? Why is it so important to the idea of higher education? What are the pedagogical challenges of bringing about this situation? This is the ground of our explorations in this chapter.

An outcome?

There is much talk these days, as we have noted, about curriculum 'outcomes': in the UK and elsewhere, there is now an expectation that curriculum units should be expressible as outcomes. Could the idea of a student offering his texts be considered an outcome? Prima facie, it has a certain plausibility. The student presents his texts at the conclusion of his module or course. Surely, that is an outcome devoutly to be prized? The essay is submitted on time, the experiment is conducted, the problem is solved, the project report is produced (and even given a warrant by the client), the examination is sat and successfully so. This is an outcome of a real kind: it has a materiality. This is a sign of the student making progress, of moving through the course in the expected way. The assignments or exam scripts are there, waiting to be assessed by the course team and they pile up in the course administrator's office. A little later, the student is given his degree certificate.

Precisely because of the power of the discourse of outcomes, we may easily be seduced into seeing the tangible expressions of the student's work in just this way, but we must beware of being so beguiled. Here, the student's performances become buried in the parallel discourse of performativity: the student's efforts are to be measured through the tangible products that emanate from him. Such a material sense of performance, that the perform-ance is only to be valued through the material outcomes that it yields, is a warped and partial valuing of the student's educational efforts. This is an economic idea of higher education, in which the student is valued only through the commodities that he produces.

'Performativity' rightly has a bad name, but much less appreciated in the higher education literature are worthwhile senses of performance. Lyotard was surely unhelpful in his (1984) use of the term 'performativity'. The sense of performance that he had in mind – that of a product having value insofar as it performed beyond itself – obscured other senses of performance and is now almost lost to sight. Two senses of performance are available that help us here. First, there is a sense of performance as evident in the world of theatre. Writing about theatre, the English director, Peter Brook asks the question: 'When a performance is over, what remains?' He goes on to answer his own question:

. . . something in the mind burns. The event scorches on to the memory an outline, a taste, a trace, a smell.

Brook also observes that:

the French word for performance [is] *representation.* A representation . . . is not an imitation or description of a past event . . . It takes yesterday's action and makes it live again . . . [it is] a making present.

(1990: 152–155)

The most powerful performances, in other words, are not just alive; they are life itself in its fullness, at once creative, engaging and significant.

Secondly, there is a parallel sense of performance bequeathed to us by J. L. Austin, one of the originators of linguistic philosophy. Austin (1975) distinguished different classes of speech acts: 'constatives' were the familiar ground in which efforts were made to describe the world; Austin, however, was more interested in 'performatives', speech acts in which actors carried out a particular performance. Austin identified a number of types of per-formative speech acts and his work gave rise to a sustained philosophical programme that led through the work of John Searle (1969) to help under-pin the system developed by Jurgen Habermas (which Habermas (1979) termed 'universal pragmatics'). For our purposes, we do not need to unpick the threads of that story. What is relevant here is simply the idea of language-in-use as performative: it does not just help us to understand the world; it also conjures into being the world itself.

Here, then, are two powerful ideas of performance that are worth hanging onto: on the one hand, the idea of performance-as-theatre, of performance as creative and as reaching out to an audience; on the other hand, the idea of language-as-performance, itself being creative, of speech as action. Connec-tions between these two sets of ideas are striking: both contain a sense of putting forward, of action, and of communication. *En passant*, we may note that this set of ideas of performance inhabits a quite different set of spaces from that of 'performativity' in Lyotard's philosophy: there, after all, we find a dissolution of inner meaning, and a separation of actor from performance. Lyotard's idea of performativity has a weak or even negative meaning, whereas both language-as-performance and theatre-as-performance are shot through with positive meaning.[1]

We must come quickly to saying more about 'meaning' – what does it mean to talk of being 'devoid of' or 'shot through with' meaning? – but let us first close the circle by returning to the ideas at the start of this section.

The manifest entities that result from a student's efforts and which are submitted to others – his tutors, his fellow students – may be considered to be 'outcomes': they are the outcomes or even, the products of his labours. However, it is surely already becoming apparent that such a language – of outcomes and products – is at best a poor description of the phenomena before us. For that language, *that* sense of performativity of outcomes and products, separates the entity – the essay, the experiment, the problem solution, the design – from its originator. In this separation is liable to be lost a sense of the involvement of the student in the work.

Pedagogical urgings

In this separation of entity from author lies, too, an educational and even a pedagogical perniciousness. Educationally, the idea of a valid act on the part of the student residing purely as an outcome not just obliterates the process leading to the outcome, but it obliterates the student himself. The student as a human being is occluded and the student as creator is neglected. Pedagogically, too, there is a further effect and it is that effect that I wish to focus on here.

The idea of outcomes, when unduly pressed, renders invisible the pedagogical context in which most student efforts have their place. By and large, even in programmes of 'independent learning', students' efforts have their place in a context of curricula hopes and even requirements: students are required to do certain things, and often in a particular set of timeframes. Again, and even where students are 'at a distance', students are held in a pedagogical frame: there are tutors or others with teaching or quasi-teaching roles with whom they are in contact. A frame of hopes and expectations and even directions encircles students.

The students' efforts, in other words, are not normally forthcoming entirely spontaneously: there are pedagogical prompts that set off those efforts and in which those efforts have meaning. A student that tried to dominate a syndicate group or continued to press particular points in a seminar, or failed to wear a white coat in a laboratory or was disinclined to respond to a tutor's advice over argumentation styles in her history essays would be misreading the pedagogical code, such that her actions would be considered to be inappropriate. Even worse, she would be liable to taking herself outside the rules of the pedagogical frame; the meaning of her continuing actions would be lessened if not nullified.

There is, then, a network of relations between the student, her tutors, the curriculum and the pedagogical frame. Together, this network of relations provides a set of pedagogical urgings: the student is expected to come forth with her work in all its manifold forms through her course of studies. There is here, to put it differently, a multitude of educational callings: the student is called to act in certain ways; other ways may lead if not to excommunication then to admonishment.

To observe that complex of relationships and its educational callings still does not give us an entrée into a proper understanding of the happening of the student's work that is made available to others. However pressing, however tight, the curricula and the pedagogical relationship may be, still there will be no work forthcoming unless the student wills it. That much we observed in our earlier explorations. Here, though, we are drawing out the shortcomings of the idea of outcomes and a further point emerges: the student's work is not disembodied and it is not itself without a will that has brought it forth, but still we are not yet home.

The pedagogical frame is replete not only with expectations (as we have just noted), but is saturated with judgement. Even if the student is working with other students, she will feel the judgemental gaze of her peers. Herein surely lies the possibility of a language that is an alternative to that of outcomes and products, a language that is testimony to the way in which the student's work is itself relational. It would be a language that acknowledges that the work emerges from the student, has the imprint of the student in it, and is presented to others for their consideration.

The offer

The language that I have in mind is one of *proffering*, of *tendering*, of *offering*, of *sharing*, and of *presenting* and *gifting*. Anthropology has devoted much effort in helping us to understand the nature of gifts: gifts are a way of establishing and sustaining social relationships. The gift giver gives of himself, but, also, in return sets up a set of reciprocal obligations on the part of the receiver of the gift. There are no free gifts. As Derrida commented more formally, 'The truth of the gift ... suffices to annul the gift. The truth of the gift is equivalent to the non-gift or to the non-truth of the gift' (in Marion, 2002: 80) It just may be, however, that higher education is a site where the rules of gift-giving are regularly broken. Rather, it just may be that – apart from the overt present giving by international students from certain cultures – higher education is not much recognized as a site *of* gift giving.

The pedagogical relationship may surely be understood in just these terms, as a setting of gift-giving that at least opens a space for mutual obligations attendant upon gift-giving (even if that space is seldom recognized as such). That, at least, is the thesis I now wish to pursue.

In the pedagogical setting, the student engages in activities circumscribed by a curriculum. Those activities are implicitly judged to be worthwhile, for the curriculum has characteristically been formally sanctioned (typically through a university's internal course validation procedures). However, those curricula activities are not just worthwhile in themselves for they are normally intended to lead somewhere. In that leading somewhere, there is something that emerges, whether it be the result of a laboratory experiment, a problem that has been solved, an essay that has been submitted or a design that has been created. These are pedagogical offerings.

Her own thinking: a student's putting forward

RB: *Here you are, you are writing an essay. You've done your research. You've more or less got an idea of what you want to say. You've got to perhaps argue for something, to develop a certain point of view. How does that feel . . . when you know this is probably quite original and it's you speaking?*

Student: *It's really exciting, and at the same time you are thinking would anyone else agree with this. And if nobody else does then obviously it's not very valid. . . . In that way, sometimes it's safer to stick to the literary criticism . . . and express the critic's point of view and put your own point forward against that.*

(Student at pre-1992 university.)

Pedagogical offerings may also be evident in more vividly performative ways: the student offers a contribution to the seminar, she works away diligently in the laboratory (even if the experiment fails) or she throws herself into her teaching practice. That the language of outcomes sits uneasily among these performances, with their lived challenges *in situ*, shows us again the limitations of the idea of outcomes.

In all of these cases, the student is offering something. She is always offering herself, in every case, but we can go further. One might be tempted to distinguish the two sets of cases: in the former set of cases, where there is something of a definite outcome of her educational labours, we might say that she is also offering the product itself – the essay, the outcome of the experiment, the design – whatever it may be. However, this would surely be a superficial reading. Again, in every case, whether there is a tangible outcome or not, the student is also offering *the act itself*. The intervention in the seminar, the work in the laboratory, the contribution to a student syndicate group, the wholehearted engagement with her teaching practice: all these are offerings too, irrespective of there being a particular outcome from such efforts.

There is, then, at least a double offer on the part of the student in any pedagogical setting: there is the labour and there is the putting forward, the commitment, of the student herself. It just may be, too, that in some pedagogical situations, there is in addition a tangible produce of her labours – evident in the data, the problem solution, the essay, the design – which the student also offers. So, we have – at least, theoretically – a *triple offer* on the part of the student: the putting forward of the student herself; her continuing efforts sustained over time and some kind of material entity that results from these labours that is presented to others. Self, praxis and materiality, then: the student's offering has this triple structure.

To speak of an offer implies that the student *tenders* the act or the entity: the intervention in the seminar, or the submitted draft essay or the action in the laboratory are ways in which the student *gives*. There is talk (and, indeed, argument) in the literature of the givenness of matters educational (of certain aspects of knowledge, of the hierarchical nature of the pedagogical relationship); there is much less talk, if any, about the *giving-ness within the pedagogical relationship*. Both the teacher and the taught put themselves forward, offer themselves, give themselves. They even, to some extent, exchange themselves.

Here, we are focusing on the student as gift giver. That which the student puts forward is an educational offer. Accordingly, those receiving the gift are put under an obligation, in the first place of acknowledging the gift as a gift. The tutor may well thank the student for her contribution to the discussion or for her essay, irrespective of any inherent qualities of the offering. In the former case, too, it is also a gift to the other students and is deserving of the tutor's thanks on behalf of the other students.

How might we understand a student's actions as a matter of gift giving and why might its simply being tendered merit thanks from the tutor? In higher education, students are present voluntarily – whatever the press of family and peers, not to mention the labour market, might be. As we have just observed, the student is involved in activities that have already been judged to be worthwhile (the course of study has been formally 'validated'). It follows that whatever the student does qua student, there is value in it – howsoever it may be judged. Its simply being proffered *is* of value.

The value lies not just for and in the student; it is not just that this proffering is a necessary prolegomenon to the student's journey along the envisaged path (implicit in the curriculum). The value lies also in its being put forward, in the student putting herself forward. For the putting forward by the student herself is an act of courage. The student puts herself out of herself. She puts herself into the open. Many students shrink from this putting forward. They remain silent in the seminar, even when given much space and gentle encouragement by a sensitive tutor, or they hold back in sharing their draft essay or thesis chapter. There is here a dual fear on the part of the student: a fear of failure, of critique; and so the hesitant student will say, as the essay is proffered, that 'I am very disappointed with it', or 'it isn't good enough, is it?' or, in advance of an assessment, 'it's not going to go well tomorrow'. The student damns herself, anticipating the failure to come.

In processes of self-assessment, students often judge themselves more severely than their tutors.

A second related fear on the part of the student is that of feeling that one has fallen short of the role in which one is cast, that one is not authentically a student. This fear is evidenced not just by those who are newcomers to higher education, who doubt their abilities; it is also apparent in research students who have already received many indications of their abilities to succeed.

There is yet a third fear at work here; namely, a fear of rejection. Since the student's offering is the student's own offering – whether in the form of the seminar intervention, the essay or whatever it may be – the student associates academic failure with personal rejection. The student feels that in whatever she does, not only is the act or the entity being judged, but that she is being judged. It is that fear of being judged as a person that may come to paralyse her into inaction and, consequently, a shrinking from making her educational offers.

Fear of freedom

We recalled earlier that Fromm famously talked of a fear of freedom: for him, a fear of freedom was one explanation of the authoritarian personality. That analysis is not without its point here. In modern society, Fromm pointed out, man 'becomes more independent, alone and afraid'. The fear arises out of 'inner restraints, compulsions and fears' (1960: 90–91). Capitalism has contributed to:

> [an] increase in positive freedom to the growth of an active, critical, responsible self . . . at the same time [however], it [has] made the individual more alone and isolated and imbued him with a feeling of insignificance and powerlessness.
>
> (Eric Fromm, 1960: 93).

Do we not see parallels with the pedagogical relationship in higher education? Here, we find a relationship that is intended precisely to help the student become independent, self-critical and self-responsible. Under those circumstances, it is hardly surprising if the student shrinks from exercising that positive freedom being extended to her, namely the freedom to venture forth, to become herself, to make something of herself. The responsibilities are too onerous: much easier is the curriculum in which her becoming is already mapped out in so many foretold 'outcomes', and so a conspiracy easily and dolefully develops such that her tutors, the course and her university (not to mention national curriculum or quality bodies) reclaim responsibility for decision-making from the student.

The analogy between Fromm's analysis of the fear of freedom and the lurch to the authoritarian personality, on the one hand, and the shifts we are surely seeing in the pedagogical relationship in Western higher education is powerful, but it should not beguile us. There is an important difference.

In Fromm's analysis, it was the individual that lurched in the direction of the authoritarian personality: the fear of freedom led the individual to yearn for security and reliance on the other that authoritarian figures and systems seemed to offer. It was, in turn, the individual whose personality become authoritarian that Fromm sought to comprehend. Here, in modern higher education, the boot is on the other foot (to coin a possibly apt metaphor). If there is an authoritarian personality lurking, it lies not in the student herself, but is surely located in the combined paraphernalia of the quality systems, the courses, the national quality bodies, and the institutions and the staff who sign up to them. In all of this, the student is rendered passive, afraid even to do the bidding of the authority figures and framework in which she finds herself.

The 'fear' here is not so much the fear of freedom *per se*, but rather the fear of rejection. To put it another way, despite the rhetoric of self-responsibility, the student does not typically feel that that is the intended character of her approach to her studies. On the contrary, she feels that her actions and her works are subject to possibly corrosive critique. She is far from free to do and say as she wishes, and in that moment, her very being is itself threatened. How can she come forth with her thoughts, her feelings, her words, and her actions when she feels so open to and so vulnerable to critique?

A will to offer

The works, interventions and actions of the student constitute, we have been seeing, a set of offers on the part of the student. The student not only puts her words, her works and her actions forwards; she puts herself forward. These are gifts from the student, gifts that take form in the dimensions of self, praxis and materiality. They are gifts because they are freely given; given, that is, without any fixed return being forthcoming.

Indeed, they have a peculiarly inverted form as gifts: these are gifts that may yield only censure, only rebuke, only critique. The critique is felt, too, in three ways (as we have also seen): as a judgement on the work, on the student qua student, and on the student as a person. In that last mode, the censures strike deeply into the student's being; the student feels herself to be put down, that she has let herself down, as well as the tutor. The student's being is deeply implicated in this gift-giving.

For Derrida, gift-giving – along with other social offerings pertinent to our theme such as friendship and hospitality – contained within it itself both a shortfall and an excess. Gift-giving appears to be without expectation of a return but usually comes with just such an expectation. However, in so doing, it reaches beyond itself, containing the hope of pure gifting. The deconstruction of gift-giving reveals its double aspect. So, too, here, in the pedagogical situation. Here are gifts given without any hope of even a 'thank-you', yet this 'gift-giving' looks for some kind of return. The feedback may come late; the marks may not be as hoped, but the expectation of some return is carried in these gifts. The student's offerings are gifts and deserve to be recognized as such, despite their hoped-for return.

Indeed, these gifts are jewels, quite often painfully won by the student from deep within himself, and hesitantly tendered, accompanied by a unsettling and troubling uncertainty as to their reception (cf. Strathern, 2004, 2007[2]). They may represent, too, only the tangible outcomes of the travail through which the student has gone. Quite often, he remained silent in the lecture or the seminar, shrinking from sharing his thoughts with the class and tutor, even though the class would have been so well served by his interventions. His contributions would have been gifts that may have lit up the class, taken the conversation forward and even caused the tutor to re-think his position.

However, it is not silence on the part of the student that has to be explained and it is not the late essay that deserves immediate attention. Rather, it is any intervention on the part of the student that has to be explained; it is the essay presented *on time* that deserves some kind of account. We account for it, do we not, by recognizing that driving the offering by the student – of whatever kind – is a will to offer. The student wills herself forward to make her offering.

Is the student's will to offer without further explanation? There is nothing that stands behind this will to offer: either the student has it or does not have it? There is, though, perhaps a little more that may usefully be observed. The student who has a will to offer, to put forward (as we have seen), runs risks of rebuke, rejection and even resentment (from 'fellow' students). In projecting herself forward, she is accepting of the possible bruising and even pain that may come in any such rejection. Whatever the outward show, the student's being is fragile. Only so much can be borne.

The student's will to offer presses itself forward. The student may deliberate as to whether she will make an intervention; she may agonize over submitting that essay. However, the will to offer is characteristically strong. The intervention comes at the last, as the seminar is ending; the essay comes in, perhaps even a little over time, but it comes in. The will to offer is strong, but it has its limits: too many rejections, too many hurting experiences in the classroom (or its equivalent in other pedagogical situations), too many failures to pick up on the interventions in the seminar and the will *will* dissipate. Such critical incidents are not always immediately evident. Two students may make contributions more or less simultaneously, and the tutor may seize on one of them to develop the point at issue and simply overlook the other one, causing the student there to feel that his offering amounted to very little, indeed. The will to offer is more fragile than might be assumed.

The will to learn, it is turning out, is nothing without a parallel will to offer. This is not necessarily a defining feature of higher education, but it is a feature of higher education, nevertheless. The pedagogical regime of higher education is a combination of voluntariness and regulation. Students, as such, are regulated probably more than in any other part of the educational system. Yet they are there out of their own volition. They are adults and can choose whether or not they stay on their course, and submit to its requirements. In such a pedagogical setting, the student is obliged to offer, to come forward with her offerings. Those offerings are expected to be the student's own and freely given. In effect, the student is being asked to have a will to offer. This is a fundamental and surely unnoticed paradox of the pedagogy of higher education: compulsion and autonomy, expectation and gift-giving.

The will to offer, therefore, takes on a strange character. It is, as we have noted, the proffering of a gift given in hostile surroundings. The gift may be followed by rejection. So the will to offer is courageous. It has its place in a characteristically threatening milieu. The offer is made despite the unpredictability of the response. After all, the internal examiners can often barely agree on the mark themselves; so how can the student be sure of the outcome? She cannot. She has to have the will to offer her work – and herself – irrespective of the forthcoming verdict. The will to offer is fearless or, rather, it overcomes its fears. It presses forward, perhaps fearing the outcome, but it presses forward nonetheless.

Without this courageous will to offer, the will to learn – in higher education – is naught. The will to learn has no substance unless it ushers forth in offerings. Not uncommonly, research students come to be passionately interested in their topic, becoming experts in their minds and in their exchanges in the supervision sessions, but at the same time, many such students find it difficult to commit their ideas to paper. One reason for this is a fear of placing their thoughts into the semi-public space – as they might judge it – of their pedagogical settings. They cannot even bring themselves to allow their supervisor to see their work. They are fearful of the ensuing judgement. Here, the will to learn has become diluted, losing its concentrated focus and its power. The will to learn is evidently present but the will to offer is sadly lacking.

Both wills are necessary conditions of student development in higher education: a will to learn *and* a will to offer. Both are fundamental and each is distinct; neither is reducible to the other. Together, therefore, the two wills constitute a dual challenge for a responsive pedagogy: students have to be affirmed in their sense of themselves, such that their will to learn is gently warmed; students have to be encouraged to come forward with their offerings, so as to submit themselves for scrutiny. Students need to believe that they have the capacity to learn and to advance themselves; *and* they need the courage to submit offerings, even if interim. The will to learn without the will to offer is jejune, is dilettante. The will to offer without a will to learn is literally pretentious; it pretends to a diligence that it does not possess. The two wills have to be present together and their nurturing is a fundamental challenge, perhaps the fundamental challenge, in higher education.

Conclusion

In higher education, the student is mandated to come forward with offerings, but the coming forward with offerings does not mean that we are in the presence of higher education. Quite the contrary; if the offerings are only tendered because they are mandated – according to the requirements set down in the regulations – no processes of higher education (worthy of the name) are before us. What is required for a process of higher education to be present is that the offerings of the student are hers. That is, she tenders her offerings on her own account. She tenders her offerings despite the regulations and not because of them.

This is the purest form of gift giving. The student puts forward her offerings – in word or deed – in the knowledge that the response may be severely critical. That the work in question 'passes' is immaterial. The student does not know in advance the response that will be forthcoming. The student places her works into the cavity that is her pedagogical situation not knowing how they may be received. They may lay there for some time, almost without being noticed on occasions. (The student waits in vain as it seems on occasions for her assignments to be returned, along with some helpful feedback.)

This proffering, this tendering, requires a considerable will. In putting her works forward, the student puts herself forward. This putting forward of the self is not confined to personal actions (in the laboratory or studio, say), or interventions in the seminar, or lecture. Even in her written assignments, the student is putting herself forward. She is investing herself in her work; she will feel any comment – whether praise or critique – as a comment on her *self*. She cannot divorce herself from her works; she is her works.

There is a will at work here, a will that is prepared to risk the vicissitudes of the critical environment that is the academic world (there are standards and there are expectations and there are judgements ahead). This is a will to offer and this will to offer is separate from, although complementary to, the will to learn. Accordingly, a dual pedagogical responsibility arises, namely that of urging forward both the will to learn and the will to offer.

The student may have to be coaxed to come forward with her offerings, to speak up in the seminar, to give in her work and engage in the clinical situation. Where such offerings are forthcoming, they are treasures, to be valued as such. The student deserves thanks for her offerings alone, even before any judgement has been made as to their intrinsic worth. The will to offer often has to be cultivated by the teacher and the student together. Another way of understanding this situation is one of the bringing forth of the student's own voice. The idea of voice, however, deserves attention on its own account, and it is to that, therefore, that we should next turn.

7

Voice

Learning is not enough!

(Nietzsche, 1968: 226)

Introduction

The student is there in the room, but yet will not utter; will not give of herself to those around her. Internally, she engages with all that is said; she thinks it through; she forms her own views; she is even critical of some of what she sees and hears; she makes her own insightful notes, but still she will not come forth so as to express any of the internal responses that are forming within her, and even on the page in front of her.

Do we have here a pointer towards what might be meant by voice, namely the projection of self into a peopled pedagogical space? Certainly, this is part of it. In a postgraduate module that I once taught, with the chairs very carefully arranged in a circle (including my own), one student attended the module diligently but spoke not a word. Doubtless, I was at fault in not making efforts to sound out the student and to see if there was some difficulty that could easily be overcome. (However, I was also concerned not to tread on the student's felt space.) The student might have had a voice, but we did not hear it.

So *public* voice is important in a pedagogical setting. Derrida sought to undermine the preoccupation – as he saw it – of Western philosophy with speech as against writing.[1] Writing can usually be rewritten whereas once the voice has uttered, it cannot be reclaimed. The latter, accordingly, has a purity that writing can hardly attain, for it always carries the hint of rehearsal, but speech remains important. It is one way in which individuals contribute to a pedagogical situation and, in the process, help to form their own pedagogical identities. It has an authenticity that writing cannot possess.

Voice, though, is more than a matter of utterances in the space of a pedagogical situation. Voice connotes a projection of the self and here there are two ideas.

On the one hand, no two voices are exactly alike. Through the voice, one becomes oneself uniquely. Through voice, the self becomes itself. This is perhaps one reason why dictatorships suppress 'free speech' for, in so doing, they hope to dampen the possibility of human beings finding their uniqueness, their special qualities. On the other hand, to say that voice connotes a projection of the self is to remind us that, through voice, the self places itself in the world. The voice is a mode of communication. Voice implies a reaching out to the world, but it is more than that. The voice looks for an audience. The voice hopes to have an impact. The self forming itself *and* having an impact on others in so doing – these are the dual possibilities opened by voice. (In exploring these matters, we shall develop our earlier reflections on voice from Chapter four.)

Two voices

Two kinds of student voice are already apparent here. First, there is the capacity or willingness of the student to give voice to her thoughts or feelings. The student has her thoughts and feelings, but can she, does she, give voice to them? Here, voice becomes almost a verb: she voices – or fails to voice – her thoughts and ideas. This is not a singing voice, but it is at least a heard voice – something is heard, or not. When she speaks, others listen.

The second voice that must claim our attention here is more a metaphorical voice. This is the voice of the student that is distinctively the student's or, at least, it is her authentically placing herself in the world. Here, the issue is not one of whether some utterance emerges, but rather as to the kind of utterance it is. Is it really the student speaking or are we simply hearing what others have said? Is the student trying to formulate her own ideas, or to impose her own orderings on the data or experiences that have come her way? Here, again, authenticity is not far from this meaning of voice.

Expressing a voice; losing a voice; finding a new voice

I've always had a huge passion for languages. But coming to [x university], I found the French and the Italian departments very different, and I did start to feel a bit bitter towards French. And I wasn't enjoying that any more. I loved it at school more than Italian. I found the French department very rigid. . . . I did feel like I was back in school, but not in the sixth form . . . I felt like I was going back to GCSE . . . I didn't feel very free to express myself in the lessons, whereas the Italian was such a small department, you got to know all the individuals . . . With the Italian classes, we all sit round a big table, or chairs without tables in front. There would be a lot more interaction . . . It was more friendly, just a liberating atmosphere.

(student just having successfully graduated)

How is it that these two meanings of voice *are* separate meanings of the one term, 'voice'? The one is vocal – does the inward murmuring turn into a heard presence? Does the student make herself heard? She may whisper something to her neighbour, but not have the courage to voice it to the wider group. At least, she shares it with her neighbour and here lies one value of small group work. The daunting prospect of voicing one's thoughts in a large group, probably in the presence of a tutor, may be diminished when only a very few of one's peer students are to hand.

The other interpretation of voice, though, is not a matter of airwaves, of physical utterance and of reception via the ear. Here, the meaning is less tangible, even metaphysical. As well as authenticity, it conjures ideas of freedom, of individuality and of distinctiveness. Here, too, lie sentiments of hope, democracy and even life itself. Connected to this more metaphysical idea of voice, after all, is the meaning implied in the idea of, say, a newspaper as 'the voice of the people'.

While these two senses of voice are – in some senses – radically different, they share much in common. In both are sentiments of courage, of being heard, of speaking out, of making an intervention and of claiming attention. In both interpretations of voice, there is a sense, too, of particularity. The student has the courage to speak in the classroom: it may not be yet fully authentic; the utterance may be a re-recording of other voices (her parents, her culture, her peers – the 'they', to use the Heideggerian term), but, even so, it is she who is doing the speaking. Both senses of voice may find their expression in all manner of modes: neither is confined to the oral voice. The student can speak out in different ways, even through her actions, say, in the laboratory or in the clinical situation, and of the speaking out, we can always ask, but is it really her voice?

The embodied and the metaphorical: both are significant voices. Both need to be present if we are to be in the presence of a genuine higher education and this tacit expectation may be especially challenging to international students from some cultures. We look to our students each to speak out, to make a contribution; we encourage them to have a voice. This is an embodied voice, visibly present in different situations. Against this, there is the metaphorical voice; the voice that is present when we can sense that this is the student's own authentic voice that shines through. This may take a little more winning; it may take several years in which the student comes gradually into his own and takes off in his own way. Here, the student acquires a trajectory of his own and gains his own voice. This is a metaphorical voice that speaks of freedom, of daring and risk taking. Here, again, is our bungee jumper, who even sings as he jumps.

Let us distinguish our two voices by naming our first voice, the embodied voice, the *pedagogical voice*. It is the voice that is manifestly present – or absent – in pedagogical settings, of all kinds. Here, the student inserts herself and makes her presence felt. Let us name our second voice, the metaphorical voice, the *educational voice*. It is in this voice, after all, that the hopes of higher education are realized. Here, the student becomes herself. If the pedagogical voice is realized through *autonomy*, the educational voice is realized through *authenticity*.

Such a distinction at once invites questions: Do these two voices characteristically have different impediments to their expression? Are they associated with different forms of encouraging in the pedagogical situation? However, the distinction, and the resulting questions, may overplay the separateness of the two voices.

Qualities of voice

Of course, the two voices are not independent of each other, but here lies a crucial difference. The expression of the pedagogical voice is a *necessary* condition of the educational voice being heard. If a student is to be authentically herself (and so demonstrate her educational voice), she has at least to utter, to project herself, to make a contribution (and so show her pedagogical voice). *However, the converse does not hold.* It by no means follows that the pedagogical voice requires the educational voice: we may be in the presence of a student speaking out, but the student may not be speaking authentically. We may not be in the presence of an educational voice.

We have here, then, the makings of a matrix: we can distinguish pedagogical voice from educational voice; they may take on different qualities, so we may also distinguish autonomous voice from authentic voice.

	Autonomous voice	*Authentic voice*
Pedagogical voice	Yes	Unknown (possibly so but not necessarily so)
Educational voice	(Yes)	Yes

The *pedagogical voice* is autonomous and visibly so. It is possible that a student, not having contributed to a seminar, feels shamed into making a contribution, even though he would rather remain silent. An insensitive tutor may turn to a particular student and seek a contribution from him. In those cases, the contributions are somewhat coerced: the student's voice is heard, but it is not wittingly heard. There is, in these cases, a limit to the student's apparent autonomy, but then, the pedagogical voice would be a *shadow* pedagogical voice; it would be half-hearted. The fully-fledged pedagogical voice is an expression of autonomy. It remains a further matter, however, whether the voice we are hearing is *authentic*. The student may speak, but may just be going through the motions, may be evincing only what she has just heard or read. She may even have a book beside her – keeping one step ahead of the tutor – and proffers a piece of that text as her own, not having thought the matter through. So pedagogical voice is not necessarily authentic.

The *educational* voice *is* authentic – and that is necessarily so. Here, the student is coming into herself; is realizing herself and is inserting herself into her offerings. Her utterances, her activities, her exchanges are manifestations of *her* voice. As for autonomy, there is an equivocation: the student may be in the company of others. What she does and says, she does and says autonomously in the sense of doing those things through her own will, but she may do and say those things by being enabled to do so by those around her who are giving her support and who are affirming her. So she is fully authentic, but she may not be entirely autonomous. In the group project, she realizes herself in new ways and is authentic, but she does so in the close company of the other students of whom she takes account and, in that sense, her autonomy is limited.[2]

Where has all this got us? What implications might arise from these points and distinctions? I want to suggest that the key distinction we have been making between pedagogic voice and educational voice is significant. It is all too easy these days to be seduced into thinking it is pedagogic voice that counts; educational voice, in contrast, is all too easily neglected.

In a performative age, in which things not only have to be done, but have to be seen to be done and done to immediate effect, attention is focused on overt actions. This is the domain of pedagogic voice, the domain in which the student has a go in front of others, in which the student makes an intervention or takes the initiative. This is the domain of so-called 'communicative skills' and it is the domain in which the self-confident student shines. This student wants to hear her own voice and wants others – student and tutor – to hear it and even to have an effect on those others.

The domain of the educational voice heralds more subtle and more significant qualities, and qualities that are surely liable to be neglected. This is the domain in which the authentic voice is encouraged, is given space and is heard. Far from being showy and from having immediate effect, the educational voice may be quiet, even apparently quiescent. It may have to be encouraged and nurtured over time.

The educational voice, we have seen, is authentic. It is that voice that has to be especially encouraged. The pedagogical voice just may be authentic, but the forces, which are nowadays subtly present in the pedagogic situation (and sometimes, not so subtly, where students' contributions in pedagogic situations are assessed) presage – do they not? – inauthenticity. The forces at work encourage the secondhand, the immediate gesture, the show for show's sake. Even assessing students' contributions in class group work, intended to have a positive educational effect, may have just such an unintended consequence – some students will speak simply to be seen and heard.

Certainly, the distinction between pedagogic and educational voice – in terms of the idea of authenticity – can be overdrawn. Whether in the studio, the laboratory, the clinical situation or the seminar, the student can be working hard to express herself, putting forward her ideas and enacting her understandings. The overt performance can be authentic or, at least, be a means by which the student comes to win her own authenticity. Ultimately, authenticity cannot be entirely internal; it has to be won in the public domain. In the educational setting, there can be no entirely private authenticity.

Students have often to be encouraged to put themselves forward and express their voice in the pedagogic situation. However, the point here is that there can be no presumption that the overt performance, of any kind, is itself authentic or even authenticity-in-the-making. The quality of authenticity has to prove itself beyond the merely performative.

'Tell me more'

Higher education does much to suppress voice. It unduly censures; it places tight boundaries – of 'disciplines' – around students' thoughts; it asserts itself in hierarchical pedagogical relationships; it even belittles self, in all kinds of subtle and not so subtle ways (from an overly powerful suggestion as to the reconstruction of an essay to an acerbic comment to the medical student on the ward round). Not surprisingly, the student sometimes submerges her voice in deference to the 'authority' of the teacher, often all too keenly asserted, or under a sea of references. With the aid of the Internet, the bibliographies grow ever longer.

Against these recollections and picking up an earlier distinction (Chapter 4), it may be felt that, in the first place, the voice has to be *recovered*. The voice *was* there, but now it is thwarted. The student fears to express his or her voice. Here, a prime pedagogical task becomes that of encouraging the voice forward through removing the impedimenta that are blocking its emergence. Pedagogy is here a matter of the recovery of voice.

However, as we have seen, the recovery of voice can take place on different levels. The hesitant student senses that she will not be belittled after all, other braver souls have even been affirmed. So she ventures forth. She makes a contribution, quietly, but sufficient so as to be heard, and all goes well. She begins to gain a pedagogic voice.

The wise teacher (whether in the classroom or, say, on the ward round), will not let things stop there. The student will be gently pressed. 'Tell me more' may be the rejoinder. Far from being marginalized, the student is now being invited to say more. What she has said is fine, but what else might be said? What other angles, or concepts or facts might come into play? An educational voice may even emerge.

In higher education, there might be a temptation to succumb to 'the principle of reason', the belief that every claim and every stance can relentlessly be pressed. Either a claim can be grounded in reason or it will be shown to be an impostor. We press the student for her reasons for saying and doing as she says and does, but, as Heidegger asked, how does the principle of reason gain its own reason? Where is its legitimacy to be found? Ultimately, reason runs out and so:

plenty of shadows are cast over the principle of reason.

(Heidegger 1996)

For Heidegger, it is not reason that stands behind reason, but *beings:*

> The principle of reason is . . . not a statement about reason, but about beings, insofar as there are beings.

Even more:

> What we bring into view is that the principle of reason speaks of the being of beings.

It is a mode of being, in which grounds and reason matter. Accordingly, the principle of reason turns out to be 'a principle of being' (p. 51). Again, then, in our inquiry, we are brought back to being and not far from being lies becoming.

The invocation to the student to 'tell me more' is now surely revealed as containing complexities for the student voice. At one level, it calls for reasons, for the telling has to be grounded. The voice is heard, being rational, but at a further level, the voice is not simply heard, but heard in an act of communication. '*Tell me* more' encourages the student to speak out; to tell *me*, to find a way of communicating to and with me. The student-as-knower is affirmed in this invitation. At yet a further level, the 'tell' contains the hope that the voice will be an authentic voice: the student is pressed for *her* stories, *her* reasoning.

However, the layers of the 'tell me more' are still not exhausted for now we have just seen – from Heidegger – that the acceptance of the life of reason is a mode of being in the world. In finding her voice, the student discloses her being.

So in responding to our entreaty to 'tell me more', the student tacitly places herself into *that* mode of being-in-the-world; a being that is in the world and yet is out of the world, as it observes the world and forms its reasons. This voice, that speaks the life of reason, is an ethereal voice, standing outside of itself, as it observes the world in order to muster its reasons. The student is, in part, *displacing* herself from herself.

Forming a voice

In forming her educational voice, then, hard work lies ahead of the student. She has to give herself to the demands of her intellectual field(s), her curriculum and her pedagogical situations. All three have their own standards or expectations, but what, then, does 'voice' mean here? If all three dimensions of the student's experience – intellectual fields, curriculum and pedagogical situation – exert demands that the student has to heed, where is 'voice'? Isn't voice necessarily particular and personal? Let us allow that the student will come to respond to her intellectual, curriculum and pedagogical situations in her own way. So there is a measure of the particular here, but what of the personal? How might that enter the fray?

An initial gambit might be to distinguish again between an epistemological and an ontological voice. In her epistemological voice, the student offers her own interpretations, her own interventions, within the demands of the discipline or professional field. Those interpretations are appraised in themselves: her essays are marked, her experiments are assessed, but her offerings are not disembodied. They come from a student and the student is a human being. Through her offerings, the student develops her voice, showing a due respect for the standards of that epistemological setting. She shows herself a historian or a microbiologist in the making. In her yet wider ontological voice, through the approval of her offerings, the student feels herself recognized *as* a person. Her immediate disciplinary or professional being is affirmed *and* her own larger being is also affirmed.

Of course, the facts of the matter often run in the contrary direction. In a mass higher education system, the affirmation levels are liable to be depleted. 'Tutorials' are held with large groups of students; essays are not marked one by one, but instead, a general commentary is made by the lecturer on the group of essays, and students as individuals go unnoticed, especially as persons in their own right. They wish to be taken seriously as persons, not just as designers or economists in the making. We might even go further and suggest that ontological voice precedes epistemological voice: unless the student feels herself to be affirmed as a person – and something of her challenges acknowledged – there is little likelihood of her giving herself to the challenges of the situations in which she is placed.

Is something of this not behind the observation by many a student who says that they became really interested in a topic or a subject as a result of the teacher in that setting? Not untypically, the student became glued to a topic partly in virtue of the teacher recognizing and affirming the student as a person, our student having in the past found little or no interest in the topic. The student was tacitly – and possibly explicitly – encouraged to engage with the world on their own terms; their being was affirmed. Through that affirmation, an interest was kindled in the topic at hand. There was a transference of interest not so much from the teacher to the topic, but from the self to the topic. The ontological voice, as we might put it, had been evoked, and so in turn it was possible for an epistemological voice to begin to develop.

Ontological voice, it is seems, is prior to epistemological voice. This way of putting the matter is significant. It reminds teachers who care about their teaching that their first duty is to engage with the student as a person, respecting her own situation. That duty is one of giving the student a sense of her own worth as a person before her own possibilities as a student. We may reflect, it is that neglect, especially under conditions of mass higher education, that leads to an intensification of self-doubt and possibly even to students withdrawing from their courses. In the pedagogical situation, the student must feel able simply to be. Ontological voice is, to repeat, prior to epistemological voice, but perhaps an even more nuanced position awaits us.

The position that I want to press for is that the student's ontological and epistemological voices are intertwined, but also, the ontological voice has the upper hand.

Characteristically, as the student gains confidence in his programme of study and in his progress on it, his wider self-confidence also grows. In turn, that growing self-belief generates new energies, a new will to learn, towards his course of study. This may seem to be an empirical claim, deserving perhaps of research in the field, but this claim surely has a philosophical component to do with human being as such. Let us entertain the thought experiment: could a student develop a strong epistemological voice, in which they were energized into offering their own bold truth claims or into throwing themselves into their practical activities (in the laboratory or design studio or clinical situation or business scenario), but yet have at the same time a weak sense of themselves? There must surely be doubt about that possibility. After all, the student's educational self is not separate from his wider self; it is part of it.

So the forming of the student voice takes place both in the student's intellectual formation (his epistemological voice) and in his being (his ontological voice). Neither is reducible to the other and each has to be held in mind for teaching to realize its potential. Successful teachers just do this, probably often without making this distinction fully to themselves. Partly, the distinction is caught by the old adage that, in higher education, the effective teacher teaches both his subject and his students. Both the intellectual and the human moments of teaching have to be present and continuously so. Neither can go on holiday (to draw on an analogy from Wittgenstein).

However, to say that the student's ontological voice and his epistemological voice have to be developed together, and to observe that the two voices can strengthen each other does not exhaust the matter. For the ontological voice is primary here, even while it may be enhanced by the student's developing capacities for innovation and even daring in his studies (his epistemological voice). It is through a sense of the student's own worth, recognized as such by his tutors, that the will to learn gains a purchase in the first place. It is the ontological voice, the sense that one's views matter, that one will be listened to, that the university affords a space in which the student can develop as a person, that makes possible the development of the epistemological voice, that emerging capacity to strike out on one's own, and to form one's own view of one's intellectual and professional field. Ontology still trumps epistemology.

Multiple voices

Of course, things aren't this simple! In today's mass higher education, students hear multiple voices and they respond by developing multiple voices themselves. We know from empirical research that a single student may adopt contrasting learning strategies in different parts of her course, in responding to the different pedagogical regimes that she experiences; the extent to which, for example, the curriculum, or the teaching approach or the assessment format encourages so-called 'deep' or 'surface' learning. In this situation, we can say that the student develops multiple identities and so forms multiple voices, marked by the extent the student mimics voices around her ('reproduces' those voices) or feels able and inspired to create her own improvizations on the themes that encircle her.

Multiple voices are not just a product of the immediate pedagogical situation. Multiple voices are present already as ideologies that pervade the pedagogical space. Students are constructed variously as units of resource, as consumers, or as potential actors in the labour market, or possibly even as 'deficient' individuals in need of agendas of compensatory 'widening participation', or even as only partly formed persons now deserving counselling and therapeutic interventions. These are, in turn, ideologies of economy, of efficiency, of marketability, of performance, of necessary participation and of therapy; they are themselves loud voices, everywhere to be both heard and seen.

As we may term them, these are *exogenous ideologies*, with their own voices, invading the campus from without, urged on by big battalions. However, while, in some places, such ideologies may find some resistance, to a large extent, they are taken up with alacrity on campus. In turn, students may even come to mimic *those* voices, but we should not be too disturbed by this situation. For this is the world today, a world of multiple voices. So students will be trying out different voices, even more or less simultaneously. Their process of becoming is a process of the trying on of voices.

Even if the student feels that she has found her own voice, is that a desirable situation? In a fluid world, does a single voice have much value? Doesn't the contemporary world require of us that we have multiple voices, a repertoire of voices indeed? The voices then become a palette that can be used to maximum effect and even mixed in different situations. Is this, indeed, not a way to read multidisciplinary courses, which bring on different voices in the individual student? A course such as Music Design Technology can have no single voice; it is even a cacophony of voices and the successful student will surely have a rich assembly of voices – at once technical, theoretical and interpersonal, and all with their different registers – on which he can call.

As well as encouraging multiple voices, do we not want to develop a *strong* voice in our students? Is strength of voice the same as authenticity of voice? It is not. One can have a strong voice, but it may still be second-hand. A task of higher education is to develop a voice of nuanced strength – we want students to think and to act, but with due reason, able to see other possibilities. The really developed voice is one that is able to express itself in a multitude of voices, but – once one voice has been determined – then sings wholeheartedly in *that* voice. Herein lies the idea of critical reason. Subtle strength, supple strength, this is the kind of voice we wish to see in our students. Authentic strength, even.

Clear voice, then? Isn't that what we expect of the accomplished singer, that she hits the intended note precisely? It was said of Bertrand Russell exactly that, that he would not hit several notes in the hope that one of them would be right; just the single note. So clarity of voice, then? After all, a temptation amid multiple voices is that of echoing many of them at one time, in the hope of reaching the diverse audiences. Especially in such a milieu, clarity of voice is surely a virtue?

Expressing a clear voice is challenging: one needs not just skills, but courage to hit a single note precisely. If one is off target, it will be noticeable, but is clarity really a virtue? Some – in a post-modern age – have urged that clarity is actually tyrannical: it pretends to an authority that is no longer available. The single position that it evinces can have no security. Fluidity, multivocality, difference within the expression of voice: these are the new virtues. The standards by which the students' texts are to be judged are changing and should change. Multimedia and even 'multimodal' texts that hold no firm narrative are to be given higher marks than the single story.

The multimodalists – at least those who would opt for this line of thinking – have an educational point. By all means, handle several vocal lines at once. Become the conductor of the orchestra, even become the composer of the piece, but here lies an alternative course of action. What is an appropriate piece of orchestral music in the twenty-first century? Should it have structure, and a definite line, and a resolution of its themes? Should it obey rules? Should it be dissonant or even atonal? On all these matters, preferences come legitimately into play, but in the end, some set of decisions has to be made. The composition has to take some form or go in some direction. It cannot be entirely shapeless or without a narrative. We look to the student essay to show a sensitivity to the multiple voices, but we still want to see a definite line of argument.

Things may be open-ended in the real world, but, in order that a course of treatment may be coherently followed through, a definite diagnosis has to be made, even if that diagnosis is open to revision in the light of further information. Let us at least have clarity here and now, even if tomorrow a new position is taken up and the evidence is subject to a different reading. Careful clarity, that is a clarity that is full of care: in a world of multiple voices, this has still to be the watchword. Of course, it is challenging in such a world, but higher education takes on a new meaning, of articulating messages in a chaotic world, messages that are at once clear and yet nuanced, and always provisional. Univocality in a multivocal world: this becomes the new higher education.

Individual voice

Through gaining her own voice, the student becomes herself. This is not to pretend that there is a single voice that awaits the student. There is no essentialism at work here. To the contrary, 'voice' is a metaphor for educational ideals such as freedom, authenticity and becoming itself. 'Voice' is a utopian concept, therefore (Batchelor, 2006a). Connected are yet further connotations of individuality and clarity, on the one hand, and of human qualities, such as courage and subtlety, on the other.

One repost to all this will be the objection that 'voice' smacks too much of individuality, when what is required today is 'teamworking'. Associated with this line of thought may also be the consideration that much human development takes place within communities, within 'communities of learning' (Lave and Wenger, 1991). Some may even advance the argument that, ultimately, there can be no private learning: a better metaphor than 'voice' would then presumably be that of 'choir', in which the achievement is precisely that of a number of singers in harmony.

The objections are misplaced. First, each member of a choir has a personal responsibility towards the other choir members. In a choir, the individual singers have to hold their own line, even while others around them are singing other parts. Furthermore, each singer is different and all will bring their own colour, their own modulations, to a part, even if the choir's director has sought to produce a particular sound. Finally, singing – even in a large choir – cannot be a matter of simply reproducing the sounds implied by the notes on the page. Each singer has to be engaged, and to bring his or her own talents to bear. This story surely holds for higher education: we look to develop the student's own clear voice, even amid inter-dependency. There is a sound to higher education (Phipps, 2007) and the sounds may even become music.

Conclusion

We may return to our opening quotation from Nietzsche: 'learning is not enough!' The student may have acquired some knowledge and skills and even some understanding, but such learning is insufficient in itself.[3] Has she emerged with a voice of her own? Is it a strong voice? Is it sensitive to other voices around her? Is it secure? Is it measured? Is it brave? Is it authoritative? Is it authentic? Is the student now ready to accept the disciplines that sustaining and developing her own voice entail? Does the student have the necessary dispositions and qualities to go on?

8
Dispositions and qualities

Introduction

In higher education, we look to develop both dispositions and qualities. Without dispositions and qualities, nothing else of any substance is possible. Learning is not possible, the acquisition of skills is not possible, and nor is any independence of action or thought possible.

Dispositions and qualities overlap in their character, but they are different. A durable determination to work things out in one's own way is a *disposition*; courage is a *quality*.

Dispositions are the expression of a will to learn. They are the orientations that a student has towards his course of studies. Qualities, on the other hand, are the form that those dispositions take. To pick up our two examples, a student may be disposed to work things out in his own way, but does he really have the quality of courage to accompany that disposition?

The *foundational* disposition is that of a will to learn. Without a will to learn, nothing else is possible. Other dispositions are built upon the will to learn. Still, all dispositions are foundational as compared with qualities. Qualities supply the character of the person that is already energized through the dispositions. Dispositions are nothing short of propensities to go on in certain ways; qualities are the character supplied to and taken on by those dispositions.

These general distinctions having cursorily been made, the more important point is that dispositions and qualities have properties in common. Through their dispositions and their qualities, students have the capacities to acquire both knowledge and skills. Through their dispositions and qualities, students become themselves. They flower not just as pedagogical persons, but as persons as such. Students *are* their dispositions and their qualities. Once these have been well enough formed, all else of importance will follow. Without them, nothing else of importance will follow.

Once formed, too, dispositions and qualities have a durability about them.

Knowledge can be forgotten and skills can atrophy without use; but dispositions and qualities are durable in their nature. They constitute the student's pedagogical being. It is they that have to be the focus of 'teaching' in higher education.

Some dispositions, some qualities

Here are some dispositions that it is especially fitting for higher education to develop:

- a will to learn;
- a will to engage;
- a preparedness to listen:
- a preparedness to explore;
- a willingness to hold oneself open to experiences;
- a determination to keep going forward.

Here are some qualities, again that have particular affinity with higher education:

- integrity;
- carefulness;
- courage;
- resilience;
- self-discipline;
- restraint;
- respect for others;
- openness.

Two health warnings are in order. First, there are more qualities than dispositions in these lists, but nothing much hangs on that, for *both* dispositions and qualities are important. Secondly, the presence of the particular items in these lists says little about their substance. Over pretty well every item there can be debate. For instance, in a world in which one arguably has to take up multiple identities – and perhaps to have several 'voices' at one's disposal (as we noted in the last chapter) – it is not clear as to what 'integrity' could mean, so we cannot be sure, without further investigation, that integrity has or should have a secure place in any educational philosophy. The presence, therefore, of particular items in those lists above should not be taken uncritically to imply that they are readily available as potential dispositions and qualities. They are, however, intended to be more than mere potentialities. I have selected them as dispositions and qualities that have the potency to make a significant contribution to students' capacity for their own becoming (cf. Macfarlane 2004).

The separate character of dispositions and qualities is apparent in these lists. Each disposition is an orientation to engage with the world in some way; a preparedness to go forward in a particular way. Each one contains the infinitive verb, 'to learn', 'to listen', 'to engage' and so forth. Each disposition points to action, even if latent.

In any disposition, there is will, will to press on in a particular way. There is a restless energy contained in each disposition. The student who has or has acquired dispositions is not completely still. This is a student who is energized and possibly even set on fire, perhaps by a newly formed love of the subjects and experiences and challenges that constitute her programme of studies. This is a student who is engaging with her studies on her terms. Through her dispositions, her studies become *her* studies. She takes ownership of her studies and imparts to it her own energies and direction. She is no longer passive.

Qualities are just that – the qualities that are evident in the way in which the student goes about her studies. In other words, qualities find their expression in the student's activities. Qualities, then, too, have an action orientation. To say of a student that she has certain qualities, but that those qualities never saw the light of day in being manifested in her activities would be nonsensical.

It may then be suggested that qualities – as well as dispositions – can be expressed in verb-like phrases. It might be urged, for example, that the quality of 'carefulness' could be expressed as a disposition 'to take care'. So it could. Similarly, say, with 'self-discipline', which could be expressed as a willingness to exercise self-discipline.

In other words, so it may be felt, there is no sharp distinction between the dispositions and qualities in those lists above. Well, there may be no sharp distinction, but that does not mean that there is no distinction. Let us follow our protestor's logic a little further. Look at another quality on the above list, that of 'integrity'. How can that quality be expressed in the form of an infinitive verb? The notion could be said to be instantiated where a student resolved to interact or to engage (with others, with her own experiences) with integrity. That is to say that, again, the supposed quality of 'integrity' could be said to be a disposition to act in a certain way. The infinitive verb is never far under the surface of the qualities we have picked out. At least, there is a potential for action within each quality.

But this argument is flimsy. There is a difference between a student's potential to act in a certain way and his preparedness to impart a certain tone to those actions. The distinction is a fine one, but it is important. I may have a preparedness to listen to others, but if I am only going to do so in a exploitative fashion – what ideas are there here that I can use later to my own personal advantage? – the disposition is tarnished by its quality.

A disposition may almost be undone by its qualities. Unless the accompanying qualities are of the right kind, a disposition may even lead to harmful or unethical outcomes. I may have an abiding will to discover the laws of nature, but if that will becomes all-powerful, I may be led into making premature announcements of 'discoveries' that turn out later to be lacking in a proper evidential basis. The disposition of enquiry is misdirected because the proper accompanying qualities – of restraint and of respect for the evidence – are absent. Instead, other qualities – of hubris and conceit and even arrogance – are present on such an occasion. Dispositions, then, while potentially valuable, may turn out to be harmful, where the appropriate qualities are missing.[1]

There is one further point to be made about dispositions. Dispositions are just that: ways in which individuals are disposed to act or even just to be in the world. That one has a disposition to go forward in some way does not entail, necessarily, that one *will* go forward in that way. A disposition is a tendency, an inclination, a potential. In its presence, there is a likelihood that one will go forward in that way; but no certainty attaches to the matter.

Different factors may intervene to stall the enactment of dispositions, some of a causal and some of a more rational basis. A mature student may be fired up by her course, but may discover that she has cancer and simply does not have the energy – either physical or psychological – to maintain her programme of work on her course. Another student may also have a very strong will to learn, but may find the teaching style of one tutor particularly off-putting (perhaps the tutor displays little respect for the students, focusing on his own interests). In such examples, the disposition is – as it were – put on hold, perhaps in a particular teaching setting (a particular tutor's lectures) or completely for a longer period of time (until the student regains her health sufficient to resume her studies). Dispositions, therefore, come with an 'all other things being equal' clause: the student is likely to act as her dispositions incline her unless there are good reasons or strong forces that dampen the acting out of those dispositions.

We may conclude here, therefore with the observation that, together, dispositions and qualities structure the student's pedagogical being. This is an unfolding being. Which being observed, the dispositions and qualities that the student is taking on *are themselves becoming firmer*. Others come into view, but may also recede from view and there may be unevenness in the journey. A student steers herself away from certain dispositions and qualities that would be liable to thwart her pedagogical becoming. She begins to arrive for meetings late or becomes careless in her work, or may interrupt others, but these may be temporary journeys, which never take a strong hold. Influences may be at work that encourage her to take on more beneficent dispositions and qualities.

The student's pedagogical being, in its dispositions and qualities, is never sure, therefore. It is susceptible to change and, that being so, is also susceptible to influences in her pedagogical situations.

Epistemic virtues: chicken and eggs

Talk of dispositions and qualities in the context of higher education may, for some, bring to mind the idea of 'epistemic virtues'. The term – around which there is now a considerable literature[2] – draws attention to connections between an interest in understanding the world, on the one hand, and human virtues, on the other hand. Two positions stand out in the debate over epistemic virtues and we can catch them in the form of opposing questions. Is it that a concern to understand the world prompts the development of certain kinds of virtues *or* is it that the possession of certain kinds of virtue orient individuals to want to understand the world? Is, for example, a concern to discriminate in a fine-grained way between one's experiences a result of an interest in acquiring knowledge about the world, *or* is it that, having a concern to discriminate in one's experiences of the world, one is likely to want to acquire knowledge of the world?[3]

One might be tempted to say that the two aspects of human nature are mutually reinforcing: having certain kinds of virtue may lead one on the arduous path of improving one's knowledge about the world, which in turn may lead to a deepening of those very virtues. This sounds like a virtuous circle: a never-ending and mutually reinforcing interaction of interest in knowing the world and of having the virtues that such an interest requires if it is to be successful.

However, such a virtuous circle may also be seen as having a vicious quality. If one wants to enhance this mutually reinforcing circle by pedagogical stratagems, where does one break into it? Is it that one attends to the student's interest in understanding the world directly? Then, if that appeals, why stop there? After all, it seems as if that interest in understanding the world is supported by the student's possession of certain ethical virtues, in which case, shouldn't one attend to the development of those virtues as a prior educational concern? Then, those virtues, so it appears, really get going where there is already an interest in knowledge, and so we are led to an infinite regress, in which one can never rationally break into this vicious circle. In such a situation, a sound pedagogical stance appears to be thwarted.

The question returns, then: which comes first on the part of the student: an interest in understanding the world or the possession of the right kind of virtues? The student will never be able seriously to acquire understanding unless she has the right kind of virtues – or dispositions and qualities, as we have termed them. But also she will not come to possess those virtues unless she has seriously applied herself to the acquisition of knowledge in her chosen field.

This line of thought requires two codicils. First, it has to be cashed out in the different domains to be found in higher education today. These processes of student becoming both hold across different domains and will take different forms in those different domains. It is immaterial to this line of thought as to whether we have in mind relatively theoretical pursuits, such as history, or physics or more practical pursuits, such as nursing studies or the performing arts. It may well turn out that each discipline or field of engagement is associated with its own set of epistemic virtues, but the difficulty that we have identified – if it is a difficulty – of making sound pedagogical interventions in favour either of an epistemic interest or of its associated virtues still remains.

The other codicil is that, so far as I can see, there is no connected issue as to the theory of truth as such. For example, nothing hangs on whether one has in mind a correspondence theory of truth or a coherence theory of truth. Whether one thinks that coming to a proper understanding of the world is a matter of that understanding 'corresponding' to the world so far as possible, or one believes that forming a proper understanding of the world is a matter of developing a coherent view of the world is immaterial. The line of thought or, indeed, puzzlement that we have just exposed holds whichever theory of truth one might favour. If truthfulness implies a serious attempt to come into a secure understanding of the world, then the relationship between that effort and the virtues that it implies remains an enigma, irrespective of the notion of truth that the truth-seeker might hold.

As stated, these two sets of considerations are just codicils to the line of thought that we have just been following through; they are not qualifications. They do not alter the line of thought that we have just pursued; they merely shed more light on it. It remains the case that there is a nice equivocation in front of us. Even if we can see merits in a pedagogy of being, it by no means follows that we should give priority to the student's being as such. It just may be the case that we will do more for the development of the student as a person by focusing on – by continuing to focus on – knowledge itself. Just focus on knowledge and the student's *being* – if that is what we are concerned about – will look after itself. The old-fashioned view just may have merit on its side.

The educational implications of such a line of thinking are clear. Those who believe that the primary responsibility of university teachers is to teach their discipline may sense here that they are let off the hook. If they wavered over the suggestion that they might have a responsibility to concern themselves with the student as such, with her dispositions and qualities, they may now feel that they can now return happily to their interests in their discipline. They can simply teach their discipline; 'teaching their students', in contrast, is not a construction that need trouble them. For now, they can content themselves with the thought that, in teaching their discipline, in focusing on that, *ipso facto*, their students will develop their epistemic virtues and so grow as pedagogic persons. By becoming expert in their own discipline, the teacher's professional task is fully identified. The student is, at most, a pedagogical *adjunct* of this disciplinary interest.

It will surely be clear that, on the argument I am pursuing here, such a line of thought should be repudiated. Let us assume, to begin with, that the student's epistemic interests – widely drawn to include practical pursuits – and her epistemic virtues are equally weighted in their mutual influencing; that neither has the greater influence over the other. In that case, the more effective strategy will be for the educator to pay equal attention to both the student's epistemic interests and her epistemic virtues – or, as we have termed them here, her dispositions and her qualities. There can be no logical or educational case for those epistemic virtues to be ignored in their own right.

However, the case I wish to make is, indeed, the stronger case that the educator should be prepared to afford the epistemic virtues a particular kind of attention.

Dispositions and qualities – again

I suggested earlier that, in relation to qualities, dispositions were foundational. It is the dispositions that carry a student forward in certain ways. The dispositions are energized: it makes no sense to say that a student has a certain disposition – say, a preparedness to explore – but that the student showed a reluctance to investigate and try to discover things in her chosen subject. The dispositions are a readiness to act, as we observed earlier. They are foundational as compared with qualities, since they are necessary conditions of the student getting off, as it were, from first base. If the dispositions supply the motive power *and* the direction of travel, the qualities supply the *style* of travel: are the qualities of good taste or bad taste? It is the qualities that determine whether the dispositions have educational value and personal worthwhileness.

Such dispositions, even though they be foundational in the sense I have just identified, can certainly be kindled by a new interest that a student may be gaining in her studies. It might be a field of study that is new to the student or it may be that the student is now seeing a subject that she previously encountered in a new light. Either way, the student has here now a burgeoning will to learn. Many, if not all, of the dispositions and qualities are beginning to appear too.

But while the student's dispositions and qualities are likely to be enhanced by a developing interest in her chosen subjects, the relationship we are examining may also work the other way around. It can also be the case that a student's interest in her subject is aided by her taking on the appropriate dispositions and qualities.

It is not unknown, we have noted, for students – after they have graduated – to remark that their interest in a subject was aroused and developed by a particular teacher. Such a remark points to the significance of the pedagogical relationship between the student and her teacher.

In such a remark, we have insight into a double faith: a confession of faith in the teacher on the part of the student, but also, by implication, a supposition that the teacher has faith in the student. Through the affirmation afforded by the teacher in the student, the student gains a new awareness of her own ability.

We shall come onto the part that teachers can play more directly in the next section of this book. For now, we are simply teasing out the relationship between a student's interest in her studies (whether they be theoretical, empirical or practical) and her dispositions and qualities. We have, I think, established that there is a dynamic relationship at work. However, what we are also glimpsing, I think, is that the dispositions and qualities can themselves help to kindle an interest on the part of the student in her studies. They constitute, as it were, an independent set of variables. There is a responsibility, therefore, on the part of the students' teachers for themselves to try to stimulate those dispositions and qualities in themselves.

The student's *pedagogical being* is turning out to be a hybrid. If she is to make progress in her studies, she has to have an interest in them. They have to capture her attention and she has to give of herself to them, but the student also has to have appropriate dispositions and qualities towards her subjects. Both the epistemic interest and the dispositions and qualities have to be present. The student, as a *pedagogical subject*, is herself a complex.

To say this, to press the point that the student's dispositions and qualities are significant in their own right, and that they can act as an independent variable (even while they may be enhanced by the student's engagements with her studies), is to add impetus to the reflection that the student's teachers have a responsibility towards those dispositions and qualities. Indeed, these considerations show that the term 'teacher' – as distinct from 'lecturer', 'tutor', 'supervisor' and so forth – turns out to have an important place in the lexicon of higher education.

The term 'lecturer' is not without its point: to give a coherent oral account of a topic can help to fire a student's epistemic interests, but it cannot fully convey the pedagogic responsibility. Even the term tutor, while it embraces a sense of the student as a pedagogic subject (for the term means 'watching over'), does not quite connote the necessary qualities of active pedagogic interventions towards the student as such. 'Pedagogue' comes itself with baggage of an expert on the science of teaching. There remains no better term than 'teacher' to conjure the dispositions and qualities required by the educator if the student's own dispositions and qualities are to be nurtured.

Ontological turns

I have been trying to establish that the student's dispositions and qualities *matter*, matter in their own right. However, even if that is now granted, our task is not yet complete. For while it surely follows that the teacher's task is in part to take seriously those dispositions and qualities on the part of the student, it is not yet clear what this means.

Crudely, even if abstractly, we can say that we are in the presence of two ontological orientations and even two ontological turns. The teacher helps the student to take on the requisite dispositions and qualities, to take on a certain kind of pedagogical being. However, in addition to the student's ontological turn, there is necessarily present an ontological orientation on the part of her teachers. They have to see themselves under this pedagogical aspect. It has to be part of their professional identity that they perceive that they have a responsibility in this way. That many 'teaching' staff in higher education do not perhaps see themselves in this way is one good reason in principle why systematic programmes of professional development for lecturers is worthwhile. That it may be unlikely that such courses pay attention to this matter, being overly concerned with matters of technique and skill, is a separate issue. A need for an ontological turn on the part of teaching staff is one thing; recognizing it and doing something about it systematically is another.

Is there anything further that may be said here? After all, the precise specification of the requisite dispositions and qualities is problematic. On the one hand, it will vary according to context. One cannot have an epistemic disposition or quality in the abstract; it has to be oriented towards a set of epistemological objects – embodied in the student's subject or study area as it is given form in the curriculum with its activities and experiences. The dispositions and qualities that will prove most efficacious for the study of anthropology, civil engineering, business management and nursing will differ. On the other hand, the specification of the desirable dispositions and qualities will differ according to value preferences. Those value preferences will be linked to a particular idea of higher education.

I have already offered my own suggestions as to the dispositions and qualities that should characteristically be developed in higher education:

- The *dispositions* are various forms of going forward (to learn, to engage, to listen, to explore, to hold oneself open to experiences, to keep going forward). They are energies to take on the world, but with an orientation to learn from the experiences it offers.
- The *qualities* are the directions and character that are given to those energies: integrity, carefulness, courage, resilience, self-discipline, restraint and respect for others. Such qualities are a mix: they help to propel one forward, and sustain one's momentum, especially in the face of arduousness (courage, resilience) and they help one do so in ways that bring discipline to those dispositions and, in the process, maintain certain value conceptions (integrity, carefulness, restraint and respect for others). There is both an outwardness and an inwardness about these qualities. 'Respect for others', for instance, acknowledges the claims of others – researchers and learners – while 'integrity' speaks to the coherence of utterances and beliefs and is more inward in its character.

Two sets of issues remain here, but I can do barely more than identify them here. First, given that there are these conceptual differences between dispositions and qualities, how in broad terms might they be encouraged? Do dispositions and qualities point respectively to different curricula and/or pedagogical approaches. Secondly, assuming answers to the first sets of questions can be forthcoming, can dispositions and qualities be assessed? Even if they can be assessed, *should* they be assessed?

On the first sets of issues, I suggest that dispositions and qualities do indeed point in different directions so far as their implications for 'teaching' are concerned. Crudely, we can say that dispositions can be encouraged by curricula arrangements and that qualities can be encouraged by pedagogical actions. Curricula that call for the student to take some responsibility for her own learning are likely to encourage dispositions of going forward, of exploration and of listening. Pedagogies that are affirming while carefully holding up critical standards, on the other hand, are likely to aid the formation of qualities, such as those of carefulness, courage, resilience, self-discipline, restraint and respect for others. This is, to repeat, a crude alignment – dispositions and curricula, qualities and pedagogies – but I believe it holds some water.

On the other set of issues, as to assessment, I would observe that characteristically – even if tacitly – both dispositions and qualities are actually assessed, but they are assessed in different ways. Dispositions are assessed simply through students' willingness to submit themselves for assessment, qualities are – *if only tacitly* – assessed through the marking schemes for different assignments. Tacitly, at least, and even not infrequently quite explicitly, assessment criteria call for judgements to be made about students' carefulness, self-restraint and respect for others. It follows that if dispositions and qualities are already being assessed, even if only tacitly, both that they can be assessed and that they could almost certainly be assessed more extensively and more systematically. Whether that would be wise is a further matter (cf. Sadler 2002).

All I would say here is by way of an assertion: that, educationally, there are benefits in worthwhile aspects of human being and becoming not being assessed. Whatever empirical evidence that there may be as to students attending only to those aspects of their own development that are assessed, a proper educational stance towards dispositions and qualities is that of softly, softly. Calling attention to them might just be counter-productive, students might be tempted to ape the desired dispositions and qualities, rather than come into them through an authentic engagement with their educational experiences.

Self-belief

There is an aspect of the student's being over which we have been silent in this discussion and yet it is crucial. It is the aspect – on which we touched in an earlier chapter (Chapter 4) – that is characterized by terms such as 'self-belief', 'self-confidence' or, as it is termed in psychology, a positive 'self-concept' (cf. Marsh *et al.*, 2005). One reason to account for this silence is that self-confidence is neither a disposition nor a quality as we have defined them here. It is neither in itself a propensity to go forward (a disposition) nor a character given to those dispositions (a quality). Rather, it is part of the ground of the student's dispositions. The student will not have dispositions to go forward if she does not have self-belief.

What, then, of the relationship between what I claimed as the foundational disposition – that of a will to learn – and the student's self-belief? Are both equally foundational? No. The student's self-belief comes even before a will to learn. That is why the idea of the student's self-belief being the ground on which dispositions are built arises. The student's self-belief is the bedrock on which the dispositions may develop. It is the nurturing of the student's self-belief that should claim the educator's first attentions, for it is a necessary condition of the student's pedagogical flourishing. To a significant degree, once the student's self-belief is in place, then the educator's task is largely fulfilled. Students are intelligent and between themselves (acting perhaps in self-organized groups), and the resources institutions have to offer, can to a large degree fend for themselves, but they need a measure of self-belief for anything much to happen. The educator has a particular responsibility to that end.

However, it is not just the educator's first attentions that should be focused on the student's self-belief; it is the educator's *continuing* attentions that should be so focused. Given that higher education is a process in which the student is constantly being stretched, and taken into new and strange places, self-doubt is always liable to break in. There is a continuing task, therefore, on the part of the educator in bolstering the student's level of self-confidence.

Summary and conclusions

A student's dispositions and qualities play a necessary and significant part in their own right in enabling the student to flourish. A student's will to learn, to acquire knowledge and skills, is founded on her dispositions and qualities. Admittedly, that formulation is a shorthand, for we have distinguished *between* dispositions and qualities. Dispositions – such as the will to engage – are propensities for action. They are like the car that is in gear at the traffic lights: they propel the student forward unless there are intervening factors. Qualities are just such intervening factors. They may slow the operation of the dispositions – such as the quality of self-restraint; or they may drive it on when challenged either by external criticism or one's self-imposed critical voices – such as the quality of courage; or they may offer a continuity and a watchfulness towards proper standards – as provided by self-discipline and carefulness.

While the dispositions are foundational and point towards certain ends, the qualities give character to the journey: the dispositions enable a student to go forward while the qualities supply a tone to those dispositions.

If the dispositions are foundational, the will to learn is at the base of the foundations: only through it are the other dispositions possible, but the will to learn is not the bedrock of the student's pedagogical being: that lies with the student's self-belief.

One merit of this view – on the relationship between dispositions and qualities – is that it indicates that the pedagogical task needs to take *both* dispositions and qualities seriously, but separately, in their own right. The student's disposition to listen carefully has to be accompanied by her also having the quality of respect for others, and both disposition and quality call for explicit attention. The listening carefully is not only a matter of attending to what is being said, but is also a matter of attending to the person who is speaking. The sensitive teacher, alert to these nuances, will help engender just such an atmosphere of solicitude and of dual respect, both for the speaker and for what is spoken.

This theory as to the nature and the relative status of dispositions and qualities, therefore, gives new meaning and validity to the idea of 'teacher' in higher education. The theory points, first, to the potential for the teacher in higher education to exemplify as a role model the dispositions and qualities that she looks to encourage in her students. However, the theory also has implications for how we may construe teaching in higher education. It is not enough for educators even to be passionate about their own subjects and to be enthusiastic in sharing those passions with their students. Rather, the students have to be recognized as beings in themselves. 'Teaching' comes, therefore, to point to pedagogies in which the students' self-beliefs, dispositions and qualities are given deliberate attention. What all this means more fully for teaching and pedagogy must occupy us in the third section of this book.

Part 3

Being a teacher

9

The inspiring teacher

True teaching can be a terribly dangerous enterprise.

(Steiner 2003: 102)

A pedagogy of inspiration

In this chapter, I want to argue that a pedagogy[1] for uncertain times has to be – whatever else it might be – a *pedagogy of inspiration*. To bring off this argument, two steps have to be accomplished successfully. I shall need to show the connections between our preceding concepts of being, will, authenticity, qualities and dispositions, and I shall have to spell out what might be meant by a pedagogy of inspiration.

In making this argument in this way, I shall also make other claims. For example, I shall suggest that inspirational teaching has to be understood as commonplace; that is to say, not that it *is* commonplace, but that the conception of higher education I am contending for in this book requires a pedagogy of inspiration to be commonplace. My point about inspirational teaching as commonplace is a conceptual point; not an empirical claim. I shall also propose that, while much of inspirational teaching is mysterious, still we are obliged to attend to it, and uncover it so far as may be possible. That there are limits to an understanding of a pedagogy of inspiration[2] in no way diminishes its significance for a worked out higher education – or, by extension, its significance for practice and policies so far as learning and teaching in institutions are concerned.

A pedagogy of air

We may recall one of our opening motifs:

But does thought need an other air than the living do? More ethereal?

(Irigaray 1992: 6)

There is not just air, but different kinds of air, and thought of the kind appropriate to higher education requires air, and new air at that; indeed, fresh air.

We know already that to be the case. The idea of inspirational teaching bequeaths to us this idea, of new air. To inspire is to make possible the intake of new air and, through that new air, new life; new pedagogic life, at any rate. In *in*-spiration, the air is taken in – and with it, too, spirit is taken in. The intake of spirit comes with the intake of air.

Air is not spirit, pedagogical air is not pedagogical spirit, but air is the carrier of spirit. To be *in*-spired is to take in air and to be energized and to be transformed.[3] For air, one needs space, space to breathe. A pedagogy of inspiration has, in the first place, to be a pedagogy of space, of pedagogical space. Each student has to be accorded his or her own space in which to gain her own air; and to feel, if only tacitly, that that is the case. Straightaway, what may seem an arcane set of considerations has practical and policy implications: to what extent can students be provided with their own space in a mass higher education system – let alone one that turns on foredisclosed 'outcomes'?

Pedagogical space itself deserves to be dissected. It is clear, is it not, that it includes not only epistemological space (the space to think the impossible), but ontological space, in which the student can bring herself into a new state of being. The inspiring teacher, accordingly, gives the student space in which she can become more fully herself, to gain her own air, to become in an authentic way.

Here arises a paradox of inspirational teaching. The inspirational teacher gives the student more than the teacher can himself control or even understand. There is no set of rules or techniques to be followed that can guarantee that a set of students will be inspired. There is an ineffability about inspiration. Inspiring a student is not a technological process: it can neither be described in advance and laid out as a set of moves to follow that will yield that kind of 'outcome', and nor can it even be fully captured after the event: the teacher cannot explain how it was that offerings on her part brought about inspiration in another. However, even the student, once inspired, cannot give a full account of such a happening, of the process that has befallen her:

> ... *I had no ... awareness of my own ability, so when you get an inspiring teacher that has faith in you, or helps you understand a topic then you know, it's amazing.*
>
> (Fourth-year student, UK post–1992 university.)

This new air, this inspiration, *comes upon* the student, takes her by surprise, unawares. She can barely understand what has happened to her. She has come into herself in new ways, but even in retrospect, the process is not fully understandable. There is a mysterious quality to inspiration. 'It's amazing.'

Being inspired, we have just noticed, is more than taking in new air, of being refreshed through that intake. Spirit is taken in, inhaled even, at that time; or, at least, it is formed. Students talk of being excited by their teachers and, in so doing, are giving testimony to the power of teachers to infuse students with new spirit:

> *You get excited . . . it makes you want to know, say, if it's about a particular topic, then you want to go and know more about it, you want to find more . . . and that way you end up learning more . . . if a teacher inspires you in a subject then you are going to pay a lot more attention, feel that drive to get involved in a way.*

(Fourth-year student, UK post–1992 university.)

In this pedagogical excitement, this infusing of new energy, this inspiration, there are four presenting elements: the student, the teacher, the subject and the inspiration itself; and there are relationships between all four elements. However, there is an unspoken element, that of air. The student goes away, to know more and to find out more. There is space between the student and the teacher, even while there is a close pedagogical relationship: the student pays attention, feels a drive and gets involved. All of these are pedagogical acts on the part of the student and they each require a pedagogical space, and in that space, the student finds air, excitement and inspiration.

The student testifies here to her being inspired: she has taken on new spirit. However, it is not simply a transmission of spirit from the teacher. The teacher is herself doubly inspired, by her subject *and* by her teaching, by her students indeed: '. . . *the teacher inspires you in a subject . . .*'. Here we have it, baldly and boldly: the student held in a relationship between the teacher and the subject. The teacher's spirit, as we may say, is caught and not taught. It is a double spirit: the teacher's spirit for his subject and for his students, but nothing will be caught of any substance without air and space.

The image of the person near drowning, pulled onto the beach, may beckon here. Through the mouth-to-mouth resuscitation, the lifeguard breathes new life back into the stranger. The onlookers say of the person prone on the sand: 'give him air'. The 'give him air' has a double meaning: give him space and do not crowd him; *and* allow him to gain air. The lifeguard gives it to him directly, but that directness is not available to the teacher; it has to be action at a distance. As we have seen, the pedagogical air has to be accompanied by pedagogical spirit.

Inspirational teaching requires that the teacher be himself inspired, in some way. There has to be a passing on of spirit or, rather, the teacher's spirit comes to be taken up in the student. The taking-up is only partly metaphorical. The spirit, evident in the teacher's *enthusiasm*, finds an echo in the student. The echo is not the original sound, but a further rendition of it. However, the student then infuses this spirit with her spirit: she fans its flames. She warms it and is warmed by it. She may even glow with excitement, seeing her curricula and pedagogical experiences in a new way.

There is no simple transfer of spirit: out of spirit is born new spirit. This *inspiration* is effected at a distance; spirit bequeaths spirit, through the air. The student has the pedagogical space to give life to this spirit in her own way.

Making connections

A pedagogy for inspiration is not a pedagogy *of* inspiration: there are, we have said, no rules or techniques that can be followed to bring it off. A pedagogy for inspiration requires an unceasing drive to bring the student to a succession of places where he or she is likely to be inspired. Some may talk, here, of 'establishing the right learning environment', but such a language is itself too redolent of systematicity. It assumes too tight a connection between 'learning environment' and inspiration. There remains an irredeemable gap – a pedagogical gap – between *any* set of efforts on the part of the educator and the student actually being inspired.

However, connections have to be made if the student is to be inspired. How might we explain this paradox: inspiration at a distance *and* inspiration through connections? We may remind ourselves that autodidacts may become excited about their own experiences. A person may become captivated by a subject purely through his own efforts, and it may come to account for much of his life. He becomes committed to this learning. Energies flow in that direction and the beginnings of such learning energy may arise serendipitously. The presence of an educator, therefore, isn't necessary for pedagogical excitement to emerge.

Correspondingly, inspiration itself may be caught at a distance. A student in nursing studies may become interested in the life and work of Florence Nightingale and may even be inspired through such historical studies. To talk of Florence Nightingale as a 'role model' here – or to construe the student as re-creating the life of Florence Nightingale – would underplay the complexity of what is happening. For in being inspired, the student not merely attempts to follow, but indeed, infuses herself into her new passions, becoming determined to understand nursing in all its contemporary challenges, and to find ways of putting that understanding into policies and practice.

Through inspiration, new being is formed, new will is taken on. The student moves herself into a new place. New connections are formed in her mind and her being. Her *being* becomes identified with its new objects, constituted by the subjects and experiences in her curriculum. Topics, concepts, techniques and experiences open up that may be completely new, or subjects that had been studied at school are suddenly seen in new ways, the student's *self* is now marked out and even filled out to a large degree by these new interests.

This pedagogical excitement propels the student forward. There is an attachment here: the student wills herself forward. More accurately perhaps, is willed forward. She has a will to learn, but the will wasn't planted there in her by herself. It came upon her.

Inspirational teaching is, clearly enough, that form of teaching that brings about inspiration. However, the paradox we noticed earlier is still before us: How can a pedagogy of inspiration be both inspiration-at-a-distance and enable connections to be made? Here, we have to distinguish two sets of connections. There is, in the first place, the set of connections that we have just been teasing out, that between the student's new epistemological interests and her state of being: her being becomes so infused with her new epistemological interests (which may well include practical interests) that her self is itself changed. However, there is, in the second place, a further set of connections that a pedagogy of inspiration opens up, that of connections being made between the teacher and the student.

We must come to this complex matter more fully in due course (in the next chapter) but, here, we must at least open the matter. What is surely clear in the idea of a pedagogy of inspiration is that the educator can be a source of inspiration. Being a source of inspiration may be achieved directly or indirectly. *Directly*, the educator may be a source of inspiration through his own qualities, dispositions or energies. *Indirectly*, the educator, as an experienced pedagogue, may displace himself into the pedagogical background and so orchestrate the students' experiences that they are much more left to their own devices and to take responsibility for their own learning.

Both sources of inspiration – direct and indirect – are important and deserve a little separate consideration.

That the educator may inspire his students directly may itself occur in a variety of ways. As remarked, his qualities, dispositions and energies may each be possible candidates for a process of inspiration to take place, but whatever qualities, dispositions and energies there may be – and even, we may add, whatever passions, excitements there may be – still, they will be a matter of sheer show unless connections are made with the students. Doubtless there are complex psychological interactions at work here. This is territory, for example, on which Lacan has touched. Under conditions of inspiration, there may perhaps be, on the part of the student, 'an identification with the Ideal' (Leader and Groves, 2003). The student identifies with the teacher, now seen in a ideal imaginary form and who has therefore become 'significant' for the student.

Such a line of inquiry may well be potent, but it is not where we need to go just now. For our speculations have opened up some searching questions. For example, does the educator have himself to be inspired in order to inspire his students? Does the educator have to have inspiration consciously in his mind as a pedagogical intention in order to be inspirational? Furthermore, does the educator have both to wish to make connections with his students *and* to succeed in doing so, if he is to effect a pedagogy of inspiration? Can one or should one set out to be inspirational? Can one even, Sartrian-like, self-consciously play the part of an inspirational teacher, and fein its presumed passion and pedagogic involvement?

We can barely do more than to lodge these questions here. All these questions are about what we may term the infrastructure of inspiration, namely the conditions of the forming of connections implied by a pedagogy of inspiration. I shall, however, baldly assert the following propositions: the educator has to be at least spirited in order for the student to take on new spirit as a direct result of that influence. It is not necessary for the educator deliberately to set out to inspire, but it will be all to the good if he does; for his pedagogical efforts may be more likely to be inspirational. For the educator will deliberately set out to make appropriate kinds of connections to that end, even though – as we have observed – there can be no automaticity about such an eventuality.

The key point to which these questions and bald responses alert us is that the educator has the potential of himself being *directly* inspiring. This direct form of inspiration is not essential to the student's will to learn being heightened [John Stuart Mill, it would seem (1989), as a supreme autodidact, got on quite nicely by himself in learning Greek], but that potential on the part of the educator, of heightening the student's will to learn, remains nevertheless. The tutor or lecturer can himself be a direct source of inspiration, whether wittingly or unwittingly. Spirit does not directly flow from spirit, but it can be engendered by it.

We noted, too, that the educator may be an *indirect* source of the student's inspiration. Connections may be made indirectly. The whole course may present the student with a dazzling array of experiences, at once galvanizing and challenging. Perhaps, too, much responsibility is placed upon the students in, say, problem-based learning, and the students come both to develop and to form a new appreciation of their capabilities. The tutor may put the students together in groups with challenging tasks such that, over a period of time, the students come to support each other and energize each other, or the students may have formed close supportive relationships with each other:

> *After five weeks, one day we turned up about half an hour later than them and they were doing exactly what they would have been doing with us. They were organizing a discussion and, of course, they didn't need us for that. We became the resource . . .*

> (Lecturer in Nursing Studies)

In circumstances such as any of these, it may be not so much that any of the tutors is inspiring or even the tutors collectively, but rather that the course itself is felt by the students to be inspiring. It is the curriculum that is inspiring. The students (plural) take on new spirit; a new and positive relationship with their pedagogical world. Collectively, the students are infused with energy and enthusiasm. They are happy in their course and look forward to the next set of experiences, even though they know that they are going to be challenged by those experiences. They enjoy being with each other. The students have taken on an *esprit de corps*. They each have a will that is urging to learn. Together, they take on a collective air.

In a pedagogy of inspiration, then, connections have to be made. The internal forming of spirit – *in*-spiration – on the part of the student is not entirely explicable; it is somewhat ineffable.[4] However, the process of being inspired does not happen in a vacuum. It occurs in a context. That context, as we have begun to see, can take a variety of forms – of the personal characteristics of a tutor or set of tutors and the immediate pedagogical relationship; or more indirectly, in the character of the curriculum; or even more indirectly still, as the student links her pedagogical experiences to other sources of meaning in her life (in her family, or work, or religion or a particular human relationship).

In any event, some set of connections has to be made. The student is able to find personal meaning in her educational experiences, and attaches her self to those experiences; she identifies with them. In the process, her pedagogical being is given new energy, new resolve. She is inspired; a new spirit has come upon her.

The ubiquity of inspiration

I said a moment ago that the process of being inspired is ineffable. We cannot hope discursively to explain completely the idea of inspiration. Always, elements of the process will remain beyond a formal description. However, this recognition of our inadequacies before a fundamental concept of much significance in no way should discourage us from trying to unravel its mysteries:

> There's no way ever to say this . . . and no place to stop saying it.
> (Traditional Eastern poet, quoted in Cooper 2002: 291)

I have also suggested – and it follows from this set of recognitions – that there can be no set of pedagogical rules that, once followed, are sure to yield processes of inspiration on the part of students. However, despite this ineffability, despite the limitations of pedagogical rules and despite – so we may add – a widespread sense that inspirational teaching is somewhat rare, I want to propose that *pedagogies of inspiration are a necessary part of the kind of higher education for which I am contending*. It follows, therefore, that pedagogies of inspiration *should* be commonplace even if, in practice, this is far from the case.

How might such a case be sustained? To begin with, we have to draw on some of the points already made. One key point already made lies in the distinction between direct and indirect forms of inspiration. To say that inspiration should be a commonplace in higher education is to say nothing about the pedagogical context in which such inspiration takes place. It could take place, as we have seen, largely through some kind of identification with the teacher – the student being inspired *by* the teacher – or it could take place more indirectly, the student being inspired by the new delights afforded her by her curricula experiences.

There is the separate point that, in higher education, students take courses in particular subjects or groupings of subjects. Even if their courses are a complex of subjects and experiences, still their will to learn is forged in relation to a particular set of educational interests on their part. Accordingly, we may observe that inspiration looks in two directions. In being inspired, a student is inspired (i) *by* her pedagogical experiences, (ii) *to do* certain kinds of things. She is willed forward to address the challenges in her immediate course of study. The will is formed in a context of particular epistemic and practical concerns. There is both a push element and a pull element at work here.

In both the push and the pull of inspiration, there may be – we should note – pain. In the pull, lies arduous standards against which the student's learning must be assessed (not least, by the student herself). In the push, lie paths to strangeness, which are likely to be disturbing and the disturbances of this strangeness occur at – as we may put it – both the micro- and the macro-levels. At the micro-level emerge the disturbances of transforming the complex of feelings and half-formed thoughts into coherent offerings, made more acute as the student wrestles with contrasting accounts of the world – whether in the form of inconsistent data or conflicting sets of ideas. At the macro-level emerge the disturbances of being itself, as the student's hold on the world is assaulted by encompassing whole new fields of understanding.

The sensitive teacher recognizes all of these elements, but is also subject to her own will to teach: the will to learn (on the part of the student) may be assisted in its formation through the will to teach on the part of the tutor:

> . . . for them to be inspired, they need to be with someone who is enthusiastic and communicative of some ideas in such a way that they know they can take them on board. And speak them through their own voice.
>
> (Lecturer, UK post–92 university)

There are three elements at work here on the part of the lecturer:

i   (Explicitly) an enthusiasm for her own subject.
ii   (Implicitly) a care for the students, and (evidently) a determination to communicate so as to enable her students to come into the issues and ideas to hand in their own way.
iii An outcome, so we might say, of the combination of the first two elements: being enthused by her subject and having a care for her students, she determines to communicate *to some effect.* That intended effect is precisely one of permitting space to the students such that they can come into their experiences authentically. The first two elements – enthusiasm for subject and care for students – are key here.

We have now, I think, the ingredients to hand for our argument that, far from being marginal, inspiration is a strong if not a necessary condition of the idea of higher education for which I am contending in this book.

The student who has a will to learn has come into herself; she is impelled forward. She can barely help herself. (We saw an example of that in the quotation from the student in reflecting on her own pedagogical 'excitement' and consequent 'drive' and involvement.) As Marjorie Reeves so nicely put it (1988) the student is 'hooked'; she is caught by her pedagogical interests. However, this is to say, surely, that she has a spirit within her; somehow or other, she has become inspired.

That nuance – 'somehow or other' – is necessary because while we have seen that the teacher can directly assist the process of being inspired, inspiration may befall the student indirectly. Even there, we may reflect that behind any such indirect process of the student's being inspired also may stand the skilful tutor who has so arranged the curricula experiences that they are likely to inspire the students.

Key concepts in the idea of higher education here are those of 'a will to learn', 'being-for-itself' and 'authenticity'. That a student is inspired is at least a strong condition of this group of concepts having application. It may not be a necessary condition, but it is a strong condition. Actually, 'inspiration' and 'a will to learn' are tightly connected: being inspired offers a strong likelihood that a will to learn will emerge. It may not be exactly a contradiction, but to say that the student was inspired, yet had no will to learn would be odd. It would imply that the inspiration was lacking in substance; it was a shadow of its real self.

In turn, a will to learn is a necessary condition both for being-for-itself and for authenticity to develop. The being of the student we encountered earlier – who had been inspired by a teacher – was a being-for-itself: it was freely willing itself forward in its own pedagogical projects. Out of such a being-for-itself, we may hope, a pedagogical authenticity may emerge, with the student's claims and actions being fully hers.

We observed earlier that there is no set of techniques or forms of curricula or even of human qualities that can ensure that inspiration will occur. However, the teacher who is wanting her students to develop a will to learn will also want to inspire them, for through their being inspired, they are likely to develop such a will to learn; and then also, in turn, develop a pedagogical being-for-itself and, ultimately, a state of authenticity in that pedagogical being. If her will to learn is to be nurtured and even enhanced, the student has to have an internal spirit. The good teacher, accordingly, is one who strives to inspire, both directly and indirectly, in the forms of pedagogy and curricula. A pedagogy for inspiration has to be a *commonplace* of a will to learn.

Degrees of inspiration

In the linguistic hinterland of 'inspiration' lie terms that are barely acceptable in the educational lexicon these days. Perhaps the idea of spirit just passes muster – we might speak of a student having lots of 'spirit' or even of a 'critical spirit', and perhaps even 'sprightliness' could, at a stretch be called into service. 'Spiritual', however, brings with it for most, surely, unwelcome and noisy suggestions of a theological perspective, but that apparently insistent association is not the pressing linkage it may seem.[5]

In his Rectoral address, Heidegger spoke (1985) of his 'commitment to the spiritual leadership of this institution of higher learning' (the institution in question being the University of Freiburg). For Heidegger, the university – his university, at any rate – had an 'unyielding spiritual mission', but he hurriedly went on to ask the question: 'Do we know about this spiritual mission?' His answer lay in a conception that again would be repudiated today, for he saw the 'will to the essence of the German university' as intimately connected with the 'historical mission of the German people as a people that knows itself in its state'. On this view, the spiritual mission of the university lay in nationalism, it would seem.[6]

If there is no way through in that vein to rehabilitate an idea of the spiritual, is another way possible, that may make sense in the fragmented world of the twenty-first century? For Paul Standish (1999), 'spirit is non-natural, non-present, out of reach, and inclined to defy measurement'. Spirit has ineffable qualities and – we have been noticing – cannot be fully described discursively. Nor are there techniques or rules – of curricula design or pedagogical relationship – that can guarantee its emergence.

Commenting on Heidegger's idea of spirit – barely worked out as it was – Derrida (1991) sees it as opening 'the possibility of questioning' (p. 43), a 'questioning that belongs through and through . . . to will . . . as the will to know' (p. 44). The being to which this spirituality points is not itself spatial, except that there is opened here a 'being of space' (p. 25) To be concerned with freedom is to be concerned with 'the freedom of spirit' (p. 43).

If we put these resources together, do we not glimpse an idea of an education for the spirit that may have some sense for us today? There can be no final position for the student whose being has been inspired. Being inflamed, excited, enthused, the student has caught fire; is newly alive, not just to his experiences, but to himself. He is free or, at least, is now working continually to realize that freedom for and by himself. This process of becoming is mysterious even to himself – recall our 'amazed' student earlier.

Such processes of human becoming are *undergone*. The student literally experiences them; *inspiration* falls upon oneself; one cannot bring one's own inspiration about in any deliberate way. However, the *spirit of inspiration* may come upon one to a greater or lesser degree; and it may deepen and become more lively over time. As the student, being inspired, moves into his own space, so that inspiration may intensify. Yet, under unfavourable circumstances, it may also dissipate. The identification with the tutor may lapse, the pedagogical situation may present with damaging experiences – the other students in the group were unsympathetic (perhaps our student was an international student where modes of self-presentation were more reticent) – and so the flame of inspiration dwindles and, if not caught in time, dies – or at least comes to lie dormant. However, it may just be caught and rekindled.

Conclusions

Through the student's own spirit, she can move into a space of her own. She can enter her own becoming. 'Inspiration' is the process in which the student begins to acquire such spirit. A pedagogy for inspiration is a pedagogy that is infused with hopes of such inspiration coming about.

Why is a pedagogy for inspiration important? Why is it important in higher education? Why is it important at the present time? A pedagogy for inspiration is important because it looks to break the bounds of conventions, whether those of disciplines or systems or even curricula. The idea of spirit looks to freedom, self-assertion and ultimately authenticity.[7] Without spirit there can be no authenticity:

> Spirit lives and moves wherever our striving for clarity is a striving for fullness of insight.
>
> (Karl Jaspers 1971: 44)

A pedagogy for inspiration is important *in higher education* because the idea of higher education looks to promote each student as a unique person, and her own powers and personal integrity. It looks to the student gaining her own air.

A pedagogy for inspiration is important *at the present time* because the contemporary world threatens to deny air, spirit and inspiration. In higher education, the bureaucratic structures – in, for instance, their insistence that learning outcomes be stated in advance – implicitly repudiate spirit. For spirit, in turn, will challenge any attempt to impose pre-ordained frameworks, but spirit is needed in the contemporary age at an even more subtle level. The modern world is a complex of conflicting currents: individualization, fluidity, risk and ideology are but some of the terms that may be called into service here. Spaces open and yet are closed all at once. The 'liquid society' (Bauman 2000) has swirling waters, but yet some are siphoned off. The individualization called for is often that of the marketplace. In such a fluidity, of mixed vortices, some more powerful than others, spirit is crucial: spirit now becomes a necessary moment of authentic self-creativity.

We have focused our attention not on 'a pedagogy *of* inspiration', but rather on 'a pedagogy *for* inspiration'. There are no quick fixes when it comes to inspiration: there can be no technology of inspiration. What is required instead is a continuing and patient effort to so configure the total pedagogical environment, such that students come into spaces of their own. The tiniest gesture can go far in creating such a space. In coming to such a space, it just may be that the students – some of them at any rate – will catch fire and be inspired.

10

A pedagogy for uncertain times

Introduction: no resting place

The main pedagogical task in higher education is both simple and near impossible; simple to state and near impossible to achieve. It is that of so releasing students that they come into themselves, in relation to their curricula challenges. They become beings-for-themselves. They engage with their educational experiences *authentically*. They have their own will to learn and, being so energized, drive themselves forward of their own volition. They are determined to come into a relationship with their experiences that is *theirs*.

It may be said that all this is characteristic of any form of education. So it may be, but – as we noted earlier – authenticity is a tacit ideal of Western higher education. This is not to say that students have to 'be themselves', as if each student had his or her own ideal state of being. It cannot be the duty of higher education to release such a state of being since, in a supercomplex age, we must doubt that such a blissful state of being is available to students, no matter how enlightened the pedagogy. There are no pure states of being available, but the idea of authenticity remains potent as states of being in which students are themselves committed to *themselves*.

There are two supplementary considerations here. First, it is a further tacit idea with Western higher education that students come to a state of self-criticality. Each student is able to evaluate his or her own position and to go on strengthening it:

consciousness critically examines itself.

(Hegel, cited in Derrida 2002: 93).

A prior condition of such criticality is that the student distances her own being from her own thoughts and actions. A state of criticality can only be reached if the student has a vantage point from which to be critical of her thoughts and actions.

Secondly, this criticality is achieved in the context of the spirit of research. This is not a point about universities as institutions themselves engaging in research, but is rather a point about the pedagogical ethos. Whether the research is conducted by the student's tutors or other staff in the department, or by other universities, or by non-university organizations, *or by the students themselves*, the student's enquiries and pedagogical acts are proffered in the context of research. Such a spirit – the spirit of research – supplies a tentativeness not just to the student's enquiries, but also to her profferings, her claims and her actions.

These two ideas – of critical being and of enquiry in the spirit of research – help to fill out the idea of authenticity. The authenticity we look for in higher education is neither given nor easily achieved. It emerges over time through arduous processes of steady engagement. Hence, our idea of a will to learn presses itself.

It presses itself forward especially because, now, in her being, her educational being at least, the student has to come to live with uncertainty. The uncertainty principle reaches deeply into the student's being (Barnett 2004). Students complain about their uncertainties, their doubts about their abilities, their concerns that everything in their minds is a muddle or just won't straighten out, but one of the achievements of higher education is precisely that of enabling students to live with their own inner turbulence and to realize that it will always hence be thus. There is no resting place from here on. Incessant turbulence is a price of realizing the idea of higher education.

Sinclair Goodlad (1976) spoke – as we observed before – of 'authoritative uncertainty'. The idea now emerging here is adjacent, but slightly apart: it is that of 'authentic uncertainty' – of being authentic amid uncertainty. The key question here that arises from such an analysis is surely this: *what kind of pedagogical relationship is likely to assist the formation of such an 'authentic uncertainty'*? I want to suggest that, at its heart (as a necessary condition) is that of what we may term *pedagogical care*.

Nurturing the student

I suggested at this chapter's outset that the main pedagogical task is that of so releasing students that they come into themselves. We may put the point starkly in the form of two questions: what kind of relationship between teacher and student is likely best to enable students to take off even amid uncertainty? What kind of relationship is going to help the formation of the kind of student being for which I am contending?

Let us start simply. The pedagogical task, self-evidently, is one of nurturing. This is almost a tautology. For 'nurture' is 'an act or process of promoting [human] development' (Oxford Shorter English Dictionary), but higher education as a 'process of human development' is a large part of the idea of higher education for which I am contending in this book.[1] So to say that the pedagogical task is one of nurture is hardly to add to what we have already been saying.

But it does add something. It adds the idea of 'act' – as in 'act of nurture' in the definition we have just encountered. Nurture is both act and process: the *process* of nurture is accomplished via the *act* of nurture.

The act of nurture entails an intention to nurture. In turn, an intention to nurture heralds a perspective of time; indeed, a dual perspective of time. On the one hand, the act of nurturing is an act – or even a series of acts – over time, but if nurturing takes place over time and if one is acting deliberately so as to nurture a student, say, then it follows that the nurturer will herself hold the perspective of time in her pedagogical deliberations. She knows that the nurturing cannot be undertaken in any satisfactory way in a brief period of time. In order to nurture with any lasting effect, the process has to endure over time, *and* the nurturer has to grasp and to accept that the process will so endure.

The educator knows all this in her bones. Called upon to provide just one or two teaching sessions in a single module, she knows that she cannot build much in the way of a relationship with the students to enable a significant process of nurturing to get going. She may give of her professional best and may even establish something of a rapport in those one or two sessions. But it can hardly amount to an enduring nurturing process. And not a process for the formation of a lifelong will to learn within her students.

However, the act of nurturing calls for yet more from the teacher. Nurturing cannot be accomplished perfunctorily. It calls not just for an enduring process, but also for an enduring commitment on the part of the teacher.[2]

What is the nature of that commitment? A typical move on these occasions is to suggest that, in higher education, the teacher has, in the first place, to be committed to her discipline; or, if the term 'discipline' is too difficult these days (for a variety of reasons), let us say that the teacher has to be committed to his or her intellectual, or professional fields. The teacher is trying to help the student come into the interior of a field of understandings and ways of engaging with the world, which has its own demands and standards. It is her field with which the teacher identifies and in which she has her professional being. This commitment arises through the pull that the field has for the teacher: she is drawn to it and even excited by it. In turn, she gives much of her life to it. She structures much of her life around its calls, its demands. Her own field of being overlaps with the field itself; her being is in-the-field (even if she journeys across its moving borders or transgresses – as it may seem to others – across to yet other fields entirely; or has increasingly a fragmented professional identity as she grapples with a range of expectations and even demands).

Others will say rather that the commitment is, in the first place, to the students. There they are: real live bodies, each with his or her own being, to be seen on the campus, with their books, their laughs, their conversations in groups, or glimpsed in the computer room, or in project groups in the library (increasingly noisy places as co-learning spaces). They look autonomous, getting on with their lives, and their educational tasks; and to see them, one would be forgiven for thinking that this autonomy was filled out with a set of educational projects that were under control, but the record is clear. Not only is progress across the class uneven; many are struggling to keep up. Some are faltering. Even those who are successful are wondering and even worrying about their next steps beyond their degree.

So each student exerts claims of different kinds. Each has his or her own being, and the sensitive teacher feels that uniqueness of each student's being drawing her forward. The teacher is committed to her students, 'to my students'. The teacher is engaged with them on a joint educational voyage. It is these commitments to each student that seriously crowd into her life. The essays sit on the coffee table at home and claim her attention, even against other commitments. Her being is partly there, in the assessing of those essays, and in the challenges which that brings, knowing that behind each essay stands a distinctive human being, and that each word in a margin scribble or in an emailed response will evoke a different response from student to student.

Yet others will say that the teacher's commitment, in higher education, is two-fold: it is both of these commitments. The teacher is committed *both* to her own field and to her students. Both the field and her students exert their claims, even though neither field nor students voice any such claims or, if they do, then it is *sotto voce*.

We must pursue this double commitment – to field and to students – in a moment, but here we are exploring the nature of nurture. Nurturing brings with it, we were observing, a time perspective and here we glimpse the structure of that temporal perspective: it has a dual structure, brought about through the claims of field and of students. Bringing the student onto the inside of a complex field – or, in a multidisciplinary course, of several fields – has to take time. But also, forming a pedagogical relationship with a student and sustaining it itself has to take place over time.

Solicitude

Part of our task here is that of deriving a vocabulary for depicting the pedagogical relationship that is adequate to our broader challenge. This broader challenge is that of understanding what it might be to be a student in an age of uncertainty (as our sub-title suggests). Just some terms that might come into view for depicting the pedagogical challenges are those of empathy, care, nurture, affirmation, encouragement, trust, respect, forgiveness, intensity, excitement, delight, generosity, reciprocity, kindliness, commitment, friendship and love. (We have touched on 'nurture' and 'commitment', but can touch on only a few of these other terms here.)

There is a further term that is, I believe, helpful to us: that of 'solicitude', a term employed by Heidegger:

> . . . there is also the possibility of a kind of solicitude which does not so much leap in for the Other as leap ahead of him in his existential

potential-for-Being, not in order to take away his 'care' but rather to give it back to him authentically as such for the first time. This kind of solicitude pertains essentially to authentic care ... it helps the Other to become transparent to himself in his care and to become free for it.

(Heidegger 1998: 159)

I regard this passage as seminal, at least for our purposes here. As well as the term 'solicitude', we see also in this passage 'care', 'authentic(ity)' and 'being', each of them concepts that have become critical in this inquiry. The dominant concept in this passage, however, is that of 'solicitude' and we may see how potent it is. It is, indeed, the pivot for the passage. In the 'possibility' that Heidegger has in mind, solicitude does not reduce the Other ('does not so much leap in for the Other'), but rather 'leap(s) ahead of him', not 'in order to take away his "care" but rather to give it back to him'.

Isn't this precisely a striking insight into the character of the pedagogical relationship at its finest? Drawing on this passage, we may say that the teacher who is intent on having a lasting effect envisages future possibilities for the student and so 'leaps ahead ... in his existentiall potential-for-Being'. This solicitude, this envisaging of future possibilities, does not stand in the way of the student's unfolding (compare 'learning outcomes').[3] This solicitude is not imposing itself; is not determining a path of becoming. On the contrary, *this* solicitude 'helps the Other to become transparent to himself in his care and *to become free for it*'. [RAB's emphasis]

Here, doors are opened for the student to pass through, in his own 'authentic care'. This is no facile process of 'knowing oneself' (as the hackneyed phrase would have it). This pedagogical process surely must be a critical process, and a self-critical process at that; and over extended time. How else could the 'Other ... become transparent to himself'?

I have dwelt on this passage and used it to explicate the concept of solicitude because I believe that it reveals the potential pedagogic value that the concept might have.[4]

Solicitude takes care because it cares (cf. Passmore 1975). It looks ahead; it has the student's longer-term interests in mind. It sees the student in a longer-term horizon. Indeed, multiple horizons – of the student's intellectual, practical and psychological well-being. It leaps ahead of the student, not so much as to determine precisely the journey that the student will take but to open up possibilities for him; for his 'existential potential-for-Being'. Through this solicitude, the teacher envisages that the student has potential for development. The teacher may not, indeed cannot, be sure what that potential might be, but the teacher firmly believes that the student's potential is nowhere near exhausted.

Solicitude does not always yield a ready response. The student may fall away, may lose heart, may lapse in some way (with the pull of the peer culture, all manner of temptations lie in wait, not to mention the sheer vicissitudes of accomplishing survival in student life, with its concerns over accommodation, fees and so forth). The challenges of the course may temporarily be too demanding. 'Temporarily' because that is how such fallings away will appear to solicitude. Solicitude urges that these lapses will be temporary and that the student can and will return.

However, solicitude does not simply assume that the student will return – whether it is a return to her studies, to her work, to her projects and to the challenges of her course, or whether it is a coming back into herself, as her personal difficulties lessen. Solicitude, being solicitude, seeks to recover the student and to help the student to make that return, and then to retain the student's endeavour.

This solicitude is sapping of the teacher's own energies. The student's will to learn calls for a corresponding will to teach among her tutors; but the will to teach, just as with the will to learn, is itself liable to falter. After all, in today's higher education, the teacher has many other calls on and shapings of her professional identity (largely hidden from students). The will to teach has to find its place among the several callings on the tutor and it can only be sustained through durable dispositions on the part of the tutor.

Solicitude need not only be a matter of personal dispositions on the part of the teacher. It can find institutional form. An institution of higher education can show its solicitude towards its students qua institution. It will wear its solicitude on its sleeve by providing support services of one kind or another. More subtly, its boards of examiners will show a receptivity towards the circumstances of each student and its departments will seek in their different ways to draw students into the mainstream of its academic life. Solicitude towards students may even be apparent in the institution's learning and teaching strategy, and in the prominence given to that strategy (alongside the institution's research strategy); for the strategy itself may be framed around the well-being of the students and their proper progression.

By *institutional solicitude*, we cannot mean that a university simply 'cares' about its students or just that its students are self-evidently important in its interior life. We must mean a more complex set of institutional dispositions in which students are enabled and encouraged to flourish over time. Such a university holds its students and supports them, as they move themselves forward. This solicitude is found in the positive way in which the senior management team works with the Students Union; it is found in the relationship that may be established in personal tutoring; and it is found more informally in the corridor, as the tutor spots one of her students and passes on a reference to a journal paper identified by chance on the previous evening.

Solicitude's care, then, is always vigilant and open actively to be called upon to work for the student in the interstices of daily academic life. It has a long time horizon, but it lives in the here-and-now.

Additional reciprocity

The French term 'l'addition' characteristically means 'the bill'. It is the addition made at the end of the meal: the account is rendered and met. In the adding up, in making the addition, nothing else should be added on. Yet, the very addition produces the bill, a claim for the restaurant's services. The addition produces a further addition: the bill itself.

So it is with teaching in higher education. Out of teaching comes more teaching. It is not just that the well known refrains hold true: 'the only way to learn something well is to teach it'; or, again, 'my students taught me more than I taught them'; or even 'many of my best ideas arose out of my teaching'. There is a reciprocity in teaching in higher education. Teachers and taught teach each other. The roles are interwoven, such that their boundaries become indistinct to some extent.

We may understand this pedagogical reciprocity as arising out of the openness of the pedagogical relationship in higher education. Of course, the extent of such pedagogical openness varies across disciplines and across institutions, and even across members of the same department. However, relatively, in higher education, the pedagogical relationship has an openness to it: teachers are open to their students even as their students are open to their teachers. In the (1996) language of Basil Bernstein, the pedagogical relationship in higher education is characterized by a relatively 'loose frame'.

Pedagogical framing: an autobiographical story (by RAB)

I like to use flip charts in my teaching as a means of engaging with my students and heightening a dialogue with them. In a heated discussion, I may simply try to capture key concepts and ideas put into the collective pool by the students themselves and try to find connections between them. In front of the students, their own conversation is relayed to us all and it takes off visibly in front of us, as the diagram becomes ever more complex – often with the use of different coloured pens. Sometimes, my notes take the form of quite abstract signs and squiggles as I try to capture nuances of the conversation. The dynamic construction of these flip chart doodlings can often help to energize even more the classroom discussion, and the students individually.

There was a party for my fiftieth birthday, organized by the students themselves. At the party, I was presented with a framed wrapped picture. On undoing the wrapping, I saw what I had been presented with: a framed example of one of my sets of squiggles many weeks beforehand (a particularly abstract set of squiggles on the sheet of paper, as it happened, with no obvious meaning at all to anyone not present at that pedagogical occasion).

The presenting back to me of my own pedagogical doodlings was a source of huge amusement all round, not least to myself. And it surely conveyed a sense of a warm interactive pedagogical relationship, working at several levels.

I want to go further, however. I want to suggest that there is a yet further form of reciprocity that we have not yet broached. At its best, the pedagogical relationship in higher education offers an infinite etceteration of interactions. The skilled teacher trades on this infinite etceteration. She engages with the class directly. She may have a loose script from which she is working, but that is all. She is prompting, encouraging, stimulating, goading, urging and exhorting. She opens herself and, in so doing, the responses come back. There is a multiple return on her efforts. As she puts herself forward, so the students return the compliment, in more than equal measure. This is even more than a 'pedagogy of recognition' or even a 'pedagogy of affirmation'; it is a pedagogy of mutuality. And it is possible through the mutual delight her teaching situations afford (but the care and solicitude is not conditional on there being some kind of pedagogical return).

This is a never ending reciprocity. Out of the giving comes more giving; out of the daring, comes more daring. This is a pedagogy of risk; the teacher can barely keep up with the flow of offerings coming her way. The will to offer has been stirred up and now won't die down. It is a cascade of mutually reinforcing offerings. The students may subtly reinforce each other. Pedagogical bungee jumping may be catching.

This we may describe as *additional reciprocity*. It is not mere reciprocity. It is reciprocity building on reciprocity. In a class in which such energies are released, pedagogical fission occurs. The students' own energies energize yet more offerings. They stimulate each other. The teacher may aid such mutual energizing among the students by placing them in groups, perhaps to work on tasks or projects over time. Out of pedagogical reciprocity may come yet more pedagogical reciprocity.

Pedagogical offerings

There is increasing talk of pedagogical friendship and even of pedagogical love (for example, Alexander, T. 2001; Burch 2002; Elton 2005), but neither 'friendship' nor 'love' seem to me to be quite on the mark here.

'Friendship' evades semantic capture. What does it mean? What can it mean? Just how could it come into play in an understanding of university teaching? Any attempt to pin it down must be accompanied by 'perhaps'. Perhaps it betokens a care *in absentia*: I think of my friend and care about him, even though he is not proximate to me, not visibly present, at any rate. Perhaps it indicates a preparedness for self-sacrifice for the good of my friend: I am prepared to do things for my friend, even though there may be a heavy cost. Perhaps 'friendship' indicates a mutuality: there can be no private friendship. 'Friendship' implies the presence of 'friends': x is a friend to y, and y is a friend to x.

We have then run into a conundrum: friendship implies both sacrifice without return and implies precisely a return, a to-ing and a fro-ing. Isn't it a consideration of this kind that leads to the stark contention: 'O my friends –

there is no friend' (Derrida, 2005: 1–2, quoting Montaigne). Friendship undermines itself. The idea of self-sacrifice is undermined by the idea of reciprocity, and so Derrida can speak of 'the politics of friendship': within friendship may lie dashed hopes, unfulfilled expectations, a plea for solitude, and the expectations of the other.

Is this, then, the semantic territory bequeathed to us by the idea of friendship? It may be a beguiling notion, the sense that the pedagogical relationship may be one of friendship. Then does it not throw up – on inspection – unsettling and contrary sentiments? The pedagogical relationship is both one of self-sacrifice and of mutuality? A difficult set of ideas to conjure simultaneously.

Practical implications are readily to hand. Does the supervisor accept a gift from an overseas student, a gift transported with some care perhaps from the other side of the world? Let us put aside any contention about role conflict as between being both a tutor and an examiner; for here, the supervisor has no examining role (the examination of research students being handled entirely by the university: in the viva, the supervisor may be present, but will also remain silent). Does the acceptance of the gift, in a spirit of pedagogical friendship, carry with it any expectation, if only of a way of going on, of conducting the relationship?[5]

From the other side of the relationship, the teacher may throw herself into her pedagogical situations with gusto. She smiles; she exudes a spirit of friendship. Even laughs are shared. Is this giving on her part not accompanied with an expectation that the students will also respond and give of themselves, and give of themselves indeed to her? Is her pedagogy not precisely built on a mutuality of engagement? Furthermore, on a mutuality infused with smiles, with affirmation from both sides? The smiles are carried over into the chance meetings on the stairs or in the corridor and in the snatched conversation. This mutuality extends over time; the relationship is sustained in all manner of ways, but this mutuality of giving of self, it is clear, is also infused with mutual expectations of a giving of self. The chance encounter is accompanied by an expectation of givingness. Mutuality and self-sacrifice dance around each other.

Friendship, then, as an idea, is a 'troublesome concept' (Land and Meyer 2006), but in a particular sense. Friendship refracts upon itself; it sets up troublesomeness as part of its own character. In higher education, in the pedagogical relationship, 'friendship' promises what it cannot deliver.

What of 'love' then? Does that fare any better? Can the idea of pedagogical love help us? Richard Rorty once observed that love is notoriously untheorizable, but here again is perhaps another matter from which we should not shrink, despite its difficulties.

We may say that, in higher education, teachers may have dual objects of love, their subject and their students.[6] How is this possible? How can the same term come into play in relation both to abstract fields and to persons? What might be meant here? A sense of love that might do justice for both modes of being – love of subject and love towards teaching – might be that of passion. The teacher is impassioned by both projects – understanding and even advancing her fields and promoting her students' learning.[7]

Passionate teaching

To me, teaching is engaging with young people who are visionaries and dreamers in vibrant spaces that resonate with the collective energies of intellectuals enriched with a wealth of prior knowledge. Teaching is a passion and a commitment that is a constant joy in my life. . . . The simple and yet complex concepts of honesty, integrity and respect are fundamental in all my professional and personal interactions with students. The value I place on my teaching and research contributes to the passion I bring to teaching and ultimately to the successful learning by students.

(Extract from personal statement by winner of
a national and a university teaching prizes
[reproduced here by kind permission].)

Pedagogical passion implies an orientation towards making connections, but this passion is about making connections with the value of the objects in mind, both the intellectual field and the student. This passion is the ability to be "magnetized toward the vision of an imagined good", however far off it may be' (Burch, quoted in Alexander 2001). Such a passion is orientated towards – as it has been put – 'the impossibly good', for it is always aspirational (Walker 2003).

How might we understand the relationship of friendship and love? They may overlap, but they also have their differences. Friendship, we have seen, is reciprocal; it implies mutuality. Love is an identity with the good of the other and wanting the best for the other; and this love may apply both to one's subject and to one's students' wellbeing. This sense of love comes close to that of 'agape', the Christian idea of selfless love, but it cannot be utterly selfless for the passion implies an engagement with the object, whether it be the study of one's field or the students in the teaching situation.

Here, we may helpfully return to the idea of 'gift', on which we touched earlier. We saw that the student gifts her offerings: so too with the teacher and connected with this notion of gifting is a sense of the student's freedom:

For any self to be free to enable another's freedom means that it must be in some way aware of the actuality, not only the possibility, of a *regard beyond desire* – and so of its own being as a proper cause of joy, as a gift.

(Williams 2003: 197, emphasis as in original.)

This will to gift fuels one's efforts. It presses the teacher forward, even when things become difficult. Being active within the field may be extremely difficult at times; correspondingly, a will to teach as offering the gift of one-self – one's values, beliefs, energies and creativity – as well as one's under-standings, may bring its own challenges.[8] As gifts, these two sets of passions (towards the field and the students) bring with them standards – of right reason and of professional care. These passions cannot be unbridled.

Principles for uncertainty

Both the ideas of friendship and love, therefore, have their attractions, but they also have their difficulties. Friendship carries with it undue overtones of reciprocity; love carries with it undue overtones of passion devoid of standards. Is there a term that will carry us forward more satisfactorily?

Can there be? In an age of uncertainty, can there be a single idea that is adequate to the challenges of a university pedagogy? Just some of the terms associated with our inquiry here – only a few to which have we been able to do any justice – are those of gift, friendship, affirmation, recognition, care, passion, empathy, love, nurture, encouragement, trust, respect, forgiveness, reciprocity, solicitude, excitement, risk, delight, generosity and kindliness. All of these are rightly aspects of a pedagogy for uncertain times for all speak to modes of being beyond reliable knowledge.

Surely, a pedagogy for uncertainty has itself to be uncertain, at least in its manifest character. A pedagogy for uncertainty will embody all of the qual-ities we have just noted and more besides. This is bound to be the case: a pedagogy for uncertainty is intent on bringing forth all manner of human dispositions and qualities (Chapter 8) that are going to be able to withstand an environment of continuing contestation. Since the world is uncertain – not just technologically, but in its systems, institutions, ideologies and ideas – and since, therefore, we have no idea what the world will throw at us each day, there can be no chance of finding a single human quality or dis-position that is going to be adequate to such a world. Destabilization lurks around every corner. Human being that is in any way capable of addressing effectively this uncertain world has itself to take on many qualities.

It would, at such a point, be easy to lurch into a plea for a 'post-modern' pedagogy: on this reading, there is no more to be said than simply 'let a thousand pedagogical blooms flower'. Perhaps an issue might arise as to whether the thousand blooms should be evident in a single university teacher or in her department or across her university, or just across the higher edu-cation sector. That would be all: simply a debate about the concentration of pedagogical diversity.

That is a debate worth having, but it would be an abandonment of the challenge of pedagogy in the contemporary age. That challenge is that of limits: are there any limits to pedagogical diversity in an age of uncertainty? From a recognition that an age of uncertainty favours pedagogical diversity, does it follow that there are no limits to pedagogical diversity? This is not an empirical question. Indeed, the question can be put another way, so as to show its non-empirical credentials: are there any pedagogic principles that might carry us forward in the contemporary age? Yet other adjacent questions, still of a non-empirical kind, flow in. Are there any guides that might help us in identifying suitable pedagogies? Are there any criteria that might act as means of demarcation, to sort out pedagogies that are suitable and pedagogies that are unsuitable?

Simply to ask these questions is surely enough to suggest that while there might be an infinite range of pedagogies that might be called upon, still some others would be ruled out as unacceptable. What might such pedagogical principles look like, that might predispose the creation of suitable modes of teaching?

Drawing on our explorations so far, I would venture the following principles – that, *all things being equal,* pedagogies for an age of uncertainty should act so as to:

- affirm the humanity of each individual student;
- encourage forward each student's pedagogical will;
- allow each student her or his authenticity-in-the-making;
- put students in touch with each other and require their inter-communication;
- have a solicitude for students over time;
- offer space to each student to forge his or her own becoming.

These may seem straightforward and uncontentious principles; indeed, vapid, such that they hardly bear weight as principles.[9] In fact, I contend that these six principles – concerned, respectively, with affirmation, will, authenticity, communication, and durability over time and space – would, if henceforth implemented across higher education, amount to a revolution in learning and teaching in higher education.[10]

Conclusion: restrained anarchy

A pedagogy for uncertain times has itself to be uncertain. It is open, it is daring, it is risky, it is, itself, unpredictable. Not matter how professional the teacher is, no matter how much she has thrown herself into 'the scholarship of teaching', her teaching, if it is truly teaching for an uncertain age, will itself embody uncertainty. How can it be otherwise? She is trying to encourage forth human qualities and dispositions that are adept at handling uncertainty and so her pedagogical situations will be characterized by uncertainty.

It may be objected that the argument is faulty. It may be said that while a pedagogy may aim to elicit forms of human being capable of thriving amid uncertainty, it by no means follows that the pedagogy itself should be characterized by uncertainty. I do not accept that rejoinder. A pedagogy for uncertainty will be ontologically disturbing and enthralling all at once. It will be electric, as one move sparks another and in unpredictable ways. The myriad of pedagogic qualities that we noted earlier – empathy, reciprocity, passion, affirmation, friendship and yet others besides – will come into play at different times; at once daring, at once careful, at once spacious, at once pressing. Here is spontaneity and, therefore, unpredictability and uncertainty.

Are there no points of security? This spontaneity is not blind. It has its own principles, principles – as we saw – embedded in the disciplines and fields to hand. The students' creativity, their utterances, their interventions, their exchanges may be of an infinite variety, but still they will have their place in the standards of the fields (standards that are themselves bound to be perpetually changing and even – for new fields – to be in the making). Those standards permit an infinite range of possibilities, but yet place limits on the student's offerings. This pedagogy is a form of restrained anarchy; even a disciplined anarchy – with its spaces and its risks.

11

Space and risk

I certainly wouldn't have got anywhere if I hadn't been willing to take risks . . .

(John Cowan 1998: 109)

Introduction: connecting space and risk

We cannot hope for a student to develop a sustained will to learn and to achieve authenticity unless she is given space, but with space comes risk. That, therefore, is the ground of this chapter: to tease out what might be meant by space and to identify its associated risks.

Risks that might arise from space being provided to students are identifiable both from the points of view of the teacher and of the student. The teacher may be afraid to let go and to allow space to the student. That particular 'fear of freedom' may take the form of a concern for the student: there may, for instance, be a sense that unless a particular topic or author is 'covered' in the syllabus, the student's development will be impaired. However, the teacher's pedagogical 'fear of freedom' may take another form: it may spring from a disinclination to surrender control. In the classroom setting, the teacher may shrink from open-ended discussion in which topics are examined without an end-point being presumed; for in such a discussion, the teacher's authority has to be constructed *in situ*, in the classroom setting itself.

The risks involved here differ. On the one hand, the risk – if there is one – is a matter of the student's own advancement. It may be limited – or so it may be felt – if certain ground is not traversed: 'if my topic is not on the curriculum, the student cannot seriously be counted as an x' (as a doctor, an engineer, a historian or whatever it may be). Here, we have what might be called the heresy of necessity.[1] On the other hand, the risk is a matter of the teacher's own identity and authority: a fluid pedagogical situation might test and even diminish his authority. This risk is internal, to the teacher's own inner *felted-ness*: his sense of himself as a teacher is liable to be impaired.

However, risk may also threaten from the stance of the student. The student herself may shrink from more open-ended curricula, where more responsibility comes her way. There may be more responsibility on the student to organize her own timetable, or to determine the topics on which she is working or to assess her own work or that of other students. Instead, the student may prefer a more structured curricula environment. A risk here is that the student may simply be not good at organizing her own efforts, and identifying personal work goals and targets, and may consequently fall behind the necessary schedule of work if she is to succeed on the course in good time. We may term this a risk of *self-organization*, a risk that emerges through *curriculum space*.

Risk to the student may also arise from *pedagogical space*. In a more relaxed pedagogical relationship, in which the pedagogical relationship between teacher and student has more to be constructed, rather than being assumed, and in which the student is expected herself partly to advance that relationship, the student may be reticent to take on that role. It may be a matter of shyness or it may be, for instance, that the student has a more instrumental orientation to the relationship, wanting the pedagogical offerings to come to her (in the form of handouts and so forth), rather than being prepared to take significant responsibility in obtaining or constructing those materials for herself.

This phenomenon may happen on a micro-scale. A teacher may have a particularly interactive pedagogical style, seeing himself partly as a resource responding to the students' needs. He comes to the class less with a precise script and more with a sense of its general architecture, wishing for a conversation. Here, the onus is on the students in part to make the running: the more the students contribute, the more they will stir up the teacher, and the more excitement and fun, as well as sheer information there will be. Some students, though, remain silent in this milieu. In this *open pedagogical space*, they run several risks, but most of all, they run the risk of limiting their personal development. We might term this an *ontological risk*.

Both with curricula space and with pedagogical space, therefore, there are attendant risks. It is such spaces and their attendant risks that I want to explore further in this chapter.[2]

Virtues of space

Before we examine the risk quotient of pedagogical space, let us identify the virtues of space.

Pedagogical space is a necessary component of a higher education. No space, no higher education (at least, of the kind being contended for here). With pedagogical space arises freedom, a key concept deep within the idea of higher education. In pedagogical space, students can take responsibility for their thoughts and the expression of those thoughts, whether in writing or in action, including the spoken word.[3] In pedagogical space, students can become authentically themselves.

In pedagogical space, students can throw themselves forward. Characteristically, for instance, in higher education, in humanities and social sciences, students are set essays as part of their assignments. Other and newer kinds of assessment approaches often extend students' space, but we may make here an observation about essays as such.

Essays are themselves spaces. In those disciplines in higher education where essays are commonplace, it is not normal for the content of the students' essays to have been outlined in advance. Essays are typically permissive spaces: students are not permitted to say false things or contradictory things, or to reason falsely or to plagiarize, but otherwise they are permitted to come at their topic or to answer the questions they have chosen in their own way. Where we might, in the role of external examiner, say, stumble across practices in those disciplines where the nature of the students' text is heavily prescribed in advance, we might start to wonder if we were in the presence of a genuine higher education. At best, we might think that the course team was overly controlling of the students' formation; at worst, we might think that the course team had been gripped by narrow sectarian definitions as to the nature of the discipline itself.

It may be commented that in some disciplines, especially those of the natural sciences and in subjects orientated towards professions involved in life-threatening situations, that there are simply matters that have to be learnt; and that assignments are vehicles for assessing the student's acquisition of such understandings. In order to be placed on the professional register (in some professions), the student – so the story goes – simply has to know certain things. There, very little space, if any, can be permitted to the student. Assignments and their assessments have to constitute a highly controlled space. Multiple choice questions and computer-marked answers are a rational and valid form of assessment in such circumstances.

Whether such an argument holds water is not to the point here, however. What is to the point is to observe that such an approach to assessment cannot constitute the sole form of assessment in higher education. Professional subjects count as suitable candidates for higher education precisely where they open themselves to multiple, competing and developing approaches. The need for and possibility of such subjects developing a research base is but one symptom of the infinite potentiality of such fields. Consequently, assessments in the field have to allow space to students to be able to form their own judgements in, say, clinical situations. Only in that way can students begin to develop the makings of their professional responsibility. Responsibility arises itself in a space in which there are choices and where one, as a result, 'takes responsibility' for one's own actions and interpretations.

Through this set of observations, something of the nature of pedagogical space and its virtues begin to reveal itself. In pedagogical space, students push off, tentatively, hoping some secure resting place can be found that they can make their own, albeit temporarily. In spacious space – as distinct from a limited space or channelled space – students cannot know in advance what they will experience. They cannot do so since even their educators cannot fully know it. The space provided is a space in which students can make their own explorations, and one of the aspects of a truly higher education is that those explorations take place almost literally in an infinite space of possible knowings and understandings. It is that quality of the infinite that marks out fields of study and experience as suitable for higher education. Accordingly, to some extent, students may explore and even occasionally open up entirely new lines of enquiry and experience. Students' work – especially at postgraduate level – may even be publishable.

In pedagogical space, therefore, a student's being and experience go hand in hand. In higher education, these days, experience is a matter both of knowing and of ways of going on in all manner of practical ways – in design, in the clinical setting, in the computer assimilation, in the studio; it is – to put it formally – a matter both of epistemology and of praxis, but the student's experience is also intimately connected with her being, and particularly so, as the student wills herself into the spaces afforded her. Does she accept the challenge hesitatingly? Does she even shrink from it? Does she go forward nervously, hanging onto whatever rails she can find (in the form, say, of other's writings, already existing data, and ideas)? Or does she hurl herself forward, 'having a go', as we might say?

Our frontispiece jumper is again surely instructive. The jumper leaps into space. The leaping is only possible in space and because of space. In the leaping, there is presumably anxiety: will the connecting thongs do their work? In the leaping, there is exhilaration and there is the exploration of personal emotions. The challenge is taken on, the wind rushes, the body plummets, the ground rushes up. There is risk here, but the risk is within bounds of acceptability: sub-consciously, the jumper has done his own 'risk audit'.

So it is with the student in pedagogical space. She throws herself forward, into she hardly knows what; but then the satisfaction comes of having tried and having emerged unscathed. In the process, she will have undergone stress and felt a range of emotions. She has developed not just epistemologically or practically, but more importantly in her being. She has developed ontologically: the being that is she has moved on. She is testimony to Heidegger's thesis: being *and* time.

There are, then, personal virtues attaching to pedagogical space and the student leaping into it. In taking up the challenges with which she is confronted, in hurling herself forward, the student experiences not just epistemological or practical challenges, but challenges to her own being. She is, perhaps, daunted by the challenges. She feels anxiety. She doubts her own capacity to succeed. Where there is a sound pedagogical relationship, she may even express her anxiety to a tutor: 'do you think I can do this?' However, suitably fortified by one means or another – not least, perhaps, by her tutor's encouragement – she has a go. She does not exactly conquer her anxiety, but she lives with her anxiety. In so doing, she moves into a new place. She is the author of her own becoming.

There are, then, epistemological and practical advantages of extending curricula space to students. They can come into new experiences that are authentically theirs, rather than merely assimilating experiences offered to them, but there are, at the same time, ontological advantages: the student becomes a new person. That is how it is possible for the student to recognize, perhaps a few years after leaving university, that 'the course changed my life'. Courage, bravery, the capacity to live with uncertainty, a willingness to step out into the unknown: all these are – as we might say – ontological virtues that curricula and pedagogical space make possible.[4]

The ontological virtues of pedagogical and curricula space are not themselves in space, however. They derive from the student's struggles in understanding matters, in acquiring new skills and in developing forms of personal expression. There are subtle interplays between epistemological, practical and ontological space; and therefore, between the risks associated with each form of space. It is to those relationships between forms of space and their attendant risks, therefore, that we must now turn.

Space and risk

We have begun to gain a sense that different spaces may be extended to students and each will have its characteristic set of risks. *Intellectual space* to follow-up one's own knowledge interests could lead to a warped perspective or a skewed understanding of a field – here would lie *epistemological risk*. *Practical space* to acquire skills in one's own way might lead to a limited array of skills or an undue dependence on particular ways of going on (for example, among midwifery students) – such we may describe as *practical risk*.

Space to engage with pedagogical challenges might lead a student lacking in self-confidence to shrink from the challenge. A class run as near as maybe to a Habermassian 'ideal speech situation', in which all were equal and all were expected to make their fair contribution to proceedings, may see one of its number as silent. In so expressing a disinclination to participate, the student may internalize the situation by thinking that he was actively participating internally within himself. However, apart from his being an 'easy rider', relying on the contribution of others, he would be failing to gain, in the development of his personal qualities and dispositions, what he might from the open-endedness of the pedagogical situation. This is a situation of *ontological risk* and the space that generates that risk is a *space-for-being*.

The structure of space and risk in higher education is now unfolding; and it takes the following form:

Space	Risk
Intellectual space	Epistemological risk
Practical space	Practical risk
Space-for-being	Ontological risk

The structure of space and risk is a little more complicated still. We have been using the terms 'curricula space' and 'pedagogical space'. The question arises, therefore, of our three spaces and their attendant risks, as to whether each space-risk complex is likely to be implicated equally in curricula and in pedagogical space. I shall assert crudely two points. First, there can be no sharp allocation of the three space-risk complexes as between curricula and pedagogical space: all three complexes can be evident in both curricula and pedagogical space. Secondly, however, the complex of *space-for-being* and *ontological risk* is especially implicated in pedagogical space. For pedagogical space is essentially a matter of the working out of the pedagogical relationship. It is there that the human dimensions, the dimensions of being and becoming or thwarted becoming are in evidence.

So the structure of space and risk takes on something like the following character:

	Space	Risk
Curricula	Intellectual space Practical space	Epistemological risk Practical risk
Pedagogy	Space-for-being	Ontological risk

Risk aversion

Two points need to be made in the light of this suggested structure of space-risk. *The first point* is a general one. To identify 'risk' as implicated in the opening of space might have unintended consequences. One might be tempted not just to limit risk to students but also, as a means of so limiting such risk, to limit the space. After all, if students are not afforded space, they can hardly fall prey to the risk that might be associated with such space.

Surely, we often see just such risk-avoidance tactics.[5] Curricula are stuffed with teaching, so reducing students' intellectual and practical spaces; and pedagogies are driven forward in a didactic manner, so limiting students' space to stretch their own pedagogical beings into a new place. The shy student remains perpetually shy, lacking any encouragement to give of himself; the 'teacher' (an honorific title now) remains in complete control, untroubled by any awkwardnesses or felt threat to his or her authority, which may arise when students are given space. Accordingly, educational risk may arise from a *risk-free* pedagogy. Lack of risk may give rise *to* risk.

One rationale for such risk-averse curricula and pedagogical stances might well be that:

> it is all in the students' interests: we are controlling their experience so that the potential risk is minimized and their progress is all the more assured and even more efficiently achieved (and, *sotto voce*, they are even more likely to be "employable" on graduation).

Another rationale is that 'these days, students are litigious. We have to specify clearly in advance the nature of the programme and then ensure that that programme is "delivered". Otherwise, if students fail, we are likely to be – literally – in the dock'.

Such rationales have to be understood as the rationalizations that they in fact are. The limitation of space allows those in positions of power to retain their curricula and pedagogical hegemony. It lets them off the hook. They retain their unassailed position, unchallenged in the presence of docile students, a docility that their 'teachers' will have brought about.[6]

So the general point is that curricula and pedagogical risk are inevitable if students are to be permitted the requisite space to grow intellectually, practically or in their own being. No risk, no space. No space, no student becoming of the kind associated with higher education.

Working for space

The second point is double-barrelled. All three forms of space – intellectual, practical and space-for-being – are necessary for students' becoming. Their achievement has to be fought for on a continuing basis, daily. Educators in higher education cannot let themselves off this particular hook.

Space is not *there*. It has to be worked at and worked for. Students may be reluctant to accept the challenges of space, preferring a uni-directional situation, in which they look to assimilate what is put before them. That they themselves might be the makers of their own experience, with all the effort and, indeed, risk to themselves that would accrue, might seem an undue set of demands. Where students are willing to open themselves to challenges, to put themselves forward and to entertain risk in the process, the educator's role is still not over. Is this student on the right track? Is she making good progress? What are her strengths and weaknesses?

It may be that the student is intellectually adventurous, but lacks the capacity to organize her own efforts in a disciplined way and so make steady progress. How might the educator intervene? Can the educator speak directly to the student about her particular weakness? Will the student lose heart? However, even her intellectual adventurousness may be lacking in the necessary care: the intellectual passion is there, but it is not yet disciplined passion. So the tutor has all the time to make judgements about how and when to intervene, to bring individuals on, to divert them into new paths of becoming, to give yet other individuals a new sense of themselves and yet others an understanding that their use of their space is not taking them forward as it should. There is an ethics of educational space, which has surely not been excavated.

It is, therefore, space as held in the pedagogical relationship that is crucial. The curriculum can be designed with all manner of spaces – through problem-based learning, group projects, student choice over the modules that form their own programme, encouragement to students to adopt creative approaches to the forming of their texts and so on and so forth, but the *spirit of space* has to be carried into the pedagogical relationship, and worked at by both students and tutors, day in and day out.

This means that risk is ever present and always liable to show itself. No matter how careful a teacher is, a word, a gesture, may be injurious to a student's being. Where she is, in her intellectual position, in her self-understanding, in her sense of her practical capacities, in her willingness to project herself, a single careless word or gesture may dislodge her. It may even shatter her.

So there is a double risk: the student is at risk, but so, too, is the educator. In living in the spaces of the pedagogical relationship, the educator risks her own sense of herself as an educator. She tries to bring the student on, but a word or a nuance is interpreted in a way that the she could not have conceived in advance.

Space, then, is accompanied by risk: multiple spaces and multiple risks. Intellectual, practical and ontological risk are opened by curricula and pedagogical space; and are borne by both student and teacher. Risk can be held in mind and the holding in mind may lead to a lessening of risk. The course team may put in place a systematic review of the progress of the students. A tutor may exercise restraint in the words employed in his margin scribbles. Rules may be established to regulate classroom discussion so that the voices of the louder students do not drown those of the quieter students. However, risk is a necessary component of higher education and the student's becoming. For the student can only become by moving into new space. And in that moving into new space, there is bound to be risk.

Letting learn

> Teaching is more difficult than learning because what teaching calls for is this: to let learn.
>
> (Heidegger, *What is Called Thinking*, 1968)

The teacher who is sensitive to these matters of space and risk, wanting to encourage her students to have a go – intellectually, practically, personally – may use just these words: 'Have a go!' She may also add: 'Nothing will happen to you; you are in a safe place', or words to that effect. The pedagogical situation is characteristically a site in which students can put themselves forward and can even leap off the platform, without experiencing harm.

An implication is that any apparent danger – as perceived by the student – is only that; merely apparent. All is under control; the student can come to no harm. The laboratory will not blow up; there is no possibility of an ideological takeover; the student cannot suddenly take on a new and untoward persona.

These perceived infrastructural risks are real, but they are not the main risk. The key risk is to the student's pedagogical being. Will she want to go on? Will she be dissuaded from doing so? Can she be inspired to go on with a new level of will?

The path between being inspired and being deflated is not especially wide. There is – as we noted in our early chapters – a fragility to most students' pedagogical being.[7] This is barely an empirical observation. It is a quasi-necessary condition of a genuine higher education. In such an educational setting, the student is perforce required to venture into new places, strange places, anxiety-provoking places. This is part of the point of higher education. If there was no anxiety, it is difficult to believe that we could be in the presence of a higher education.

Risk in higher education, therefore, is more a matter of possible angst within and a connected fragility of the student's pedagogical being than it is a matter of the infrastructure of the student's educational situation. Yes, given that the estates strategy has not kept pace with the deterioration of the buildings, it could just be that a classroom will suddenly have to be closed for emergency refurbishment. It may also be that the impending national quality assurance evaluation will find matters not entirely to its liking: the library and the information and computing services are found to be wanting. However, the key risk is the student's own pedagogical being: is it going forward? Is it flourishing? Or is it regressing? Not only is the student's appreciation of key concepts actually receding, but is the student herself contemplating leaving the course altogether?

Can, then, indeed dare, the teacher let his students learn? To do so involves a pedagogical sacrifice on his part:

> The teacher is ahead of his apprentices in this alone, that he has still far more to learn than they – he has to let them learn . . . The teacher is far less assured of his ground than those who learn are of theirs.
>
> (Heidegger, ibid: 240)

To let his students learn is to let go, to allow the student as bungee jumper to take off. His job is to ensure that the ropes will hold; that is all. He has to then cede control, to stand back. The teacher has to learn to lose control, to sacrifice control. Actually, like all such analogies, the image of the bungee jumper, for all its potency, is misleading. After all, the bungee jumper is held.

Suppose he wasn't held? It may be that, with the right encouragement, with self-belief, he just may take off and fly.

Under these circumstances, there is one question, therefore, that each teacher must ask himself and to do so continually: Is my presence here in the pedagogical situation helping the students? It just may not. The students may be better off – at this moment – by themselves. In higher education, after all, the students are characteristically intelligent and have available to themselves rich resources in their universities (in the library, in the electronic resources) and, in any number, share between themselves considerable resources (of different capabilities and mutual support). Learning communities, by definition, will learn by themselves. The teacher, accordingly, should not assume that his interventions are necessarily worthwhile.

The injunction of 'let learn' is a salutary reminder of the teacher's beckoning redundancy.[8] The teacher's presence may serve perniciously to reduce the students' space: why, therefore, put that at risk? The precautionary principle, applied here, would surely suggest caution: that a teacher's presence should only be permitted where it can demonstrably do no such harm.

A spatial tension

The pedagogical task has now become three-fold:

i   to design curricula spaces in which the student can make her own explorations – often with her other fellow students;
ii   to encourage the student actually to make those explorations;
iii to bring the student to a realization of the standards embedded within the intellectual and professional fields in question in her programme.

There is here a key spatial tension: to let learn, to let go, implies *singularity*. By this I mean that the student is to be permitted to become what she wishes, to pursue her *own* intellectual inclinations, to identify sets of skills that she wishes to acquire and to come into her own voice. However, the teacher in higher education has a kind of tacit ethical code of ensuring that that student comes to live in keeping with the standards of her intellectual and practical fields. The student is going to be judged by those standards, in any event, but standards of this kind imply *universality*. The presence of a field in higher education is testimony to its being a form of life that is open to progressive judgement through which it advances. So *singularity and universality*: this is perhaps the fundamental tension embedded within the pedagogical relationship within higher education.

This tension – between singularity and universality – is felt in the micro-practices of the relationship and it is exacerbated by considerations of space. We afford space to students in higher education to become themselves in new ways and separately; so *singularity* is there. Given spaces in which to explore and to develop, students will become more differentiated from each other. We also look to students to become themselves authentically; so singularity is there too. A student's authentic state – of knowing, of doing, of being – is hers alone; it cannot be replicated by another student. So singularity is a necessary outcome of space. In encouraging students to take advantage of the spaces extended to them, we are encouraging them to become themselves. Our encouragements, even if delivered to the whole class, in course handbooks and orally, are nevertheless that each student should respond in his or her own way. Our concerns are for each student, as a separate point of being.

But then we have to guide those endeavours by the light of the standards in the fields in question. Faced with the essay, and its awkwardnesses, precisely how does one word one's comments? A comment, meant to be helpful, may be read quite differently by different students. That is not just their right, but it is a necessary outcome of each student feeling him or herself into her own educational space. Their hopes, their abilities and their background all predispose each student to fill out his or her own space, in his or her own way, but the standards are universal. Can I find a form of words that will do justice both to the standards of the field and to the singularity of this particular human being? The same dilemma holds whatever the pedagogical situation, in the laboratory or the clinical situation no less than the essay.

This is why the phrase 'the pedagogical relationship' is telling, in a way. A relationship is never finished; it is always in the making. It is in and through the relationship that one comes to judge what might be possible. The singular-universal tension will be resolved differently with different students. It will be resolved differently for the same student both across her different subjects, and it will be resolved differently for the same student over time. At the start of a pedagogical relationship, one may have to be more sensitive to singularity, to the student as a being in herself. Over time, as the pedagogical relationship develops, one's remarks may more firmly and directly take their bearings from the standards of the field as such. One is able to do this – to be more direct in one's judgements – precisely because a felt and trusting relationship has been built over time with the student in her singularity.

However, the singularity-universal tension never dissolves; it is always there, waiting to emerge. The student may suddenly feel hurt, bruised, not listened to, as the heavy weight of universal judgements descends. To repeat, this singular-universal tension is itself heightened by the wish that students should have space extended to them and that they should come into those spaces in their own way. Giving space to students, therefore, brings into play ethical dilemmas, as the singularity-universal tension itself becomes necessarily apparent.

Conclusion

Extending space to students in higher education is a necessary condition of their 'higher' education. Without space, they cannot come freshly to their experiences under their own volition. Without space, they cannot come authentically to their judgements, findings, observations, actions and exchanges, but with space comes risk. There is a risk that the student's educational diet will be skewed: perhaps she shrinks from practical challenges that properly should be part of her programme or perhaps she has suddenly latched onto a writer whose entire corpus she now tries to devour, or she becomes obsessed with the structure of a compound or organism to the near exclusion of other important matters.

Space and risk has its structure in higher education and a complex structure at that. We may differentiate spaces that are intellectual, practical or more personal in character; and each space possesses its characteristic set of risks. Of the several sets of spaces and attendant risks, it is the pedagogical space and its associated risks that are the most potent. For it is there, in that space, that a student can most vividly come to have a good sense of herself, become inspired and will herself forward in new ways. The handling of that pedagogical space by her teachers, therefore, is critical in that unfolding.

There are, therefore, considerable professional challenges for tutors and others who form the student's pedagogical relationships. Encouraging a student forward through his self-doubts is challenging in itself. Part of the student's difficulties, after all, may have arisen precisely as a result of the space – the freedom and the choices – extended to him. However, encouraging a student forward with an eye also on the standards embedded in the immediate fields of the student's programme produces a tension: singularity and universality are present in and have to be worked out in the pedagogical relationship on a daily basis.

Recall our main concern in this book. It is that of the student's will to learn in an age of uncertainty. The will may be cautious or it may be fairly uninhibited. In either case, the educational task is to bring it into a state in which it becomes a disciplined will-for-itself, a being in the active making, struggling to come forward and to work progressively. Space is necessary, but it has to be a controlled space. The student's efforts should be not just effective but also efficient. Those efforts should be repaid with success at the highest standards and without undue time being spent. (A student's educational being is only part of her being.) So the spaces that are necessary for the student's own authentic unfolding should be controlled spaces. The tension between freedom and control is another tension, therefore, that arises out of the presence of educational spaces.

In space, there may be collisions. Both in the classroom and in the tutorial, there is a not infrequent frisson, as ideas conflict and a rawness results. Interchanges, therefore, are fraught with risk. The presence of risk is a necessary part of a genuine higher education. It cannot be risk-audited away. A teacher's professionalism may limit the level of risk, but it cannot be extinguished.

An indication of the presence of space is the asking of critical questions and it is to that, therefore, that we now turn.

12

A critical spirit

Introduction

The idea of critical thought has been central to the idea of higher education for a very long time. It has been part of the heritage of the Enlightenment, even if the Enlightenment, as such, largely by-passed the universities. Through critical reason, humankind can truly develop. Not only can it free itself from enslavement to prejudice, bigotry and idolatry; it can more positively purchase new ways of thinking that more assuredly approach a true and objective reading of the world. Through critical reason, humankind and the world can be joined harmoniously.

In the post-modern world, however, this set of ideas has to be abandoned. In the post-modern world, reason undermines itself. The principle of reason takes no prisoners. Every utterance, every framework, every offering – of any kind – comes under its critical gaze. This principle seems to be invulnerable. However, as Heidegger (1996) observed, that means that even the principle of reason falls victim to itself – and finds itself wanting. For the principle of reason is without reason: it cannot itself be underpinned by reason. *This* is supercomplexity, an irredeemable complexity born of incessant critique. In it, there is no resting place, not even in the principles of critique. For they are subject to critique. That is why Habermas (1991) cannot find any secure foundation – in his inner 'validity claims'.[1]

In such a world of irredeemable critique, the pedagogical challenge is twofold. It is, in the first place, to open the student to an understanding of the rival frameworks in the fields in question, to an insight into the main conflicts. It used to be said that the absence of conflict was a sign of the maturity of the field. Now we can – and should – say that the absence of conflict is a sign of the *im*maturity of the field. No wonder if students find their programmes of study boring when they are not introduced to and enabled to understand their field(s) as sites of controversy and even radically opposed viewpoints.

However, in a world of radical dispute (that is to say, a world which we now know to be of incessant and never-ending differences), the pedagogical challenge has a second challenge. In such a world, succour is neither to be had merely through the acquisition of critical viewpoints, nor even through the critical standards underlying those contrary viewpoints. For critical standards are rooted in an epistemological way of living in the world; of knowing the world. In a destabilized world, the concept of critique has itself to be critiqued if it is to offer pedagogical resources (if not to say pedagogical comfort). The concept of critique has to be put on a different ground; that is to say, other than the epistemological.

Critique as alternative space

In an age of supercomplexity, the main pedagogical challenge of critique cannot be that of inserting critique as such into the curriculum. Supercomplexity, after all, is supersaturated with critique! The curriculum can and should display critique; the current vogue for 'research-led' and 'research-based' curricula can help in such an endeavour (cf. Healey, 2005), but this is icing on the cake. Critique heaped upon critique. The main challenge lies elsewhere.

The main educational challenge of critique amid supercomplexity is precisely that of living with critique, with the destabilization that arises through a situation in which there is no sure ground, in which every move, every framework, every value, every working assumption can be and is critiqued. This situation has both curricula and pedagogical implications.

One is surrounded by alternative frames of understanding and rival perspectives.[2] For example, is chemistry a means of understanding the structure of the world or of manipulating the world? Is it a means of harnessing to good effect the raw materials of the world or is it a vehicle for polluting the world? Is it a way of revealing in relatively simple structures the composition of the world or is it a means of producing risk in the world, through the unpredictable impacts of multiple new compounds and drugs? Is its research a neutral field or do even its concepts and the structures to which they speak represent the interests of the global pharmaceutical companies? These are rival frameworks for understanding a field: some are simply different and are not incommensurable; merely difficult to hold together in the same countenance. Some, however, are mutually conflictual, a conflict that arises out of separate and rival value structures.

In such a world of competing and even inconsistent frameworks, the formation of criticality is not a matter of giving oneself up to or even of yielding to different standards. Reason itself cannot arbitrate between disparate and rival frameworks. Criticality, cannot even resort to a Kierkegaardian (2001: 105) assumption of faith, for why should one framework be favoured over others?

Accordingly, the development of criticality is no longer a matter of the acquisition of critical reason but now becomes a matter of the formation of the *critical spirit*.[3] In higher education, criticality is no longer only, or even primarily, an epistemological matter; it is now in the first place an onto-logical matter. It is an issue of how the student is in the world, of her being in the world (to use again the term of Heidegger's that we encountered earlier), of her 'comportment' in such an unstable world.

To be critical now is to let live. That is, it is to have the *preparedness* to open oneself up to frameworks that run counter to those in which one has invested one's own pedagogical being.[4] It is not just a matter of assimilating another theory, or another way of going on, where there are just technical differences across frameworks. It is now a matter of *being*, the students' being, being capable of being other than it is and has become. For this being now has to be able to embrace, or at least be sensitive to, contending values, and orien-tations in the world.[5] One person's benign influence in the world is another person's dangerous manipulation of the world. It is to stand differently in the world. It is to be other than that which one is.

Contending modes of understanding are both internal and external. For example, the study of leadership in MBA programmes is variously pur-sued through sub-disciplines such as social psychology or organizational behaviour, through case studies of 'great leaders' or through scenarios in which students are encouraged to take on leadership perspectives.[6] Hardly yet present on MBA programmes, and for understandable reasons, is an overtly critical perspective, in which the concept of leadership – as character-istically understood in the business world – is subjected to a critical interro-gation, as to its assumptions and implicit values. These approaches may be situated in a triangular space, with 'education about leadership' at one corner, 'education for leadership' at another and 'education in contention with leadership' at the remaining corner. However, to enter imaginatively into those curricula perspectives is to enter – on the part of the student – different, even contending modes of educational being.

My point here is three-fold. *First*, a genuine higher education will seek to open alternative spaces through which a topic or subject may be approached – and experienced. *Second*, some of those frameworks may be external to the field in question; and it is there that the most searching critique will be found.

By themselves, however, these two points are inadequate to confront the situation that we are addressing here. For both of these two points spring from an epistemological viewpoint, a sense that provided critique is thor-oughgoing, is untrammelled, all will come out well, but what does it mean for things to come out well, in a situation in which every framework can be contested and may even be incommensurable with another? A framework may take for granted that leadership is a matter of securing assent to strat-egies worked out by the management team and that, therefore, 'leadership education' is a matter of identifying operational means of achieving that end. Such a framework is logically inconsistent with a framework that under-stands leadership as an art form in which narratives of organizational being are jointly worked through.

The incommensurability in play here is not only epistemological. It is also a matter of being in the world. Enabling a student to comprehend such conflicting frameworks cannot be understood only as a cognitive challenge.[7]

My third point, therefore, is precisely that the pedagogical challenge here is one of being, and in two senses. First, the frameworks call for different modes of pedagogical being – ranging from the operational, to the cognitive through to the critical. These are contrasting modes of pedagogical being that the student is being asked to take on. Secondly, the student is brought into a mode of being in which the different frameworks can be assimilated; a kind of pedagogical meta-being. Here, the student wills herself to take on differing frameworks, even though they may jolt her out of her present mode of being. It is the second of these forms of pedagogical being that is the more important – the pedagogical meta-being that wills an accommodation with diverse pedagogical forms of being – and it is largely unnoticed.

A critical attitude

In a study of critical thinking among midwives, Cheng[8] has distinguished no less than four modes of criticality:

i *Logical mode* – in which midwives reveal their capacity for making valid logical moves in their clinical reasoning;
ii *Framework mode* – in which that capacity for critical thinking is put into practice via separate perspectives that may shed light on a situation within midwifery practices (alternatively, scientific, sociological, managerial, humanistic and so on);
iii *Pragmatic mode* – in which the midwife's capacities for critical thinking are worked out in particular contexts (and here, Cheng has shown how different frameworks come into play according to the extent to which the situation is variously loosely or tightly structured);
iv *Attitudinal mode* – through which the midwife takes on dispositions for critical thinking, in forming a preparedness to interrogate her beliefs and her understandings.

Cheng observes that each of the modes of critical thinking may be exhibited in stronger or weaker forms; and that some midwives may be strong in some modes and others strong in yet others. However, Cheng also observes that the attitudinal mode forms a kind of substrate for the other modes of critical thinking. That is to say, without the midwife having a preparedness to take up critical stances, such critical orientations simply will not get going.

This empirical case study supports our general thesis. Criticality shows itself in two levels of *critical being*.[9] At one level, critical being moves into and through different spaces, from which the object of attention is viewed or experienced. This is the relatively familiar sense of critique opened up by multi-disciplinary enquiry. A situation is viewed or experienced through a range of different disciplines or fields. Critical being allows itself to wander through different spaces and, in the process, a situation is engaged in contrasting perspectives. This critical being is cognitive and experiential all at once. The spaces are lived; the student takes on the identity afforded by the frames.

At a more fundamental level, however, the student has a *prior* disposition to take up such critical stances. For the taking up of such critical stances does not come lightly. On the contrary, criticality lays open the possibility of being dislodged, of destabilization. The student's hold on her world – at least, that of her studies – may be turned upside down, as she dares to enter another frame that tacitly undermines her existing frame. So the prior disposition to take on critical perspectives is crucial. Through this prior disposition in favour of the critical life, new frames may be entered and lived in. The student has acquired a disposition *for* destabilization.

In Cheng's language, it is the attitudinal mode of criticality that makes possible all the other modes of criticality, but strictly speaking, what is before us here is a *disposition* in favour of criticality. This disposition – for destabilization – is a superordinate form of criticality. It is a condition of criticality – as the taking up of alternative frames – ever being present. This is a general open space that makes possible the *particular* spaces. It is a large, even an infinite, space, into which other spaces – the singular forms of critique – may show themselves.

On the one hand, then, the *restricted spaces* – the particular frameworks that come into a much less restricted space – that come to form a student's critical being. On the other hand, the *unrestricted space* itself – a potentially limitless space – that is critical being.

Infinite possibilities

These two forms of critical being, understood as living at two levels of critical space, may be aligned to pedagogy and curriculum respectively:

unrestricted space	critical being as such	pedagogical challenge
restricted spaces	forms of critical being	curriculum challenge

The *curriculum challenge* of such a view of criticality lies in a range of singular spaces being opened to the student. The *pedagogical challenge* lies in the student's will being so formed that she wills herself to go forward into those spaces, which may well challenge her being itself.[10] It is the formation of an unrestricted general space that becomes the student's being and, potentially, her homelessness.

Since the spaces for critical engagements that may be opened to the student are limitless, the curriculum itself stands in the realm of the infinite. That is why curriculum design is a tough matter and far harder than many realize. Curriculum design for criticality is not merely putting together a number of pre-existing blocks from a limited array of such blocks. It is itself a journey into infinity.[11]

To design a curriculum is to be imaginative, to shape spaces that have hardly been dreamt of. Curriculum designers would do well to have poetry in their souls. They are asked to play with the infinite. Characteristically, today, after all, a curriculum invites a complex of intellectual and action-oriented engagements on the part of the student. Which forms of knowing? Which forms of action? Which forms of design – in engineering, transport or management studies – might come into play? What is their combination to be?

My point here is not about curriculum design itself, but about the character of the spaces that are involved here and their relationship to criticality. They are infinite in their possibilities, in their shape, their extension and their relationships with other shapes in the curriculum. On that set of infinite possibilities turns the infinity of the critical spirit.[12]

Another way of putting the educational challenge of criticality, therefore, is that of enabling students to live in and with infinity. They may rest a while in one space but they come to know their sojourn is temporary; other spaces affording alternative perspectives await to claim their attention. These successive visitations can go on forever. Whatever they are interested in, they can come at it from an unending series of viewpoints. The spaces, the viewpoints, are implicitly critical viewpoints: they shed new light on previously encountered framings.

Heidegger saw in the multifarious viewpoints that the modern university offered a sign of the ending of the university; it was losing its potential unity in its connection with Being as such. My contention here is to the contrary: the many viewpoints that the contemporary university opens up – now immeasurably extended since Heidegger's time – offer sites of potential new Being. Heidegger (1985) saw the university as a site in which Being, as such, could be reclaimed. Instead, I suggest, we should see the university as a site of infinite spaces for infinite being; even infinite forms of being. This is not only an educational project more in keeping with the complex character of post-modernity; it is actually a richer educational project for it liberates Being.[13]

Now, understood as a movement through potentially infinite spaces, the student's being is opened and challenged. The student is encouraged, through imaginative framing of curricula, to come into new forms of being. One day, she will be challenged by giving a presentation to her fellow students; another day, she will be grappling with new concepts; another day, she will be tacking a project with any number of new interactive dimensions in it; and on yet another day, she will acquire new research methodology skills. In the following week, she may encounter an entirely new epistemological framework that dislodges all that she has painstakingly come into over the previous days and weeks. There are signs that students find such destabilization understandably difficult to which to accommodate (cf. Miller, 2007).

If the curriculum challenge of criticality is the design of spaces into which the student can move and experience the world in new ways, the pedagogical challenge is that of prompting the student to take up such a disposition. The disposition here is that of a readiness to open oneself to new experiences. In turn, surely, the pedagogical challenge of encouraging such a disposition of openness on the part of the student raises an issue as to the openness of the teacher. If we want our students to open themselves, do their teachers not need to show a corresponding openness?

Basil Bernstein characterized the pedagogical relationship in terms of the tightness and looseness of the pedagogical frame. Some teachers in higher education allow a wide range of human being – feelings, reflections on emotions, self-disclosure, hopes, challenges and aspirations – to come into their exchanges with the student; they may even open themselves up to their students in parallel ways. Other teachers maintain a tight relationship with their students, sticking only to the formal curriculum, and seeing their task purely in cognitive and practical terms and never allowing their students to see them as full persons.

However, we surely need to go further in capturing the heart of the pedagogical relationship. For the tightness or looseness of the pedagogical frame is willed by the teacher. Does the teacher wish to give of herself, to engage wholeheartedly with her students and to share emotions with them? Are there to be mutual excitement and smiles in the classroom? Is mutual disappointment to be made apparent? To what degree and in what ways is the teacher energized? Does some of that energy flow from her encounters with her students? The openness of the pedagogical relationship is a self-willed openness, invested with will on the part of the teacher. This will is infectious; and is liable to be caught by the students.

How are these reflections pertinent to our immediate theme, that of the forming of the critical spirit? The links are close at hand. The forming of the student's critical spirit can be immeasurably aided by the teacher. That is, perhaps, self-evident, but in what ways and how might the critical spirit be caught? What is the character of the pedagogical relationship that is liable to prompt its emergence?

To answer those questions, we have to return to some of our earlier observations. The critical spirit is a preparedness on the part of the student to move into new spaces. Being new spaces, they are spaces of uncertainty, anxiety and risk; and voyaging into such spaces requires courage and wonderment on the part of the student. It requires, too, a preparedness on the part of the student to enter otherness; new understandings, new positions in the world. The teacher can help the student to form these qualities of courage, wonderment and a willingness towards strangeness that are part of the dispositions of critical being. However, it is self-evidently true that the teacher is not going much – if at all – to aid the formation of such dispositions and qualities on the part of the student by maintaining a tight pedagogical relationship, in which its scope is only the intellectual and practical territory of the curriculum.[14]

Let us summarize our position. The formation of criticality within the student is not the movement of the student into this or that so-called critical framework; after all, one person's critical framework is another's apologia. Rather, the formation of criticality is, in the first place, the formation of critical being, of the student's *preparedness* to venture into unknown and probably discomforting frames.

Criticality is fundamentally ontological in its nature; it is not intellectual or epistemological or even practical. It is a disposition that sits relatively easily with the infinite scope of the potential frames ahead. A pedagogy for critical being, therefore, is the formation of this *spirit-for-openness*. As well as any intellectual capacities that it may call for, a necessary condition of its enactment lies in the teacher's own disposition to encompass new forms of being and to share that disposition with the students. A pedagogy for critical being is a voyage-of-being undertaken by both teacher and taught.

On the edge

The teacher cannot hope his students to become critical beings if he himself does not openly exhibit such a mode of being and share it with his students. Criticality has to be *lived*.

It is lived in the pedagogical relationship. It is so lived that the phrase 'the pedagogical relationship' is put under strain. The phrase *does* do helpful work (as we have been witnessing). It suggests an interaction between teacher and taught, it says that there is something special about the context of teaching, and it points to a mutuality of expectations and responsibilities developed over time. However, the phrase does not distinguish between different kinds of pedagogical intent and sits happily with didactic teaching approaches, and to closed relationships, built around taken-for-granted frameworks of understanding and practice.

In the context of a pedagogical intent towards criticality, however, the phrase 'the pedagogical relationship' falls short as a term of art; and for four reasons. *First*, it is too dry; it fails to capture the pedagogical excitement that is characteristic of a shared atmosphere of criticality. Teaching for criticality is alive; it exudes life.[15] *Second*, it omits any hint of the reflexivity that is part of a critical pedagogy.[16] Teaching that is infused with the critical spirit has to open space that turns upon itself: here, every utterance is made with an inner hesitancy, no matter how much outward bravado there may be. *Third*, the phrase contains no sense that the relationship is pointed outwards: both parties are exploring possibilities beyond the relationship. *Finally*, a pedagogy orientated towards criticality is necessarily on the edge.

Teaching for criticality is open to itself. It is open to itself, we have seen, not just intellectually, but in its being. We can talk of and ask questions about the being of the pedagogical relationship. Is it alive? Are the parties engaged with their objects of attention and with each other? Is there personal investment here?

Just as the image of our frontispiece leaper may be potent for our understanding of the student's being, so it may also be potent for our understanding of the pedagogical relationship. The pedagogical relationship is itself on the edge or, indeed, it may leap into the unknown. Will it save itself?

The student is held in the pedagogical relationship. The student takes risks but is safe, but what of the pedagogical relationship itself? Is *it* held? What if it leaps? Perhaps it won't be held – or caught.

And yet a pedagogy for critical being has to leap. It has to transgress (hooks 1994). It has to go beyond boundaries, into the unknown, not just intellectually, but in its pedagogical being, and so we can talk, we have to talk, of the *being* of the pedagogical relationship itself. What is its felt character? Is it alive? Does it pulse? Is it daring? Does the teacher open himself up to his students? Does he disclose his vulnerability? Does the teacher reveal a sense of his own limitations? Does the teacher show his trepidation about venturing forth into what is, *for him,* a new domain? Dare he do so? Unless the pedagogical relationship is one of openness, of daring, of leaping into the unknown, how can we have a realistic expectation that the student might take on these characteristics?

A pedagogy for critical being, therefore, has its own being. It has its fortitude and its reticence; its daring and its hesitancies; its struggles and its delights, as new boundaries are crossed, and new patterns, shapes and understandings revealed through the relationship itself. It is a relationship of joint enthralment, wonder, voyaging and learning. It is a pedagogy of joint discovery. It is a pedagogy that becomes itself daily; which is to say, it is always becoming itself.

Critical standards

In this near-final section, I want to return to the notion of standards (on which we touched in this and earlier chapters). So far as I can see, texts on teaching and learning in higher education, especially those that are somewhat radical in their orientation, tend to be silent on the matter of standards. This is not just a neglect; it is a scandalous neglect.

In this book, in trying to unravel what it is to be a student, I have tried to bring forward the student's being and becoming. A motif in our explorations has been that of the bungee jumper. Can the student let go? Does she have the will not merely to keep going, but to go forward into the unknown? Can she throw herself forward and emerge possibly a new person? Can she become herself anew? Can she come into a new state of being? Perhaps for the first time, a being-for-itself?

Amid such talk, there is a temptation – and, so we may say, even a danger – of gaining a sense that throwing oneself forward is all that matters. Howsoever the throwing of oneself is accomplished and wheresoever the throwing of oneself takes one can easily be neglected. Herein lies the matter of standards; the criteria by which the putting of oneself forward are to be judged. The leaping has its standards.

Judgement is part of criticality: to be critical is to judge. To travel into new spaces is, *ipso facto*, to set up a reflection on the space just left behind, but getting the student to be self-critical even within a given framework is also to call up judgement. So whether on a weak *or* a strong form of criticality, judgement and standards have to be in the offing.

Standards, judgement and criteria are, therefore, a necessary part of higher education. There should be no squeamishness about this. The students may be set off on a voyage of delight, and there may be smiles and even laughter, but the students' offerings have to be held to account.

In short, the commas matter. Being precise and being clear in one's utterances – of any kind, whether in propositional or performative variety – is part of one's criticality. If being critical is to move into a new and authentic mode of being, then precision and clarity are necessary concomitants of that journeying. The student cannot authentically come into a new space unless that position is won and secured satisfactorily. It can only be won and secured through precision and clarity. Through her precision, the student can achieve some firm ground, albeit temporarily. Through her clarity, she can demonstrate that sure ground to others. Through her offerings, she can come to embody a live and critical spirit.

So, in encouraging forward the student's criticality, the teacher will be bound to have an eye on standards. Standards are almost entirely context-dependent. They are held within any academic form of life, although the strength of and consensuality in any such standards will vary across different academic subjects. The well-known disciplines have their own fairly well developed standards; the newer fields much less so. In the interdisciplinary and cross-practical programmes of study that are developing (for example, in enquiry across the humanities and medicine), in effect new regions of inquiry are being opened and the standards in question are having to be created *in situ*. Even so, even in the well-established subjects, there is room for dispute over the interpretation of and priority to be given to the different criteria.

My point here is that standards are essential for the formation of critical being. There is, as it were, a quadrilateral set of relationships between critical being, becoming, authenticity and standards. Becoming authentic in higher education is none other than the formation of critical being; and for that, the student is having to intuit subtle sets of standards; critical standards, no less. Here is one reason why higher education – a genuine higher education – is an arduous experience. The student comes to an appreciation of the critical standards in question and so becomes self-critical; the critical voices are internalized, but in the process, those critical voices may bear in so penetratingly that they thwart just what is struggling to form itself, namely authentic being.

In higher education, the formation of critical being can undermine itself. Often, it is the most sensitive, most diligent and even – dare one say it – the most intelligent students that are prone to suffer this paralysing syndrome. Self-doubt moves in the student's being such that he can barely get anything down on paper, or he can hardly utter anything in the seminar.

Against this potential situation the sensitive teacher contends by being explicit about these internal challenges that students may face. The pedagogical task becomes, yet again, ontological, rather than epistemological or practical in nature. The teacher brings out into the open such challenges that those internal critical voices will bring with them. She helps the students form self-help groups so that they may support each other, as each one grapples with his or her internal assailants. She shares her own corresponding self-doubts in contending with her own internalized critical voices.

Together is formed a new kind of self-critical community, one in which the participants share with and support each other, in their own struggles towards authenticity, even though no-one puts it quite like that. The private becomes semi-public; the struggles intersect. In the process, critical standards are brought somewhat into the open within this learning community, even if they remain partly submerged, as they must do.[17] This learning community, inspired by the teacher, takes off; it has its own critical being.

Conclusion

The term 'critical thinking' does more harm than good. It renders the idea of criticality far too much an intellectual matter. It cuts away the ontological presence in criticality. Even the term 'presence' underplays the matter. Criticality is, in the first place, a critical *spirit*. It is a mode of being; of critical *being*. It is a set of dispositions on the part of the student. In order to be critical in any form – including being self-critical – the student has to be so placed as to have a will towards criticality.

This will is not easily forged. For criticality can be disturbing. It opens up the possibility of ontological disturbance. The student is liable to dislodge herself in the critical moment. A favoured position, or orientation, is suddenly seen anew; and perhaps in an unfavourable light. It may have to be abandoned, and that abandonment may be like leaving home, with all its associated trauma.

But, still, criticality is possibly the greatest of all educational achievements embedded in the idea of higher education. How is the matter of curriculum design for criticality to be construed? I have suggested that the opening of spaces offers a helpful metaphor. Spaces not for learning as such but for critique. The student is beckoned into a new room and can view the room that she has just left with a new perspective. The room may be in the existing house or it may be in another house altogether, but some alternative perspective there has to be, through which the object of the student's attention may be critiqued and the student is prompted into a more general set of dispositions for criticality afforded by the critical spirit.

Critical spaces may, accordingly, be 'hot' or 'cold' (cf. Strathern 2007). Cold spaces are largely internal; they may bring a new alignment, an adjustment of the student's position. Hot spaces are largely external; they offer the possibility of an about-turn. The student moves into a new universe. Both sets of critical spaces have their part to play; for both together offer a path to authenticity.

The pedagogical task here is two-fold. It is to cool passions, through the opening up of critical standards. Passion is brought under control. The commas matter; the links between the sentences are made clear; the work of each utterance is restrained. Through such self-critique, the student is able to eke out a new level of integrity, but the pedagogical task is at the same time to inflame passion. It is to engender the critical *spirit*. Revolutionary critique catches fire in hot pedagogies. The teacher gives of herself, bringing all manner of new frames of experience and understanding to her students; they are encouraged to work together to uncover even yet other such transforming perspectives. Critical beings tumble over themselves. This is a pedagogy on fire.

Coda: puzzles and possibilities

Two puzzles

At the outset of this inquiry, we identified two puzzles:

i Is the will to learn *particular* or *general?* In having a will to learn, is the student driven forward on the one hand towards certain kinds of knowledge and to satisfy *particular* kinds of learning interests *or*, on the other hand, is her will to learn *general* in character? Is it that the student simply has taken on a general will to learn and, perhaps fortuitously, that will, that spirit, just spills over into her particular studies so that she becomes enthused about them? Is the will to learn particular or general?

ii So far as learning itself is concerned, how might the idea be justified that ontology trumps epistemology? Is it really the case, as I have been urging, that a student's being and becoming is more significant than her developing knowledge and understanding in a particular field? There are intricate interactions between the student's being and her knowing – which we have encountered frequently in our conceptual explorations here, and seen exemplified in the voices of students – but, in the end, are being and becoming *more* significant than knowing?

We could not have solved the two puzzles at the outset of our inquiry but I believe that solutions have emerged. The two solutions can be set out in the form of a single matrix (see Figure 1).

		Specific	General
Student's will to learn	Epistemology	✓	✗
	Ontology	✓	✓

Figure 1 The will to learn – a philosophical schema

Let us begin with the top line, in relation to the dimension of knowledge ('epistemology'). In higher education, students are expected to come to know things. That knowledge is not to be superficial but is supposed to have qualities of personal insight and understanding. 'Learning', therefore, becomes a complex matter. It is to have '*depth*' and is certainly not to be a mere acquisition of knowledge; 'understanding' becomes an important dimension of this learning.

Any effort to take teaching seriously has also, on this view, to take learning seriously; '*learning*' becomes complex in its own right. However, the tutor who wants to be more effective may legitimately concern himself with his student's knowing efforts in the field that he is teaching, for the student is trying to advance her understanding in that field and, at that time, not in any other field. If the veterinary student is grappling with an understanding of animal anatomy, it is her understanding of that field that is in question. Issues therefore arise for the reflective lecturer as to how to aid *that* understanding (not an understanding in anthropology, or economics or music or any other field). Such an understanding poses its own problems; knowing and learning are *significantly* particular to a field:

> *I will never get used to the smell of the anatomy laboratory – the cadavers hanging from hooks in plastic bags. . . . The putrid smell of decaying dogs is stomach turning . . .*
>
> [Nearea Fletcher (2006), prize winner essayist,
> Higher Education Academy, Medicine, Dentistry
> and Veterinary Medicine, Subject Centre
> Autumn/Winter newsletter, p15.]

Both the student's and the lecturer's attentions are focused on the knowing and learning tasks to hand, and legitimately so. This is not to deny that there isn't value also in understanding teaching and learning across the different fields, but there is a *strong specificity* about knowing in higher education. Accordingly, in our table, against 'Epistemology', we are drawn to place a tick under the 'specific' category and a cross under the 'general' category.

With ontology, or the student's being, however, matters are different. Certainly, the student's being has a specificity about it. We want the student to become personally involved in her studies; we want her offerings – whether in textual form or in the form of action – to be shot through with her authenticity. Her passion, care and leaping – to use three terms from this inquiry – are specific in their orientation. Her will to learn has a definite orientation towards certain kinds of study. We noted, for example, how a modern languages student, studying French and Italian, found her will to learn being enhanced in relation to Italian, but being diminished in relation to French (which had been her stronger subject, but towards which she came 'to feel bitter'). That will to make progress in the student's own intellectual or professional field is crucial – a 'necessary' condition of the student's flourishing – but it is contained. Accordingly, we may say that the student's will to learn is specific; and so we may place a tick firmly under the 'specific' category alongside 'Ontology'.

But, we are not done yet, in relation to 'Ontology' in our table. Yes, the student is here, on *this* course, in *this* institution, with *these* students and *these* lecturers. This is the specific context for her will to learn: her will to learn is shaped and supported (or not) here, through these particular influences. The student has her pedagogical being and becoming here and now. Our tick under the '*specific*' heading alongside 'ontology' is justified, but the student also has a wider being that comes into play.

It is not just that the student invests time in going to the gym or swimming pool, and finds that those activities fuel her epistemic energies. Nor is it even that the student has friendships outside of her course and may – increasingly these days – have a family in whom she invests much of herself, or even that the student has worries over her financial situation or her accommodation, all of which may well be the case. Rather, it is that the student has *being* as such, with its trajectory full of possibilities. In turn, her educational achievements may entirely change her entire sense of herself. The student's being as such is implicated here. Unless her whole being is right, she cannot be expected to commit herself to her studies; her progress will remain in doubt. Being and becoming, accordingly, are significant concepts for higher education. This wider being is itself – as we have observed – fragile. So, alongside 'Ontology' we should also place a tick under the '*general*' category.

We have, therefore, in this table, a summary and a confirmation (if somewhat crude) of the thesis that we have been developing: that the student's being and becoming is more significant than the student's knowing efforts. In higher education, ontology does indeed trump epistemology. *It follows that – even in higher education – it is the student's being that should occupy her teachers' primary attentions.*

Trajectories of becoming

It becomes the task of a genuine higher education, therefore, to ensure that those possibilities for the student's becoming are opened out. The bungee jumper takes off; and, miraculously, even breaks her own bonds, and flies by and for herself. Her thinking becomes *hers*. [1] This higher education lives in the future at least as much as here-and-now. It censures 'outcomes' thinking, which lives in the here-and-now.

We can depict this set of reflections in Figure 2.

The lower trajectory, we may say, is a trajectory in which the student moves steadily forward. Here, the risks are low. If she falls to earth, little damage will have been done. She sticks to the well-known authors and scholars, and familiar positions and understandings, and offers sound and careful analyses of all of that information. Her moves are hers and hers alone, but they are kept within limits. Her pedagogic being is authentic, but it is a limited authenticity.

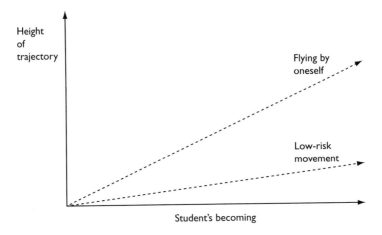

Figure 2 Two trajectories of becoming

The higher trajectory, with its steeper gradient, is the trajectory in which the student takes off, free of the 'they' of her surrounding voices. Here, the student comes into her own. She reaches out and up; she becomes herself. She not merely uncovers, but discovers her own voice. This is a pedagogical self that is now 'for itself'; the former trajectory was merely 'in-itself' (a situation not at all to be repudiated). In this higher trajectory, the student makes her own possibilities: she goes beyond the given situation. The distinction here is between, as it were, a first class honours degree and a good second-class degree, but the risks are higher.

It is possible, we may conclude, not only for there to be different trajectories of becoming, but also for there to be *degrees of authenticity*, which are associated with those higher or lower trajectories.

In the upward trajectory, the student reaches into infinity. Faced with epistemological and ontological uncertainty, the student creates her own new uncertainties, and thrives in them. Here, our distinction between the epistemological and the ontological dimensions of the student's pedagogical being is again surely potent.

Through authentic being, the student takes off and journeys among the infinite. Here, there is *epistemological courage* in coming to believe in her beliefs, but there is also, and fundamentally so, *ontological courage*. It is the belief in herself that will fuel her will to learn, to press herself into the day, bending those experiences to further her own learning projects. The student puts herself forward; she leaps forward. She even flies by herself. This is not fantasy. It is achieved day in and day out, even in mass higher education; and even against the odds.

Emancipation – and Robinson Crusoe

In an earlier (1990) book, *The Idea of Higher Education,* I set out what might be termed a philosophy of higher education based on the idea of emancipation. In that book, my explorations of emancipation turned doubly on (a) an intellectual freedom deriving at least in part through (b) an educational process pursued as an open dialogue. Arising from our inquiry here, though, we may perhaps glimpse a different insight into emancipation. Now, we may say instead that emancipation is to be won through the student's own will to learn. Through that will, ultimately, she is able to project herself forward, even into the void as it may seem.

There are two obvious objections to *this* conception of the student winning her own emancipation. The first is that it is unduly heroic; that it calls for students to be Nietzschean super-students, as they stand out bravely and leap off, fearlessly, committing themselves to nothing but their own courage. The objection exaggerates my position. The bungee jumping metaphor is a metaphor and should not be taken too literally, but it surely contains the truth that in higher education worthy of the name, we precisely want students to attain a situation of their own, in part of their own realization on which they stand by themselves; in short, as I have been urging, to attain their own authenticity.[2]

The second objection is that the idea of emancipation that I am now putting forward is a kind of 'Robinson Crusoe' position. Here, it would be urged that my argument neglects the several ways in which the establishing of a position in academic life is necessarily conversational. There can be no suggestion of the student as her or his own islander.[3] How, indeed, it may be asked does the version of emancipation I am now suggesting square with my earlier version – drawn from Jurgen Habermas – of emancipation deriving from an unfettered dialogue? Isn't a lively engaged experience of higher education to be derived in exchanges not only with tutors but also with other students? Dialogue is crucial in higher education.[4]

My response to *this* line of thinking and the objection is two-fold.

First, my view is that emancipation understood as unfettered dialogue underplays the element of the personal, of human being as such. Such a conception surely neglects the point that it is individuals who contribute – or fail to contribute – to the rational life [a point to which Habermas' predecessor, Horkheimer (2004), was alert]. We need, therefore, to a philosophy of communication, to add a philosophy of being.

Of course, we cannot simply retreat to Heidegger or Sartre, much as they may be helpful to us. Being has itself to be reinterpreted in the ever increasing complexity of today's world and that is why I have talked in this study of 'being-for-complexity'. Being is now called forward unremittingly, day in and day out. And this is the world that graduates especially will go into, as they grapple with the competing demands of professional life (both internally within professional life itself and between professional life and their own lifeworlds). However much individuals draw on others and grow through their associations with others, ultimately we are each faced with a particular set of challenges and have responsibilities to ourselves. There is a sense in which each of us is, as Camus (2000) put it, an 'Outsider'.[5]

Second, nothing I have said here denies the role of communities in the development of the student's becoming and here I want to make two points. On the one hand, rule following, turn taking, sincerity, truthfulness and appropriateness: all the ingredients of the Habermassian ideal speech situation I am happy to endorse. Each of these dimensions have a necessarily social aspect, but what has not often been noticed about this form of life is that it is *personally* arduous.

Engaging in a conversation in which there are many competing and contradictory voices calls for courage, a willingness to put oneself forward, a preparedness to be criticized, and to secure and to hold one's ground. It calls for a personal responsibility for one's offerings and interventions.[6] The critical dialogue – precisely through its being genuinely interactive while incredibly complex – calls for extraordinary qualities and dispositions on the part of the participants. We have to reminded ourselves of the students who would prefer to remain silent, though doubtless for different personal and cultural reasons. So, again, a philosophy of communication, if carried through, will lead us surely to a philosophy of being. It is this ontological turn that is now needed; and, in an age of utter uncertainty, desperately so.

On the other hand, the student's putting herself forward, her having the courage to do so itself has a social aspect. She does so often in front of the other students, who in turn may lend her their support. Our frontispiece leaper leaps precisely as a member of a community in which the leap has significant social meaning; but it is *his* leap and no-one can do it for him. Personal becoming and social meaning: these are not necessarily cleft apart. They can support each other. Even the personal becoming supports the community: the individual student's achievements are often celebrated by her classmates. Through her achievements, the other students affirm themselves.

Language, risk and (even) terror

Language

In this book, I have contended that our contemporary language in higher education is totally inadequate to the situation – at once of closure, complexity, and ideology – that faces us. In developing my argument, I have drawn on a vocabulary barely seen in debate on higher education these days – of being, becoming, authenticity, commitment, passion, air, spirit, criticality, inspiration, care, dispositions, faith, travel, voice and will. It is a language that speaks to personal qualities and to pedagogical qualities. This language looks to the student's becoming.

I have pressed this language in the context of a set of threats of closure and of self-censure that is upon us. The closure comes through risk aversion in an era of accountability, consumerism and litigiousness. *Accountability* – in the UK at least – has taken a particularly strident form in a heavy-handed quality assurance regime (admittedly now having given way to a much lighter regime); *consumerism* arises as students – now fee-paying – redefine their relationship with their institution; and *litigiousness* arises in a heightened pedagogical climate of consumer 'rights'. The self-censure arises not only because academics constrain themselves in taking on controversial topics – even in the sciences, for example, in the teaching of Darwinianism – but they constrain themselves too in the pedagogical relationship. The curriculum is now more managed and presented to the students for their assimilation.

So arises a new need for a wider sense as to what a curriculum and a pedagogy can offer. As it has been put (Council for Industry and Higher Education 2005), 'higher education is more than a degree' and there are challenges on curricula designers to have such a wider view in mind, but a curriculum is a dead thing unless it is supported by a sense of the student's becoming. For that, we need – I have argued here – a pedagogy that breathes, that allows the student air; a pedagogy in which students are encouraged to fly by and for themselves; a pedagogy in which student's own will is encouraged, a pedagogy of air.

Risk

This is, as we have noticed, a pedagogy of (some) risk. The student may try to take on an unrealistic task, or may become undisciplined or may lack courage. These are – we may note – risks within the pedagogical situation itself. They are forms of *self-induced risk*: the student risks herself, but there are other kinds of risk that may open in a pedagogy of air. These are the risks, essentially, of ideological take-over or – as we may term them – of *discursive risk*. Being in her own space, the student is open to becoming snared by a particular set of ideas, or framework or way of being.

Such *ontological corruption* would be ironic. In trying to become herself and free herself from the dominance of the conventional frameworks, the student may become susceptible to the lure of a new current of air (if only in the student societies). The student may feel energized anew. Uncertainty may have been replaced by a new certainty, but this new certainty would be a result of the student having been so beguiled as to invest herself *unduly* in a new framework. The 'they' of the conventional frameworks will have been replaced by a new 'they' – of the glitzy avant-garde frameworks.

(Even) terror

Here, too, and we should admit this, lies the possibility of terror. After all, if students are encouraged to fly, might they not fly into the arms of those who would offer them the home of terror? For, paradoxically, terror may seem to offer a home to those who are troubled by uncertainty.

But ideological take-over and beguilement by the lure of terror are not part of the pedagogy of air that I have proposed. The windhover flies and hangs in the air, but it only does so through holding itself in and through the air. The air is a condition of its flying. The windhover feels and uses, and even plays with its context. Its surrounding context is not abandoned and so, if the student is to fly and maintain her trajectory, she will draw support from all the resources around her – her literatures, models, perspectives, traditions and routines. It is through the pedagogical context that the student may take off and fly, may become herself. Space and support, as well as self-propelled will, are necessary for this flight.

The alleged dangers of succumbing to terror(ism) are, in any case, actually trivial.[7] The main dangers remain those of consumerism, over-weaning audit, risk-averseness and timidity: all of these may readily infect the pedagogical relationship at the present time. To these, both student and educator may contribute in more or less equal measure. There springs up a conspiracy of quietism. As a result, what emerges is a pedagogy-for-the-easy-life. The will to learn is vanquished. After all, what need is there for a will to learn in such a pedagogy, a pedagogy of conformism?

Finale

My fundamental thesis in this book has been very simple. It is that students count not *en masse* or, even as course cohorts, but as individuals. What matters supremely is their separate becoming, and their becoming requires the formation and the sustaining of their will to learn. However, in turn, implications arise for the pedagogical relationship: tutors and lecturers bear a heavy responsibility in bringing about the necessary dispositions and qualities on the part of the student. Care and passion together are called for in bringing about a continuing pedagogy of air.

A pedagogy of air is, admittedly, fragile. Uncertainty calls *for* uncertainty, but what alternative is there?

Notes

Introduction

1 http://www.vanuatutourism.com/vanuatu/cms/culture/nagol.html
2 Paul Gibbs' book (2004) is a rare exception to this observation.
3 For Mary Warnock (1970: 1), '. . . the common interest which unites Existentialist philosophers is the interest in human freedom.' However, see also David Cooper (2000) for whom existentialism – as I read him – is characterized by a penumbra of interlinked concepts, including becoming, being and authenticity. Such a set of interests, taken up as a kind of philosophico-practical project, constitutes, as Simon Critchley (2001: 48–9) puts it, a philosophical 'culture' distinct from philosophy of the English-speaking world.
4 Compare the approach taken here with the kind of inquiry and data offered in a recent report (HEPI 2006). We are told (para 21) that 'half (of the students surveyed) considered (some aspects of their experience) to be worse than expected. Amongst that group, disappointment with academic provision was much stronger than disappointment with other aspects of the university experience.' This leaves open the matter of the disappointments in question. However, even if we knew that, further questions would open as to any implications for curricula and pedagogical action, and no survey could tell us that. For implications reside in the realm of values and it remains notoriously difficult to extract 'values' from 'facts'.
5 In Heidegger's terminology, students in conceptions of these kinds become a kind of 'standing reserve', a resource to fill others' purposes. See Fitzsimons (2002).
6 See Haggis (2004), who urges a wider conception of what matters in understanding learning in higher education beyond that of 'approaches to learning'.

Chapter 1: Where there's a will

1   An answer that Alison Phipps would give to this question is that of 'desire'. See her (2006) book on *Learning the Arts of Linguistic Survival*, wherein we are given rich insight into the 'long arduous process of learning' that the tourist language learner sometimes pursues in 'the will to relate, the desire to make meaning'.

2   To say that the will and the intellect work in different planes is not to deny that they are inter-related; indeed, much of my inquiry here is an attempt to explore that relationship in the pedagogical situation. We should note that there is an influential strain in contemporary philosophy that has been examining the relationship between the will and the intellect, a strong strand of which debate is precisely that they are intertwined. See, for example, Derry (2004). What I am concerned to do here is to emphasize the autonomy and fundamental significance of the will as such. In this, I follow Schopenhauer, for whom 'will . . . is installed . . . as the realm of the free 'thing-in-itself', the unique site of authentic Being in the world.' (Roberts, 1990: 182).

3   There are complex inter-connections here between 'will' and 'freedom'. Neither is reducible to the other, but a strong thesis that I would wish to assert is that the university is a space in which both the will and freedom are formed (cf. Frankfurt 2005).

4   See Janaway (2002) and Young (2005) for very clear introductions to Schopenhauer's thought. Magee (1987, chapters 6 and 7) is also helpful here.

5   'Weakness of will is always possible' (Searle, 2001: 25).

6   On the over-close association of the university with knowledge, Heidegger (2002b: 31–32) was very clear on the matter: 'From its beginning, then, the university got off on the wrong foot by instituting itself as the privileged site of access to what is real, where all things submit to the theoretical gaze . . . [to the contrary] Its beginnings originates in mood . . . springing from . . . astonishment . . .'

7   See Parker (2003) for a way of 'reconceptualising the curriculum' so as to lead 'from commodification to transformation'.

8   For a careful discussion of the inter-relationships of some of these concepts, see Dunne (1993).

Chapter 2: Being

1   Even though we cannot escape the matter of 'being' in these inquiries, I am conscious that I do not attempt to define it. Perhaps I may be forgiven: 'Being is everywhere . . . [but] Being is nowhere . . .' [Inwood, in commenting on Dasein and Being in the work of Heidegger (Inwood, 2000: 21).]

2   On the weakness of the will, see Henden (2004), in which is explored the matter as to whether the weakness of the will is or is not to be associated with a positive evaluation on the part of the individual to the course of action or non-action in question.

3   For an exploration, among other things, of the implications of the Heideggerian distinction between 'ready-to-hand' and 'present-at-hand' for science education, see Roth (1997). For a wide-ranging exploration of 'the sociocultural and psychosocial order of practical understanding and interpretation that rests upon and resumes the . . . structuring of being', see Keller (2005).

4 cf. Ashworth (2004), who, also drawing on Heidegger, argues for a conception of understanding as the transformation of what is already known. For Ashworth, we may note, however, such a learning process has to be conversational in character. Cf. also Husserl's awareness of 'the intuitive presence of the object of knowledge' (Bernet, 2003).

5 John Macmurray is hardly ever read these days, but he drew attention to the connections between reason and emotion quite some time ago: indeed, for him, 'reason is primarily an affair of emotion, and . . . the rationality of thought is the derivative and secondary one.' (Macmurray 1995/1935: 11).

6 I am conscious that much of what I say in this book comes close to the idea of 'embodied knowing', on which see Dall'Alba and Barnacle (2005; in press), who have drawn especially on the thinking of Merleau-Ponty (for example, 1994/1962). I haven't felt drawn explicitly to pursue the idea in this book, but I am sure it is important.

7 Anxiety among students is almost certainly a fact of student life. Probably, the first major empirical study of such matters was that of Zweig (1963). Zweig notes that students 'struck me as old, laden with responsibility, care and worry, with night-mares and horror dreams. "It is difficult to be young in our present-day society", they said.' (Zweig 1963: xiv) More recently, we learn that 'Almost six in ten (58%) students now agree that *since being at university I feel under a lot more stress than before* – this ha[d] increased by five percentage points since the question was first asked in (2001)' (UNITE/HEPI report 2005).

8 For a sociological working out of the ideas of Kiekegaard and Heidegger, in so far as they bear upon anxiety in modern society, see Giddens (1995: Chapter 2).

9 I use the phrase 'the Western idea of the university' from time to time in this volume because it seems to me that the set of concepts that I am articulating here are in a sense precisely that.

10 'We sail within a vast sphere, ever drifting in uncertainty, driven from end to end. . . . Nothing stays for us. This is our natural condition, and yet most contrary to our inclination . . . Let us therefore not look for certainty and stability' (Pascal 1947: 19–20).

11 'What we can do is learn to live in a radically contingent and infinitely pluralistic universe' (Garrison 2004: 106).

Chapter 3: Authenticity

1 For a recent exploration of the idea of authenticity, see Guigon (2004). Guigon brings to light what for him is 'the social embodiment of authenticity', especially its involving 'deliberation about how one's commitments make a contribution to the good of the public world . . .' (Guigon 2004: 163).

2 I associate closely this text with what I term the 'Western idea of higher educa-tion'. Many will feel uncomfortable with this identification, but the themes – explicit and tacit – of this book of personal authenticity, freedom, emancipation and criticality seem to me to be inescapably part of the Western idea of higher education (see Barnett 1990). Whether or not, deep down, there are also connec-tions to specific Christian beliefs as to self-management and 'inner turmoil' at work here, I am not sure. See Zizek (2002: 128–9).

3 See Bonnett and Cuypers (2003) for a further analysis of differences between the

concepts of authenticity and autonomy. See Christman (1989) for a set of essays on individual autonomy and see Dearden (1972) for a classic paper on 'Autonomy and Education'.

4 Cf. 'To know the truth means to acknowledge it deeply and completely, to allow it to permeate one's being.' (Furtak 2005: 43). Also, 'Reason, in short, constructs the personality in a very deep way, shaping its motivations as well as its logic'. (Nussbaum, (2000: 29).

5 In a detailed commentary on Hegel, Heidegger brings out how knowledge involves consciousness, which separates the object from being, but which, in the process, enhances being; raises being into 'being for' as distinct from mere 'being itself' (Heidegger 2002a: 125–131).

6 It should not be thought here that this line of thinking, if it has merit, applies only to studies involving human being; I am offering observations that appear to me to apply in every field of knowing. Another way of making the point is to draw on Gadamer, for whom creative interpretation was at the heart of understanding texts. I would want to say that all understanding takes this form, for an access to understanding in every field is, in part, via texts. See his magnum opus (1985/1965: e.g. 162–170).

7 The virtues that I identify for students are likely to have their counterparts as virtues for teachers. For example, drawing on Macfarlane's analysis (2004: 129), the teaching virtue of 'restraint' has as its 'defect' the vice of 'evasiveness' and as its 'excess' the vice of 'self-indulgence'.

8 For example, in *The Concept of Anxiety* (Kierkegaard 2001: 201).

9 '. . . you must wager. It is not optional' (Pascal 1947: 66).

Chapter 4: Becoming

1 On the theme of 'Becoming what you want to be', see Batchelor, 2006b. The paper presents what we may term the strong argument for supporting the student's 'voice for being and becoming'.

2 Connected to the idea of personal development is the idea of personal growth, on which concept see Ventimiglia (2005), who articulates 'growth' and its educational implications as worked out by Charles Peirce. Much of Peirce's philosophy that is articulated in that paper chimes with what I offer in this book, for example, the sense that there is a felt dimension to ideas [which, we are told (p296), Peirce called 'quale']. Correlatively, Peirce suggested that 'great respect should be paid to the judgements of the sensible heart', a position close to that of Schopenhauer, on whom I have lent in these enquiries.

3 'The concept of becoming is not only a central Deleuzian concept . . . it can also be seen . . . to contain in germ the entirety of his philosophical perspective.' (May, 2003). For Colebrook (2002: 4), for Deleuze, becoming is 'not just another word but a problem . . .'

4 Hence, we may speak of 'phenomenological time': see Roth (2002: 14).

5 Cf. Rowan Willliams (2005: 25) writing on faith in the university: 'To live in faith is to be conscious at some level . . . that your being there and your being who you are, are not under threat; your existence and your identity have roots and solidity.'

6 For instance, Marsh *et al.* (2005).

7 'The notion of the primal nature of the will is the connecting link between Nietzsche and Schopenhauer' (Dolson, 1901: 244).

8 In placing stress in this book on individuals and their becoming, I am not wanting to imply that individuals are Robinson Crusoes, having entirely to make their own way in the world. On the contrary, I continually draw attention to both the desirability and the need for students to engage with their educational environment, including those others that help to constitute that environment, including teachers and students. For Herbert Marcuse, we may note, 'inwardness and subjectivity may well become the inner and outer space for the subversion of experience, for the emergence of another universe' (quoted in Brookfield, 2002). On the wider issues as to the relationships between becoming, freedom, autonomy and relationships with others see, for example, Glynn (2006: 372–3): '[individuals'] self-consciousness presupposes other, essentially similar, subjects' and it is through such structures and individuals' capacities for self-reflection that we can understand such individuals' 'freedom'. See also Devine and Irwin (2005: 329) who, in articulating the work of James Marshall, argue that 'Agency is not individuated freedom of will . . . By entwining raised consciousness into already existing language, discourse can exceed the prevailing ways of imagining ourselves and our world'.

9 Cf. 'Learning is not only about the acquisition of skills or knowledge . . . What is called for, rather, is a passionate commitment to the object of study, and a readiness to have one's thinking and one's life-view transformed . . .' (Rae 2004: 101)

10 The extract is taken from the contribution by Eirini Spentza, as part of the chapter by Ahearn *et al.* (2007).

Chapter 5: Travel broadens the mind

1 See Lilge (1974) for an examination of the relationship of Hegel's philosophy to his educational ideas.

2 Unfortunately, 'the present education system colludes in a mass deflection from "the self" '.

3 The will here, therefore, is – to a significant extent – focused, even if the will plays itself out in the horizon of the infinite. Cf. Kierkegaard (1956: 61): 'Now, willing one thing does not mean to commit the grave mistake of a brazen, unholy enthusiasm, namely, to will the big, no matter whether it be good or bad.'

4 Cf. W. R. Niblett (1974) *Universities between Two Worlds*.

5 For a demonstration as to how travel may broaden the mind, see Phipps (2006).

6 Precisely on the matter of the academy and hospitality, see Bennett (2005).

7 There are issues here as to the meaning of 'strangeness' in a pedagogical world, not least in a global age, in an age where there is talk of students being encouraged to become 'global citizens'; and of otherness, including the Cultural Other (Sanderson, 2004). Raised here too is not only the question as to who is to count as a stranger, but who is to count as homeless, see Michael Ignatieff (1984).

Chapter 6: A will to offer

1 Michael Peters (2004) has pointed, in the later work of Derrida, to a promise of 'a positive rehabilitation of the concept of performance that elevates it from its

neo-liberal managerialist appropriation to its more human and enabling sense: a shift from "the logic of performativity" to the "culture of performance" '. A separate sense of 'performance' in a context of learning is to be found offered by Newman and Holzman (1997: 115 *et seq*) in their idea of 'performed conversations'.

2   Cf. the depiction by Marilyn Strathern (2004a), in drawing on Miyazachi of the Fijian gift, 'when the givers' side "subjects itself to the gift-receivers' evaluation, and quietly hopes that the other side will respond positively". Motionless, the givers' spokesman holds the object in front of him until a recipient steps forward and takes it. "In this moment of hope, the gift givers place in abeyance their own agency . . ." '

Chapter 7: Voice

1   For an exploration of Derrida's suggestion that 'being as *logos* is something that is *heard*' see Backman 2006, whose paper traces Derrida's analysis of Heidegger on the matter.

2   This distinction between pedagogic voice and educational voice, and their respective relationships between autonomy and authenticity allow us to be consistent with the distinctions we made earlier (Chapter 3) between autonomy and authenticity, including the reservations we made about autonomy in the context of higher education.

3   In a world dominated by large and unequal forces, learning is liable to be insufficient also because learning itself may be deprived of its autonomy, as individuals are compelled not only to learn, but to learn in prescribed ways (see Lambeir 2005).

Chapter 8: Dispositions and qualities

1   Even the 'right' dispositions and qualities can undo themselves if they are pressed unduly. See, for example, Cox, Caze and Levine (2003), who point out that the quality of integrity can be held in an excessive way.

2   See the edited volumes by Crisp and Slote (2000), and by Brady and Pritchard (2003). For a recent and authoritative exploration of 'virtues' in the context of higher education, see Macfarlane (2004). See, too, a paper by Gibbs (1996), which in the context of Lyotard's critique of a performativity at the heart of higher education, argues for a 'reconstituted Aristotelian virtue model of self'.

3   There are a host of related issues that we cannot go into here, such as the significance, for her epistemic virtues, of a person being successful in reaching understanding, of rules and procedures, of internal and external factors, and of the relationship of epistemic virtues to one's overall goals. On these and other issues, see Eflin (2003).

Chapter 9: The inspiring teacher

1   I am conscious that I commit the sin in this book of not defining what I mean by 'pedagogy' (see Ireson *et al.* 1999: 212). If I was pressed to offer one, I would say I

mean nothing more than a deliberate approach to teaching and I try to set out here what, for me, that deliberate approach might be.

2 One limitation is that 'inspiration' here does not entail 'charisma'. Indeed, it will be noticed that the term 'charisma' is absent from this chapter. See Moore (2004) for a critique of teaching as charisma.

3 On connections between air and mind, see Abram (1996: 237–238).

4 Cf. '. . . the teacher must help students to . . . realize their own mystical vocation, for we are all mystics in the making' (Gruba-McCallister 2002: 85).

5 Why this pressing towards 'spirit' in *this* text? If not far from 'spirit' lies spirituality, is there lurking in this book a sense or a hope that a higher education as argued for here is a substitute for religiosity, at once educational and therapeutic; a kind of educational form of the sacred? On these large themes of the therapeutic and the sacred, respectively, see Rieff (1987) and Ben Rogers (2004). For a discussion of the spiritual in higher education, see Robinson (2005: 235–240).

6 In the context of higher education and the university, Heidegger's remains surely the most famous, not to say, infamous account of the spiritual in education. For a more recent account, see Alexander, H. (2001). On the connections between the idea of the university and the formation of national identity, see Readings (1997).

7 For a thesis as to the way in which the spiritual may be taken up by the university, see Bussey (2004).

Chapter 10: A pedagogy for uncertain times

1 Related to these ideas are the separate concepts of *Bildung* and 'liberal education', on which relationships see Lovlie *et al.* (2003). However, I deploy neither concept myself in this book, one reason for which is that I do feel that we need to bring in imaginatively a new language for our efforts in higher education.

2 See Macfarlane (2006: 124–125) for a related discussion, on the 'benevolence' that tutors may show towards their students.

3 Linked to this care for the student's future lies a pedagogy of hope: see Shade (2006). Linked also to 'solicitude' is the idea of empathy, but we should note that empathy can bring with it insidious psychological dimensions, in which the student's being may be mis-represented through processes of 'projective identification'. See Richmond (2004).

4 Related to the concepts of solicitude and care is the concept of stewardship, on which concept and its implications for higher education, see Gillespie (2003).

5 Bruce Macfarlane has dealt explicitly – through an imaginative scenario – in his (2004) book on *Teaching with Integrity* (pp. 79–80).

6 Cf. the offerings of Elton and Rowland, respectively (2005).

7 'There is no technological substitute for passion' (Bearn 2000: 412). For a defence of passion in teaching, as to both its need and its value, see Day (2004). Also, on passion in teaching, see bel hooks (1994, chapter 13).

8 Perhaps a further helpful idea here in construing the pedagogical relationship is that of 'the sacred' in the sense advocated by Ronald Dworkin (2004: 142), for whom 'to regard something as sacred implies *something* about how it should be treated: that it must not be destroyed . . .'

9 In a commentary on the manuscript of this book, Alison Phipps has suggested a

seventh principle: 'In a destabilized world, provide some rest for the teacher and her/his students.'

10 As it seems to me, these six principles 'bear witness to the different, to a form of education based on difference' (Peters 1995: xxxii), but also embrace a sense of mutuality amid difference. They also perhaps do some justice to the idea of therapeutic university, as advanced by Richard Smith (2004: 83–87) and which may even stand 'in opposition to the various forms of fragmentation that increasingly threaten the very idea of a university and . . . the values and purposes of higher education'. (Smith 2004: 87)

Chapter 11: Space and risk

1 The idea of 'heresies' in the university and higher education, I take from Goodlad (1995). Goodlad identified 16 (other) heresies.
2 For a thorough exploration of different kinds of 'learning spaces', see Savin-Baden (2007).
3 Practical expression to ideas of this nature are to be seen in the work of Carl Rogers (1983).
4 Melanie Walker offers a conception of a higher education pedagogy that – as it seems to me – is in the spirit of what I am saying here, but is, in its 'capabilities approach', even more ambitious.
5 For a philosophical commentary on 'an education without risk', and its association with a conception of teaching as technology, see Blake *et al.* (2000, Chapter 1).
6 'Docility' I take from Foucault (1977).
7 A concept related to that of fragility is that of vulnerability, on which matter see Batchelor (2006a). The paper associates vulnerability with the student's 'voice' and identifies different kinds of such voice; and, in keeping with the argument here, proposes that the student's 'ontological voice' is fundamental to the winning of the student's epistemological and practical voices.
8 On the pedagogical and educational implications of 'letting learn', see Gibbs and Angelides (2004) and Gibbs *et al.* (2004). For a Marxist, such letting learn and such hopes for transformation may point to a 'dialectical' account of 'non-directive' and 'self-management' pedagogies: see Gadotti (1996, esp Chapter 3).

Chapter 12: A critical spirit

1 This chapter may be read as a way of wrestling with this issue: what is higher education to be in an age where epistemological authority is in doubt? How does educational 'responsibility' gain a foothold in such an age? On these matters, see O'Byrne (2005).
2 Or at least, this should be the case. In their (2006: 150) book on *Why Truth Matters*, Benson and Stangroom remind us how, even in universities, there are partly lines and students are denied exposure to frameworks that go against a departmental orthodoxy.
3 Precisely on 'critical spirit', see Passmore (1969). Cf. Pavlich (2005) who offers a critique of critique as emerging out of 'disciplinary truth regimes' and turns to a

'different grammar of critique as an *experience* of imagined prospects . . . This experience is structured through the impossible . . .'

4 Cf. Brookfield's (2002) analysis of some of the features of Marcuse's thinking as to criticality and their implications for adult education: 'an apparent engagement with diversity can be manipulated to reinforce dominant ideology'. Accordingly, to exploit the ambiguity of the term, we may say that some frameworks may be more 'critical' than others. See Hinchcliff (2006) who has taken up the idea of criticality in relation to lifelong education, drawing *inter alia* on Heideggerian ideas of being-in-the-world and comportment.

5 '. . . what we call "understanding" . . . may be a matter of being open to the world, and becoming consciously aware to that to which we have opened ourselves' (Sotto 1994: 78).

6 I draw these references to leadership in MBA programmes from the work in progress of a PhD student, Eric Garcia.

7 There are related issues here of interdisciplinarity, the potential 'uselessness of knowledge and the educational value of ignorance'. See Strathern (2005).

8 These ideas on critical thinking are drawn from work in progress of a PhD student, Mong Chue Cheng.

9 I developed the idea of 'critical being' in my (1997) book on *Higher Education: A Critical Business*.

10 See Alexandra (2005) for a conception of curriculum that, as it seems to me, is much in the spirit of what I am contending for here: a 'meaningful account of curriculum . . . requires students to recognize that . . . they have the capacity to err in what they think, feel and do, but that they can also change course and make a difference. This is a source of fear and trepidation, but also of great joy. Cultivating this sort of existential joy is, to my mind, the highest aspiration of any curriculum'.

11 'Critical Pedagogy never arrives, it continually takes us beyond our own boundaries and beyond ourselves . . .' (Phipps and Guilherme 2003: 168)).

12 For explorations into ways in which the 'abundance' of the world is all too often tacitly denied by limiting frameworks placed upon the world, and the potential richness of being is lost, even by 'intellectuals', see Paul Feyerabend's (2001) last book, *Conquest of Abundance*. For a linking of the realm of the critical with the realm of the infinite, see Gary (2006).

13 See Marks (2005) for what I regard as a fascinating account – built on Heidegger's conception of space – of the way in which universities tacitly open up local and 'exclusive' spaces. One issue – for me – that insight opens up is the possibilities that the university may open for global and even infinite spaces. Marks looks to the possibilities of the Internet, but on the distinction I mention here, we may be placed there in the realm of the global but is it necessarily the realm of the infinite?

14 For an account of a practical working out of a curriculum and a pedagogy that is in keeping, as it seems to me, with the spirit of these remarks here is the offering by Canaan (2005). Indeed, in drawing on Freire and suggesting that students can link their curricula experiences with practical action in the wider world, the paper goes further, in some senses, than I propose here. It remains a further issue how far that form of criticality has application across the various disciplines and fields of knowing.

15 This connection of criticality and life was a point on which Leavis, the English literary critic, was insistent (see Leavis 1969).

16 The idea of 'critical pedagogy' is, of course, yet a further idea over which there is dispute. See McClaren (1995) for a politicized conception of it.
17 Such a sense of collective criticality has implications especially for the local unit, typically the department that has responsibility for a programme of studies. See Trowler, Fanghenel and Wareham (2005) – on *Freeing the chi of change* – for ways of releasing blocked energies at that 'meso' level.

Coda

1 The bold lines of the diagram are at once misleading and, I believe, informative. This book has been, in a sense, an inquiry into the manifold inter-relationships between will and intellect, between the student's being and her epistemic interests. However, each is different and is not reducible to the other. The will enables the intellect to take off, to become an independent intellect, but the will has to be ever present for that trajectory to persist. At this point, my view departs from Schopenhauer, for whom such will-dependency was a mark of intellectual 'vulgarity' (2004: 94), but I do not see how such a pure intellect can otherwise sustain itself.
2 Cf. Taylor (1991: 29) on *The Ethics of Authenticity*: 'Being true to myself means being true to my own originality, and that is something only I can articulate and discover. In articulating it, I am also defining myself.'
3 It is one of the insights of post-structuralism that 'we do not become anyone at all unless we are spoken to and spoken about'. (Blake *et al.*, 1998: 13).
4 Dialogue is important not only within the pedagogical situation but between academics as teachers. See Walker (2001) for an account of a dialogical but also critical professionalism between colleagues across the disciplines.
5 In this way of thinking, 'In a world that is radically meaningless the subject can heroically, through the experience of dread, assert its freedom.' (Critchley, 2005: 26). That would be an extreme view, but precisely in a world that is characterized by surveillance, bureaucracy and powerful battalions, it may be time to re-visit the existentialists and see their relevance for us today.
6 Cf. Martin Buber (2002, p81) on 'the Single One, that is, the man living in responsibility'. Cf. also, George Steiner (2003: 101): 'In the end, responsibility does lie with the individual spirit . . .' See also Barbour (2004) for a detailed examination of *The Value of Solitude*.
7 Even if terror – in whatever form – is a real presence on campus, the challenges to pedagogy arguably point in directions not much different from those enunciated here: a pedagogy of tolerance does not entail a toleration of the intolerant (Badley 2005). Although we should note Lyotard's bleak warning (or is it an observation?): 'All education is inhuman because it does not happen without constraint and terror.' (1991: 4–5).

Bibliography

This bibliography contains a limited number of items not cited in the text or the notes, but which are pertinent to this inquiry.

Abouserie, R. (1995) Self-esteem and achievement motivation as determinants of students' approaches to studying, *Studies in Higher Education*, 20(1): 19–26.

Abram, D. (1996) *The Spell of the Sensuous*. New York: Vintage.

Adorno, T. (2003, orig. 1973) *The Jargon of Authenticity*. London: Routledge.

Ahearn, A., Broadbent, O., Collins, J. and Spentza, E. (2007) Being an Undergraduate Student in the Twenty-first Century, in Barnett, R. and Di Napoli, R. (eds) *Changing Identities in Higher Education: Voicing Perspectives*. Abingdon: Routledge.

Alexander, H. (2001) *Reclaiming Goodness: education and the spiritual quest*. Notre Dame: University of Notre Dame.

Alexander, T. (2001) Eros and education: postmodernism and the dilemma of humanist pedagogy, *Studies in Philosophy and Education*, 21: 479–496.

Alexandra, H. (2005) Human agency and the curriculum, *Theory and Research in Education*, 3(3): 243–269.

Arnheim, R. (1988) *The Power of the Centre: a study of composition in the visual arts*. Berkeley: University of California.

Ashworth, P. (2004) Understanding as the transformation of what is already known, *Teaching in Higher Education*, 9(2): 147–158.

Astley, J., Francis, L., Sullivan, J. and Walker, A. (eds) (2004) *The Idea of a Christian University: essays on theology and higher education*. Bletchley: Paternoster.

Austin, J.L. (1975) *How to do Things with Words*, 2nd edn. Oxford: Clarendon.

Backman, J. (2006) *The (Con)text of Being: Heidegger, Derrida and the deconstruction of logos*, research seminar, Department of Philosophy and Social and Moral Philosophy, University of Helsinki, 23 March, 2006.

Badley, G. (2005) Against Fundamentalism, for democracy: towards a pedagogy of tolerance in higher education, *Teaching in Higher Education*, 10(4): 416–419.

Barbalet, J. (ed.) (2002) *Emotions and Sociology*. Oxford: Blackwell.

Barbour, J.D. (2004) *The Value of Solitude: the ethics and spirituality of aloneness in autobiography*. Charlottesville: University of Virginia.

Barnett, R. (1990) *The Idea of Higher Education*. Buckingham: Open University Press.

Barnett, R. (1997) *Higher Education: a critical business.* Buckingham: Open University Press/SRHE.

Barnett, R. (2000) *Realising the University in an Age of Supercomplexity.* Buckingham: Open University Press.

Barnett, R. (2003) *Beyond All Reason: living with ideology in the university.* Buckingham: Open University Press.

Barnett, R. (2004) Learning for an unknown future, *Higher Education Research & Development,* 23(3): 247–260.

Barnett, R. (ed.) (2005) *Reshaping the University: changing relationships between teaching and research.* Maidenhead: McGraw-Hill/Open University Press.

Barnett, R. and Di Napoli, R. (eds) (2007) *Changing Identities in Higher Education: voicing perspectives.* Abingdon: Routledge.

Bataille, G. (1988) *Inner Experience.* New York: State University of New York.

Batchelor, D. (2006a) Vulnerable voices: an examination of the concept of vulnerability in relation to student voice, *Educational Philosophy and Theory,* 38(6): 787–800.

Batchelor, D. (2006b) 'Becoming what you want to be, *London Review of Education,* 4 (3): 225–238.

Bauman, Z. (2000) *Liquid Modernity.* Cambridge: Polity.

Bauman, Z. (2005a) *Liquid Life.* Cambridge: Polity.

Bauman, Z. (2005b) The liquid-modern challenges to education, in Robinson, S. and Katulushi, C. (eds) *Values in Higher Education.* St Brides Major: Aureus and the University of Leeds.

Bearn, G.C.F. (2000) Pointlessness and the university of Beauty, in Dhillon, P.A. and Standish, P. (eds) *Lyotard: just education,* chapter 13. Abingdon; Routledge/Falmer.

Bennett, J.B. (2005) *The Academy and Hospitality.* Available at: http://www.crosscurrents.org/Bennett.htmm (accessed 3 May, 2005).

Benson, O. and Stangroom, J. (2006) *Why Truth Matters.* London: Continuum.

Bernet, R. (2003) Desiring to know through intuition, *Husserl Studies,* 19: 153–166.

Bernstein, B. (1996) *Pedagogy, Symbolic Control and Identity.* London: Taylor and Francis.

Blake, N., Smeyers, P., Smith, R. and Standish, P. (1998) *Thinking Again: education after postmodernism.* London: Routledge Falmer.

Blake, N., Smeyers, P., Smith, R. and Standish, P. (2000) *Education in an Age of Nihilism.* London: Routledge.

Blake, N., Smeyers, P., Smith, R. and Standish, P. (2003) *Blackwell Guide to the Philosophy of Education.* Oxford: Blackwell.

Bone, J. and McNay, I. (2006) *Higher Education and Human Good.* Bristol: Tockington Press.

Bonnett, M. (2002) Education as a form of the poetic: a Heideggerian approach to learning and the teacher–pupil relationship, in Peters, M. (ed.) *Heidegger, Education and Modernity.* Lanham: Rowan and Littlefield.

Bonnett, M. and Cuypers, S. (2003) Autonomy and authenticity in education, in Blake, N., Smeyers, P., Smith, R. and Standish, P. (eds) *Blackwell Guide to the Philosophy of Education.* Oxford: Blackwell.

Brady, M. and Pritchard, D. (eds) (2003) *Moral and Epistemic Virtues.* Oxford: Blackwell.

Brook, P. (1990) *The Empty Space.* London: Penguin.

Brookfield, S. (2002) Reassessing subjectivity, criticality, and inclusivity: Marcuse's challenge to adult education, *Adult Education Quarterly,* 52(4): 265–280.

Buber, M. (2002, orig. 1947) *Between Man and Man*. London: Routledge.

Burch, K. (2002) The love problem in liberal pedagogy, *Studies in Philosophy and Education*, 21: 497–503.

Bussey, M. (2004) *Homo Tantricus: tantra as an episteme for future generations*. Available at: http://www.gurukul.edu/pubs_journal_homotantricus.php (accessed 28 July, 2004).

Camus, A. (2000) *The Outsider*. London: Penguin.

Canaan, J. (2005) Developing a pedagogy of critical hope, *Learning and Teaching in Social Science*, 2(3): 159–174.

Christman, J. (ed.) (1989) *The Inner Citadel: essays on individual autonomy*. New York: University of Cambridge.

Colebrook, C. (2002) *Gilles Deleuze*. Abingdon: Routledge.

Cooper, D.E. (1983) *Authenticity and Learning: Nietzsche's educational philosophy*. London: Routledge and Kegan Paul.

Cooper, D.E. (2000) *Existentialism*, 2nd edn. Oxford: Blackwell.

Cooper, D.E. (2002) *The Measure of Things: humanism, humility and mystery*. Oxford: Oxford University Press.

Cowan, J. (1998) *On Becoming an Innovative University Teacher*. Buckingham: Open University Press.

Cox, D., La Caze, M. and Levine, M.P. (2003) *Integrity and the Fragile Self*. Aldershot: Ashgate.

Crisp, R. and Slote, M. (eds) (2000) *Virtue Ethics*. Oxford: Oxford University Press.

Critchley, S. (2001) *Continental Philosophy: a very short introduction*. Oxford: Oxford University Press.

Critchley, S. (2005) Conversation with . . ., *Naked Punch*, 4. London: Forum for European Philosophy.

Dall'Alba, G. and Barnacle, R. (2005) Embodied knowledge in online environments, *Educational Philosophy and Theory*, 37(5): 719–744

Dall' Alba, G. and Barnacle, R. (in press) Embodied knowing in higher education,

Day, C. (2004) *A Passion for Teaching*. London: Routledge Falmer.

Deleuze, G. (2001 [1994]) *Difference and Repetition*. London: Continuum.

Dearden, R. (1972) Autonomy and education, in Dearden, R.F., Hirst, P.H. and Peters, R.S. (eds) *Education and Reason*. London: Routledge and Kegan Paul.

Derrida, J (1991, orig. 1987) *Of Spirit: Heidegger and the Question*, transl. Bennington, G. and Bowlby, R. Chicago: University of Chicago.

Derrida, J. (2001) *Deconstruction Engaged: the Sydney seminars*. Sydney: Power Publications.

Derrida, J (2002, orig. 1967) *Writing and Difference*. London: Routledge.

Derrida, J. (2004) *Eyes of the University: right to philosophy 2*. Stanford: Stanford University.

Derrida, J. (2005) *The Politics of Friendship*. London: Verso.

Derry, J. (2004) The Unity of Intellect and Will, *Educational Review*, 56(2): 113–120.

Devine, N. and Irwin, R. (2005) Autonomy, agency and education: he tangata, he tangata, he tangata, *Educational Philosophy and Theory*, 37(3): 317–331.

Dolson, G.N. (1901) The influence of Schopenhauer upon Friedrich Nietzsche, *Philosophical Review*, 10(3): 241–250.

Dunne, J. (1993) *Back to the Rough Ground: 'Phronesis' and 'Techne' in modern philosophy and in Aristotle*. Notre Dame: University of Notre Dame.

Dunne, J. and Hogan, P. (eds) (2004) *Education and Practice: upholding the integrity of teaching and learning*. Oxford: Blackwell.

Dworkin, R. (2004) The concept of the Sacred, in Rogers, B. (ed.) *Is Nothing Sacred?* Abingdon: Routledge.

Eflin, J. (2003) Epistemic presuppositions and their consequences, in Brady, M. and Pritchard, D. (eds) *Moral and Epistemic Virtues*. Oxford: Blackwell.

Elton, L. (2005) Scholarship and the Research and Teaching Nexus, in Barnett, R. (ed.) *Reshaping the University: new relationships between research, scholarship and teaching*. Maidenhead: McGraw-Hill/Open University Press.

Engestrom, Y. (1999) Activity theory and individual and social transformation' in Engestrom, Y., Miettinen, R. and Punamaki, R-L. (eds) *Perspectives on Activity Theory*. Cambridge: Cambridge University Press.

Feyerabend, P. (2001) *Conquest of Abundance: a tale of abstraction versus the richness of being*. Chicago: University of Chicago.

Fitzsimons, P. (2002) Enframing education, in Peters, M. (ed.) *Heidegger, Education and Modernity*. Lanham, Maryland: Rowan and Littlefield.

Foucault, M. (1977) *Discipline and Punish: the birth of the prison*. London: Penguin.

Frankfurt, H. (2005) Freedom of the Will and the concept of a person, in Atkins, K. (ed.) *Self and Subjectivity*. Oxford: Blackwell.

Freire, P. (1978) *Pedagogy of the Oppressed*. London: Penguin.

Fromm, E. (1960, orig. 1942) *Fear of Freedom*. London: Routledge and Kegan Paul.

Furtak, R.A (2005) *Wisdom in Love: Kierkegaard and the ancient quest for emotional integrity*. Notre Dame: University of Notre Dame.

Gadamer, H-G. (1985, orig. 1965) *Truth and Method*. London: Sheed and Ward.

Gadotti, M. (1996) *Pedagogy of Praxis: a dialectical philosophy of education*. New York: State University of New York.

Gardiner, P. (2002) *Kierkegaard: a very short introduction*. Oxford: Oxford University Press.

Garrison, J. (2004) Dewey, Derrida and the 'Double Bind', in Trifonas, P.P. and Peters, M.A. (eds) *Derrida, Deconstruction and Education*. Oxford: Blackwell.

Gary, K. (2006) Spirituality, critical thinking, and the desire for what is infinite, *Studies in the Philosophy of Education*, 25: 315–326.

Gibbons, M., Limoges, C., Nowotny, H., Schwartzman, S., Scott, P. and Trow, M. (1994) *The New Production of Knowledge: the dynamics of science and research in contemporary societies*. London: Sage.

Gibbs, P. (1996) Whose life is it any rate? Of virtue, temporality and vocational education, *Quality in Higher Education*, 2(2): 155–164.

Gibbs, P. (1999) Competence or trust: the academic offering, *Quality in Higher Education*, 4(1): 7–15.

Gibbs, P. (2004) *Trusting in the University: the contribution of temporality and trust to a praxis of higher education*. Dordrecht: Kluwer.

Gibbs, P. and Angelides, P. (2004a) Accreditation of knowledge as being-in-the-world, *Journal of Education and Work*, 17(3): 333–346.

Gibbs, P., Angelides, P. and Michaelides, P. (2004b) Preliminary thoughts on a praxis of higher education teaching, *Teaching in Higher Education*, 9(2): 183–194.

Giddens, A. (1995) *Modernity and Self-identity: self and society in the late Modern Age*. Cambridge: Polity.

Gillespie, K.H. (2003) Rumination: the concept of stewardship applied to higher education, *Innovative Higher Education*, 27(3): 147–149.

Glynn, S. (2006) The atomistic self versus the holistic self in structural relation to the other, *Human Studies*, 28: 363–374.

Goodlad, S. (1976) *Conflict and Consensus in Higher Education.* London: Hodder and Stoughton.

Goodlad, S. (1995) *The Quest for Quality: sixteen forms of heresy in higher education.* Buckingham: Open University Press/SRHE.

Gruba-McCallister, F. (2002) Education through compassion: cultivating our mystical vocation, in Mills, J. (ed.) *A Pedagogy of Becoming.* New York: Rodopi.

Guignon, C. (2004) *On Being Authentic.* London: Routledge.

Guattari, F. (2005) *The Three Ecologies.* London: Continuum.

Gur-Ze'ev, I. (2002) Martin Heidegger, transcendence, and the possibility of counter-education, in Peters, M. (ed.) *Heidegger, Education and Modernity.* Lanham: Rowan and Littlefield.

Habermas, J. (1979) *Communication and the Evolution of Society.* London: Heinemann.

Habermas, J. (1991) *The Theory of Communicative Action: reason and the rationalization of society.* Cambridge: Polity.

Haggis, T. (2004) Meaning, Identity and 'Motivation': expanding what matters in understanding learning in higher education, *Studies in Higher Education*, 29(3): 335–352.

Hassan, R. (2003) *The Chronoscopic Society: globalization, time and knowledge in the network economy.* New York: Peter Lang.

Healey, M. (2005) Linking research and teaching: exploring disciplinary spaces and the role of inquiry-based learning, in Barnett, R. (ed.) *Reshaping the University: changing relationships between teaching and research.* Maidenhead: McGraw-Hill/Open University Press.

Hegel, G.W.F. (1977) *Phenomenology of Spirit*, transl. Miller, A.V. Oxford: Oxford University Press.

Heidegger, M. (1968) *What is Called Thinking?* New York: Harper & Row.

Heidegger, M. (1985) The self-assertion of the German university, address, delivered on the solemn assumption of the Rectorate of the University, Freiburg, 1933–34. *Review of Metaphysics*, 467–502.

Heidegger, M. (1996) *The Principle of Reason.* Bloomington: Indiana University Press.

Heidegger, M. (1998, orig. 1962) *Being and Time.* Oxford: Blackwell.

Heidegger, M (2002a) *Off the Beaten Track.* Cambridge: Cambridge University Press.

Heidegger, M. (2002b) Deposition submitted before the Committee on the De-Nazification of the Albert Ludwig University, Freiburg im Breisgau, July 23, 1945, excerpt edited and translated by Valerie Allen and Ares D. Axiotis, as 'Heidegger on the Art of Teaching', in Peters, M. (ed.) *Heidegger, Education and Modernity.* Lanham, Maryland: Rowan and Littlefield.

Henden, E. (2004) Intentions, all-out evaluations and weaknesses of the will, *Erkenntnis*, 63(1): 53–74.

Hinchcliff, G. (2006) Re-thinking lifelong learning, *Studies in Philosophy and Education*, 25: 93–109.

hooks, bel (1994) *Teaching to Transgress: education and the practice of freedom.* New York: Routledge.

Horkheimer, M. (2004, orig. 1947) *Eclipse of Reason.* London: Continuum.

Ignatieff, M. (1984) *The Needs of Strangers.* London: Vintage.

Inwood, M. (2000) *Heidegger: a very short introduction.* Oxford: Oxford University Press.

Ireson, J., Mortimore, P. and Hallam, S. (1999) The common strands of pedagogy and their implications, in Mortimore, P. (ed.) *Understanding Pedagogy and Its Impact on Learning.* London: Paul Chapman.

Irigaray, L. (1992, orig. 1982) *Elemental Passions*, transl. Collie, J. and Still, J. New York: Routledge.

Irigaray, L. (1999, orig. 1983) *The Forgetting of Air in Martin Heidegger*, transl. Mader, M.B. Austin: University of Texas.

Irigaray, L. (2002) *The Way of Love*. London: Continuum.

Janaway, C. (2002) *Schopenhauer: a very short introduction*. Oxford: Oxford University Press.

Jarvis, P. (1992) *Paradoxes of Learning: on becoming an individual in society*. San Francisco: Jossey Bass.

Jaspers, K. (1971) Philosophy of existence, in McNeill, W. and Feldman, K. S. (eds, 1998) *Continental Philosophy: an anthropology*. Malden, Mass: Blackwell.

Keller, K.S. (2005) The corporeal order of things: the *spiel* of usability, *Human Studies*, 28: 173–204.

Kierkegaard, S. (1956) *Purity of Heart is to Will One Thing*. New York: Harper & Row.

Kierkegaard, S. (2001) *The Kierkegaard Reader*. Oxford: Blackwell.

Kierkegaard, S. (2004) *The Sickness unto Death*. London: Penguin.

Lambeir, B. (2005) Education as liberation: the politics and techniques of lifelong learning, *Educational Philosophy and Theory*, 37(3): 349–355.

Land, R. and Meyer, J. (2006) *Overcoming Barriers to Student Understanding: threshold concepts and troublesome knowledge*. Abingdon: Routledge.

Lave, J. and Wenger, E. (1991) *Situated Learning: legitimate peripheral participation*. Cambridge: Cambridge University Press.

Leader, D. and Groves, J. (2003) *Introducing Lacan*. Cambridge: Icon.

Leavis, F.R. (1969) *English Literature in Our Time and the University*. London: Chatto and Windus.

Levinas, E. (2005, orig. 1969) *Totality and Infinity: an essay on exteriority*. Pittsburgh: Duquesne University.

Lilge, F. (1974) Philosophy and education in Hegel, *British Journal of Educational Studies*, 22(2): 147–165.

Lovlie, L., Mortenson, K.P., and Nordenbo, S.E. (eds) (2003) *Educating Humanity: bildung in postmodernity*. Oxford: Blackwell.

Lyotard, J-F. (1984) *The Knowledge Condition: a report on knowledge*. Manchester: University of Manchester.

Lyotard, J-F. (1991) *The Inhuman*. Cambridge: Polity Press.

Macfarlane, B. (2004) *Teaching with Integrity: the ethics of higher education practice*. London: Routledge Falmer.

Macfarlane, B. (2006) *The Academic Citizen: the virtue of service in university life*. Abingdon: Routledge.

Macmurray, J. (1995, orig. 1935) *Reason and Emotion*. London: Faber and Faber.

Magee, B. (1987) *The Philosophy of Schopenhauer*. Oxford: Oxford University Press.

Marcoulatos, I. (2003) John Searle and Pierre Bourdieu: divergent perspectives on intentionality and social ontology, *Human Studies*, 26: 67–96.

Marion, J-L. (2002) *Being Given: toward a phenomenology of givenness*. Stanford: Stanford University Press.

Marks, A. (2005) Changing spatial and synchronous structures in the history and culture of learning, *Higher Education*, 50: 613–630.

Marsh, H.W., Trautwen, U., Ludtke, O. and Baumert, J. (2005) Academic self-concept, interest, grades and standardized test scores: reciprocal effects models of causal ordering, *Child Development*, 76(2): 397–461.

Marton, F., Hounsell, D. and Entwistle, N. (eds) (1997) *The Experience of Learning:*

implications for teaching and studying in higher education, 2nd edn. Edinburgh: Scottish Academic Press.

May, T. (2003) When is a Deleuzian becoming?, *Continental Philosophical Review*, 36: 139–153.

McLaren. P. (1995) *Critical Pedagogy and Predatory Culture: oppositional politics in a postmodern era*. London: Routledge.

Merleau-Ponty, M. (1994, orig. 1962) *Phenomenology of Perception*, transl. Smith, C. London: Routledge.

Mill, J.S. (1989, orig. 1873) *Autobiography*. London: Penguin.

Miller, L (2007) Scenes in a university: performing academic identities in a university, in Barnett, R. and Di Napoli, R. (eds) *Changing Identities in Higher Education: voicing perspectives*. Abingdon: Routledge.

Mills, J. (ed.) (2002) *A Pedagogy of Becoming*. New York: Rodopi.

Moore, A. (2004) *The Good Teacher: dominant discourses in teaching and teacher education*. London: Routledge Falmer.

Mortimore, P. (ed.) (1999) *Understanding Pedagogy and Its Impact on Learning*. London: Paul Chapman.

Naidoo, R. (2005) Universities in the Marketplace: the distortion of teaching and research Barnett, R. (ed.) *Reshaping the University: changing relationships between teaching and research*. Maidenhead: McGraw-Hill/Open University Press.

Newman, F. and Holzman, L. (1997) *The End of Knowing: a new development way of learning*. London: Routledge.

Niblett, W.R. (1974) *Universities between Two Worlds*. London: University of London Press.

Niblett, W.R. (ed.) (1975) *The Sciences, the Humanities and the Technological Threat*. London: University of London Press.

Nietzsche, F. (1968) *The Will to Power*, Kaufmann, W. (ed.). New York: Vintage.

Nillsen, R. (2004) Can the love of learning be taught? *Journal of University Teaching and Learning Practice*, 1(1). Available at: http://jutlp.uow.edu.au/

Nussbaum, M. (2000) *Cultivating Humanity: a classical defense of reform in liberal education*. Cambridge: Harvard.

O'Byrne, A. (2005) Pedagogy without a Project: Arendt and Derrida on teaching, responsibility and revolution, *Studies in Philosophy and Education*, 24: 389–409.

Parker, J. (2003) Reconceptualising the curriculum: from commodification to transformation, *Teaching in Higher Education*, 8(4): 529–543.

Pascal, B. (1947) *Pensées*. London: Dent/Everyman's Library.

Passmore, J. (1969) On teaching to be critical, in Peters, R. S. (ed.) *The Concept of Education*. London: Routledge and Kegan Paul.

Passmore, J. (1975) A note on care, in Niblett, W.R. (ed.) *The Sciences, the Humanities and the Technological Threat*. London: University of London Press.

Pavlich, G. (2005) Experiencing critique, *Law and Critique*, 16: 95–112

Peters, M. (1995) *Education and the Postmodern Condition*. Westport: Bergin and Garvey.

Peters, M. (2002) *Heidegger, Education and Modernity*. Lanham, Maryland: Rowan and Littlefield.

Peters, M. (2004) The university and the new humanities: professing with Derrida, *Arts and Humanities in Higher Education*, 3(1): 41–57.

Peters, R.S. (1969, orig. 1958) *The Concept of Motivation*. London: Routledge and Kegan Paul.

Peter, R.S. (1970) *Ethics and Education*. London: George Allen and Unwin.

Peters, R.S. (1975) Subjectivity and standards, in Niblett, W.R. (ed.) *The Sciences, the Humanities and the Technological Threat.* London: University of London Press.

Phipps, A. (2006) *Learning the Arts of Linguistic Survival: languaging, tourism, life.* Clevedon: Channel View Publications.

Phipps, A. (2007) The sound of higher education, *London Review of Education.* 5(1) 1–14.

Phipps, A. and Guilherme, M. (eds) (2003) *Language and Intercultural Communication,* Special issue on Critical Pedagogy, 3(3).

Phipps, A. and Gonzalez, M. (2004) *Modern Languages: learning and teaching in an intercultural field.* London: Sage.

Plato (1966) *Meno,* transl. Guthrie, W.K.C. London: Penguin.

Popper, K. (1975) *Objective Knowledge.* Oxford: Oxford University Press.

Prosser, M. and Trigwell, K. (1999) *Understanding Learning and Teaching: the experience in higher education.* Buckingham: Open University Press.

Quinn, J., Thomas, L., Slack, K., *et al.* (2006) *Re-thinking Working Class Drop-out.* Stafford: Staffordshire University (originally published by Joseph Rowntree Foundation).

Rae, M.A. (2004) Learning the truth in a Christian university: advice from Soren Kierkegaard', in Astley, J., Francis, L., Sullivan, J. and Walker, A. (eds) *The Idea of a Christian University: essays on theology and higher education.* Bletchley: Paternoster.

Readings, B. (1997) *The University in Ruins.* Cambridge: Harvard University.

Reber, A. (1993) *Implicit Learning and Tacit Knowledge: an essay on the cognitive unconscious.* New York: Oxford University Press.

Reeves, M. (1988) *The Crisis in Higher Education: competence, delight and the common good.* Stony Stratford: Open University Press/SRHE.

Richmond, S. (2004) Being in others: empathy from a psychoanalytical perspective, *European Journal of Philosophy,* 12(2): 244–264.

Ricoeur, P. (1994) *Oneself as Another.* Chicago: University of Chicago.

Rieff, P. (1987, orig. 1966) *The Triumph of the Therapeutic: uses of faith after Freud.* Chicago: University of Chicago.

Roberts, J. (1990) *German Philosophy: an introduction.* Cambridge: Polity.

Robinson, S. (2005) Values, spirituality and higher education, in Robinson, S. and Katulushi, C. (eds) (2005) *Values in Higher Education.* St Brides Major: Aureus and the University of Leeds.

Robinson, S. and Katulushi, C. (eds) (2005) *Values in Higher Education.* St Brides Major: Aureus and the University of Leeds.

Rogers, B. (ed.) (2004) *Is Nothing Sacred?* Abingdon: Routledge.

Rogers, C. (1983) *Freedom to Learn for the 80s.* New York: Merrill.

Rorty, R. (1980) *Philosophy and the Mirror of Nature.* Oxford: Blackwell.

Roth, W-M. (1997) Being-in-the-world and the horizons of learning: Heidegger, Wittgenstein and cognition, *Interchange,* 28(2/3): 145–157.

Roth, W-M. (2002) *Being and Becoming in the Classroom.* Westport: Ablex.

Rowland, S (2000) *The Enquiring University Teacher.* Buckingham: Open University Press/SRHE.

Rowland, S. (2005) Intellectual love and the link between teaching and research, in Barnett, R. (ed.) *Reshaping the University: changing relationships between teaching and research.* Maidenhead: McGraw-Hill/Open University Press.

Sadler, D.R. (2002) Learning dispositions: can we really assess them? *Assessment in Education,* 9(1): 45–51.

Salecl, R. (2004) *On Anxiety: thinking in action.* London: Routledge.

Sanderson, G. (2004) Existentialism, globalisation and the cultural other, *International Education Journal*, 4(4): 1–20.

Sartre, J-P. (1973, orig. 1948) *Existentialism and Humanism.* London: Methuen.

Sartre, J-P. (2003a) *Basic Writings*, Priest, S. (ed.). London: Routledge.

Sartre, J-P. (2003b, orig. 1943) *Being and Nothingness.* London: Routledge.

Sartre, J-P. (2004, orig. 1940) *The Imaginary.* London: Routledge.

Savin-Baden, M. (2007) *Learning Spaces: creating opportunities for knowledge creation in academic life.* Maidenhead: McGraw-Hill/Open University Press/SRHE.

Schopenhauer, A. (1997) *The World as Will and Idea.* London: Dent.

Schopenhauer, A. (2004, orig. 1850) *On the Suffering of the World.* London: Penguin.

Searle, J.R. (1969) *Speech Acts: an essay in the philosophy of language.* Cambridge: Cambridge University Press.

Searle, J.R. (2001) *Rationality in Action.* Cambridge: MIT

Shade, P. (2006) Educating hopes, *Studies in Philosophy and Education*, 25: 191–225.

Smith, R. (2004) Thinking with each other: the peculiar practice of the university, in Dunne, J. and Hogan, P. (eds) *Education and Practice: upholding the integrity of teaching and learning.* Oxford: Blackwell.

Sotto, E. (1994) *When Learning Becomes Teaching: a theory and practice of teaching.* London: Cassell.

Standish, P. (1999) The spirit of the university and the education of the spirit, in Crawley, F., Smeyers, P. and Standish, P. (eds) *Universities Remembering Europe.* Oxford: Berghahn Books.

Steiner, G. (2003) *Lessons of the Masters.* Cambridge, Mass: Harvard.

Strathern, M. (2004a) *Commons and Borderlands: working papers on interdisciplinarity, accountability and the flow of knowledge.* Wantage: Sean Kingston.

Strathern, M. (2004b) *A community of critics? Thoughts on new knowledge*, the Huxley Memorial Lecture. London: Royal Anthropological Institute.

Strathern, M. (2005) *Useful Knowledge*, the Isaiah Berlin Lecture. London: British Academy.

Strathern, M. (2007) Knowledge Identities, in Barnett, R. and Di Napoli, R. (eds) *Changing Identities in Higher Education: voicing perspectives.* Abingdon: Routledge.

Taylor, C. (1991) *The Ethics of Authenticity.* Cambridge: Harvard.

Taylor, C. (1992) *Sources of the Self.* Cambridge: University of Cambridge.

Taylor, R, Barr, J. and Steele, T. (2002) *For a Radical Higher Education: after postmodernism.* Buckingham: Open University Press.

Thomson, I. (2001) Heidegger on ontological education, or: how we become what we are. *Inquiry*, 44: 243–268.

Trifonas, P.P. and Peters, M.A. (eds) (2004) *Derrida, Deconstruction and Education.* Oxford: Blackwell.

Trowler, P., Fanghanel, J. and Wareham, T. (2005) Freeing the chi of change: the Higher Education Academy and enhancing teaching and learning in higher education, *Studies in Higher Education*, 30(4): 427–444.

Tubbs, N. (2005) Philosophy of the Teacher, *Journal of Philosophy of Education*, 39(2): Special Issue.

Ventimiglia, M. (2005) Three educational orientations: a Peircean perspective on education and the growth of the self, *Studies in Philosophy and Education*, 2: 291–308.

Walker, M. (ed.) (2001) *Reconstructing Professionalism in University Teaching: teachers and learners in action.* Maidenhead: McGraw-Hill/Open University Press/SRHE.

Walker, M. (2003) 'Beyond the Impossibly Good: Developing University Teaching through Research.' paper given to conference at Institute of Education, University of London, April 2003.

Walker, M. (2006) *Higher Education Pedagogies: a capabilities approach.* Maidenhead: McGraw-Hill/Open University Press/SRHE.

Walker, M. and Nixon, J. (eds.) (2004) *Reclaiming Universities from a Runaway World.* Maidenhead: McGraw-Hill/Open University Press/SRHE.

Warnock, M. (1970) *Existentialism.* Oxford: Oxford University Press.

Watts, M. (2001) *Heidegger: a beginner's guide.* London: Hodder and Stoughton.

Williams, R. (2003) *Lost Icons.* London: Continuum.

Williams, R. (2005) Faith in the university, in Robinson, S. and Katulushi, C. (eds) (2005) *Values in Higher Education.* St Brides Major: Aureus and the University of Leeds.

Wyatt, J. (1990) *Commitment to Higher Education.* Buckingham: Open University Press/ SRHE.

Young, J. (2005) *Schopenhauer.* Routledge: Abingdon.

Zizek, S. (2002) *On Belief: thinking in action.* London: Routledge.

Zweig, F. (1963) *The Student in an Age of Anxiety.* London: Heinemann.

Reports

Bone, J. and McNay, J. (2006) *Higher Education and Human Good,* Report of a Consultation, Sarum College, Salisbury, inspired by the work of Professor Roy Niblett. Bristol: Tockington Press.

Council for Industry and Higher Education (2005) *Higher Education: more than a Degree.* London: CIHE.

Higher Education Academy and Open University/CHERI. (2006) *What is Learned at University: the social mediation of university learning,* Working Paper 3. York: HEA.

Higher Education Policy Institute (2006) *The Academic Experience of Students in English Universities.* Oxford: London.

NCIHE (1997) *Higher Education in the Learning Society,* Report of the National Committee (Dearing Inquiry). Norwich: HMSO.

NFER (2005) *Plain Guide to the Education Act 2005,* authored by Fowler, J. and Waterman, C. Slough: NFER.

UNITE/HEPI (2005) *The Student Experience Report, 2005.* Bristol: UNITE.

Websites

http://www.vanuatutourism.com/vanuatu/cms/en/culture/nagol.html

Subject index

This book involves an interweaving of a number of concepts, which occur throughout; and this index therefore picks out the main instances of those concepts. They include:

Authenticity
Becoming
Curriculum
Energy
Learning
Pedagogy
Students
Teaching
Will

Being
Care
Disposition
Higher education
Ontology
Space
Risk
Voice
Will to learn.

Bold entries are to key references. Page numbers in italics refer to instances of items that appear in the endnotes.

Name index

The Society for Research into Higher Education

The Society for Research into Higher Education (SRHE), an international body, exists to stimulate and coordinate research into all aspects of higher education. It aims to improve the quality of higher education through the encouragement of debate and publication on issues of policy, on the organization and management of higher education institutions, and on the curriculum, teaching and learning methods.

The Society is entirely independent and receives no subsidies, although individual events often receive sponsorship from business or industry. The Society is financed through corporate and individual subscriptions and has members from many parts of the world. It is an NGO of UNESCO.

Under the imprint *SRHE & Open University Press*, the Society is a specialist publisher of research, having over 80 titles in print. In addition to *SRHE News*, the Society's newsletter, the Society publishes three journals: *Studies in Higher Education* (three issues a year), *Higher Education Quarterly* and *Research into Higher Education Abstracts* (three issues a year).

The Society runs frequent conferences, consultations, seminars and other events. The annual conference in December is organized at and with a higher education institution. There are a growing number of networks which focus on particular areas of interest, including:

Access	FE/HE
Assessment	Graduate Employment
Consultants	New Technology for Learning
Curriculum Development	Postgraduate Issues
Eastern European	Quantitative Studies
Educational Development Research	Student Development

Benefits to members

Individual

- The opportunity to participate in the Society's networks
- Reduced rates for the annual conferences
- Free copies of *Research into Higher Education Abstracts*
- Reduced rates for *Studies in Higher Education*

- Reduced rates for *Higher Education Quarterly*
- Free online access to *Register of Members' Research Interests* – includes valuable reference material on research being pursued by the Society's members
- Free copy of occasional in-house publications, e.g. *The Thirtieth Anniversary Seminars Presented by the Vice-Presidents*
- Free copies of *SRHE News* and *International News* which inform members of the Society's activities and provides a calendar of events, with additional material provided in regular mailings
- A 35 per cent discount on all SRHE/Open University Press books
- The opportunity for you to apply for the annual research grants
- Inclusion of your research in the *Register of Members' Research Interests*

Corporate

- Reduced rates for the annual conference
- The opportunity for members of the Institution to attend SRHE's network events at reduced rates
- Free copies of *Research into Higher Education Abstracts*
- Free copies of *Studies in Higher Education*
- Free online access to *Register of Members' Research Interests* – includes valuable reference material on research being pursued by the Society's members
- Free copy of occasional in-house publications
- Free copies of *SRHE News* and *International News*
- A 35 per cent discount on all SRHE/Open University Press books
- The opportunity for members of the Institution to submit applications for the Society's research grants
- The opportunity to work with the Society and co-host conferences
- The opportunity to include in the *Register of Members' Research Interests* your Institution's research into aspects of higher education

Membership details: SRHE, 76 Portland Place, London W1B 1NT, UK Tel: 020 7637 2766. Fax: 020 7637 2781. email: srheoffice@srhe.ac.uk world wide web: http://www.srhe.ac.uk./srhe/ *Catalogue*: SRHE & Open University Press, McGraw-Hill Education, McGraw-Hill House, Shoppenhangers Road, Maidenhead, Berkshire SL6 2QL. Tel: 01628 502500. Fax: 01628 770224. email: enquiries@openup.co.uk – web: www.openup.co.uk

Related books from Open University Press
Purchase from www.openup.co.uk or order through your local bookseller

BEYOND ALL REASON
LIVING WITH IDEOLOGY IN THE UNIVERSITY

Ronald Barnett

> A major work . . . provocative, unsettling and profoundly challenging. I think it should be prescribed reading for all vice-chancellors.
> > Colin Bundy, Director of the School of Oriental and African Studies,
> > University of London

> Ron Barnett's latest book lives up to, and possibly exceeds, the high standards he has set himself in his previous books – which are now established as the premier series of reflective books on higher education.
> > Peter Scott, Vice-Chancellor, Kingston University

Beyond All Reason argues that ideologies are now multiplying on campus and that, consequently, the university as a place of open debate and reason is in jeopardy. The book examines, as case studies, the ideologies of competition, quality, entrepreneurialism and managerialism. All of these movements have a positive potential but, in being pressed forward unduly, have become pernicious ideologies that are threatening to undermine the university.

Ronald Barnett argues that it is possible to realize the university by addressing the ideals present in the idea of the university, and so developing positive projects for the university. These 'utopian ideologies' may never be fully realized but, pursued seriously, they can counter the pernicious ideologies that beset the university. In this way, it is possible for the idea of the university to live on and be practised in the twenty-first century.

Beyond All Reason offers a bold optimistic statement about the future of universities and offers ideas for enabling universities to be 'universities' in the contemporary age. It will be of interest and value not just to students of higher education but also to vice-chancellors, administrators, academics generally and those who care about the future of universities.

Contents
Introduction – Part 1: The end of the matter – The ends of reason – A complex world – The states of higher education – The end of ideology? – Part 2: Pernicious ideologies – 'The entrepreneurial university' – Anything you can do – Never mind the quality – 'The academic community' – Part 3: Virtuous ideologies – Communicating values – Engaging universities – Uniting research and teaching – Reasonable universities – Prospects – Appendices – Notes – Bibliography – Index – The Society for Research into Higher Education.

192pp   0 335 20893 2 (Paperback)   0 335 20894 0 (Hardback)

RESHAPING THE UNIVERSITY
NEW RELATIONSHIPS BETWEEN RESEARCH, SCHOLARSHIP AND TEACHING

Ronald Barnett

What is the emerging shape of the University? Are there spaces for present activities to be practised anew or even for new activities? If these questions have force, they show that the metaphors of shapes and spaces can be helpful in understanding the contemporary university.

Research, teaching and scholarship remain the dominant activities in universities and so it is their relationships that form the main concerns of this volume. Are these activities pulling apart from each other? Or might these activities be brought more together in illuminating ways? Is there space to redesign these activities so that they shed light on each other? Is there room for yet other purposes?

In this volume, a distinguished set of scholars engage with these pertinent but challenging issues. Ideas are offered, and evidence is marshalled, of practices that suggest a re-shaping of the University may be possible.

Reshaping the University appeals to those who are interested in the future of universities, including students, researchers, managers and policy makers. It also addresses global issues and it will, therefore, interest the higher education community worldwide.

Contributors
Ronald Barnett, David Dill, Carol Bond, Lewis Elton, Mick Healey, Mark Hughes, Rajani Naidoo, Mark Olssen, Bruce Macfarlane, Kathleen Nolan, Jan Parker, Michael Peters, Alison Phipps, Jane Robertson, Peter Scott, Stephen Rowland.

Contents

2005   240pp   0 335 21701 X (Paperback)   0 335 21702 8 (Hardback)

ENGAGING THE CURRICULUM IN HIGHER EDUCATION

Ronald Barnett and Kelly Coate

There is greater interest than ever before in higher education: more money is being spent on it, more students are registered and more courses are being taught. And yet the matter that is arguably at the heart of higher education, the curriculum, is noticeable for its absence in public debate and in the literature on higher education. This book begins to redress the balance.

Even though the term 'curriculum' may be missing from debates on higher education, curricula are changing rapidly and in significant ways. What we are seeing, therefore, is curriculum change by stealth, in which curricula are being reframed to enable students to acquire skills that have market value. In turn, curricula are running the risk of fragmenting as knowledge and skills exert their separate claims. Such a fragmented curriculum is falling well short of the challenges of the twenty-first century.

A complex and uncertain world requires curricula in which students as human beings are placed at their centre: what is called for are curricula that offer no less than the prospect of encouraging the formation of human being and becoming. A curriculum of this kind has to be understood as the imaginative design of spaces where creative things can happen as students become engaged.

Based upon a study of curricula in UK universities, *Engaging the Curriculum in Higher Education* offers an uncompromising thesis about the development of higher education and is essential reading for those who care about the future of higher education.

Contents

Acknowledgements – Introduction – Part I: The possibility of curriculum – Curriculum: a policy vacuum – Understanding curriculum – Higher education for a new age – Framing curriculum – Part II: Signs of curriculum life – Conjectures – Knowing – Acting – Being – Part III: Prospects for Engagement – Engaging the Curriculum – Engaging Students – Engaging Academics – Summary and Reflections – Appendices – Bibliography – Index.

160pp   0 335 21289 1 (Paperback)   0 335 21290 5 (Hardback)

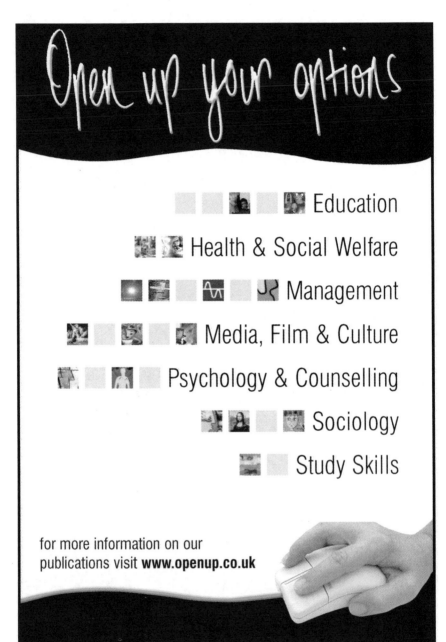